A Fleeting Improvised Man

on the quest for enlightenment

DJ

I0142406

Published in 2013 by
DJ

Cover Design
DJ and Esther H

Canadian Cataloguing in Publication Data
****
ISBN 978-0-9919954-0-0

Dedication

To Nemo for simply Being. I wouldn't be here without you.

Acknowledgements

Veronica T.
David B.
Esther H.
Caroline M.

Table of Contents

Introduction

Hey, want to hear something funny? In fact it's the most hilarious thing I ever heard. I expect you do, what with all the seeming financial woes, environmental problems, wars and energy concerns highlighted so eagerly in the media these days. Let's temper all this for a moment with a little jocularity, shall we?

There was a chap who took himself to be a relatively well-adjusted sort of person. I mean no more dysfunctional or neurotic than the average Joe. While certain of his outlooks differed from those of the norm, or the "sheeple" as he occasionally called them, his views could not be construed as terribly extreme or significantly out of place. He thought of himself as a free thinker, a pragmatist with a fundamentally prosaic outlook on life. In practice he spent most of his time contemplating the arcane; finding knowledge, spiritual or otherwise, wherever he could uncover it. However, he never followed any kind of practical experiential spiritual path. For all intents and purposes, he was an armchair mystic.

At this point the material may not appear to be groundbreaking comedy club fodder but it gets better. Hold on—I promise it's worth it.

This chap, in all his warehousing of information, in his quest to find answers—to find THE ANSWER—one day set out on a journey across a continent. Eventually securing refuge, he simply woke up. He saw that what he took to be a "life" was nothing more than a grand illusion, a dream plain and simple. He burst out laughing. To be accurate, it was more akin to a momentary, uncontrollable, hysterical fit emerging from the very depths of his being. Or, more pointedly, just pure enlightened BEING itself, devoid of any sense of self whatsoever. He inexplicably found that what he had always taken himself to be was totally removed from the picture. It was the funniest darned thing he had ever experienced and most assuredly ever would. This is what happens when the

1

curtain comes down, the play ends and one is left wondering, with jaw agape, how the hell it was possible to confuse that farce for REALITY. He was, as the British are fond of saying, truly gobsmacked. It was the mother of all jokes, the great cosmic epiphany laid bare and manifest, and man was it a hoot.

For you see, I was that guy! I was the actor who decided to shuffle on HOME after the curtain fell and get, or rather simply BE LIFE. HOME and LIFE being among the many terms one can use to describe the ineffable. It turns out LIFE, not a life but LIFE proper (the thing that remains once Elvis has left the building), is much broader, more peaceful and settled, than could ever be imagined while embroiled in the vagaries of dreamlike existence all of us vagabond thespians typically must endure. From the moment I took up the search in a totally motivated, do-or-die fashion, about one year passed until awakening from the dream state seemingly occurred. If a befuddled, ignorant and delusional (as far as true reality goes) seeker such as myself can awaken, surely anyone can. From that initial awakening things got even weirder.

In fact the whole journey, from the moment I decided to abandon everything and take up the search to find the ultimate nature of reality, has been much like a trip down Alice's rabbit hole or a conversation with Morpheus of *Matrix* fame. Before setting off on the journey, I knew little to nothing about the disparate elements that could contribute to one's final awakening. Things like profoundly mind-expanding and healing natural substances (e.g., *ayahuasca* and magic mushrooms) were mere legend to me. Buddhism, Advaita Vedanta (non-dualism) or even meditation were completely foreign. This whole enterprise has not been stranger than I imagined, it has been stranger than I ever could have imagined. To quote Oz's Dorothy, "I've a feeling we're not in Kansas anymore."

All concepts and reference points eventually vanish as one discovers them to be completely fictitious constructs to begin with. What remains is inexplicable. What you find everything, self included, to truly be isn't anything in particular at all. A single vast, seamless, unbroken field of *Beingness* presents itself with no centre to be found anywhere. Everything and nothing at the same time. Paradox is your true nature. It has been labelled many things including *Non-duality, Now, Void, Oneness, Emptiness, Buddha Nature, Beingness, Presence, The Infinite, No Mind, Spacious Awareness, Non-conceptual Reality, The Absolute* or simply *Spirit* or *God*.

Introduction

The famous Chinese Taoist sage, Lao Tzu, put it well when he began his masterwork, *The Tao Te Ching*, with the following admonishment: "The Tao (Ultimate Reality) that can be spoken of is not the real Tao." The truth of all cannot be conceptualized in any meaningful fashion. In a similar way, Buddha is quoted as saying, "All Dharmas are empty." This explains the multiplicity of terms used to describe Reality. It must be experienced for oneself. The best that words can do (including the ones in this book) is point in a very limited way to what is actually true. Never confuse the map for the landscape, the list of ingredients on the box for a chocolate chip cookie. And on that note let's get back to mundane reality shall we, as I formally introduce myself.

For the record (how I used to define myself) my name is DJ (I prefer spinning my own tunes, thank you very much). I'm a Canadian country boy through and through. Farming has been a big part of my life. I did have occasion to spend some years teaching English as a second language and studying mar-tial arts overseas. I was also a correctional officer for a spell and a few other things as well, but that hits the major points of interest regarding *the DJ Story*.

In reflection, as far
seems that some of my
conducive to providing
environment for self-
was pretty much oblivious

as spiritual matters go, it
preoccupations were very
a good foundation/
realization to occur, but I
to this fact at the time. I never

purposely cultivated experiences or career choices for any spiritual gain. But now I wonder if they were somehow echoes of a past life or linked to previous Karma in some way. Or perhaps my subconscious knew what it was doing all along. I travelled and lived exclusively to/in countries that were predominantly Buddhist but never clued in to that fact until recently. These, and other occurrences, seemingly eased me down the path without *me* really being aware of what was happening at the time.

I would like to make it clear, before we proceed, that the following story is true as far as any story can be. None of the following can be considered *real* in any meaningful way. It is, after all, just a story (as is the fictional nature of all reality), so it is safe to say that none of what follows reflects the truth. Experiences occurred, people were met, things seemingly happened, but ultimately they were no more real than my illusionary self I have come to know recently. However, as far as tall tales go, it ain't so bad. Perhaps it's even in the same league as a

Paul Bunyan or Robin Hood fable—at least in its comparable level of *authentic* truth telling.

Now let's turn attention to my long-held interest in the manmade creation of illusion and subterfuge, here in our very own consensual reality. In this category falls my experience in the visual arts, particularly filmmaking. My university education comprised earning a BA (Honours Arts) in Film Studies as well as an Honours BSc in the Natural Sciences.

With regards to filmmaking, I found that once I had immersed myself in the art and science of motion picture creation, I could never actually experience cinematic reality in quite the same way again. It was much more difficult to suspend my disbelief and get lost in the narrative on hand. My attention was often drawn to the lighting, sound, editing or perhaps even finding continuity errors that filmgoers, who have not studied filmmaking, are completely oblivious to.

The mainstream Holly-wood filmmaking style is sometimes referred to as *the dream factory*. It is a very seductive form of storytelling and it turns out that the narratives of our lives unfold in much the same manner. To become an accomplished filmmaker you must understand inti-mately how this process works.

Consequently, one cultivates a sort of natural filmic *mindfulness practice*. This is comparable to the way spiritual mindfulness practice works, but *filmic* awareness is limited to this one specific realm only. I see quite clearly now that the main preoccupation in my life has been one of cutting through the crap and peeling back as many layers of illusion as I could find. From a philosophical viewpoint, I searched fairly diligently, but for a long time didn't get close to the core of the matter.

My passion for film was tempered with a long-held interest in science. I guess this was also an attempt to figure out if there actually was any *gnosis in the machine* but from another angle altogether. Of particular interest to me was rooting out phenomena that existed, for the most part, totally obscured to the casual gaze. Using the scientific method to probe life's mysteries was interesting, to say the least, but ultimately it proved an unsatisfactory method to investigate what I was looking for. Few secrets were divulged. I realized things were not as they appeared, but I seemed to progress no further than that. Admittedly, a few groundbreaking scientists were beacons of hope as far as investigating the mystical nature of science was concerned. Though I doubt they would consider their work anything but hard-hitting science. These were men like alternating-current inventor and visionary Nicola Tesla, homeopathic investigator Jacques Benveniste or biochemist Rupert Sheldrake, who proposed the morphic field theory — loosely speaking a kind of *etheric* unseen organizing field which shapes and conditions all things.

If anything, quantum mechanics held out the most promise. Here physicists like Niels Bohr and David Bohm discovered that *high strangeness* was woven throughout the fabric of reality at least at the sub-atomic level. Einstein coined the term *spooky action at a distance* to describe physicists' prediction of non-local effects at the quantum level. Certain physicists extrapolated, from the results of later experimentation, that everything is entangled or interconnected to some degree and thus essentially one. This really perplexed physicists. Equally baffling to them was the *measurement problem* which demonstrated that an atom only appeared in a particular place when it was measured. In other words it took an act of conscious observation to bring an atom, and by wider abstraction seemingly our whole universe, into existence. Consciousness was making its presence known in processes which common reasoning dictated impossible.

But one could find weirdness down other avenues as well. Turning to matters of the occult, which originally didn't carry connotations of the supernatural or paranormal, but simply meant things that were hidden or obscured from normal view, I sought out answers.

As a youngster I was intrigued with anything that could excite a young boy's imagination. UFOs, ghosts, Sasquatch, Loch Ness monster, etc., were material for my consideration. Fortean mysteries (Charles Hoy Fort was an American author and researcher interested in anomalous phenomena) were a passion. From here I branched out into more complex subjects such as philosophy, psychology, mysticism, quantum physics, conspiracy research and the machinations of the Illuminati. Apparently I held in the back of my mind Hamlet's remarks to the rationalist Horatio, "There are more things in heaven and earth, Horatio, than are dreampt of in your philosophy." It turned out that waking up was many factors stranger than the esoteric interests mentioned above. After all, at least those peripheral investigations had to do with phenomena ostensibly occurring in our so-called normal reality.

High strangeness may have been hard to fathom but not impossibly so. Enlightenment, well that was simply *far out man*. I mean really really out there. In fact, it was so out there that it completely transcended my ego's *event horizon*. That is the region marking the outer boundary of a black hole, inside which the gravitational force is strong enough to prevent matter or radiation from escaping. For a graphical representation of what is involved, take a look at the front cover of this book and you will see what I am alluding to. In one sense the Yin/Yang interplay is representative of the opposing dichotomies of dualistic everyday reality, i.e., male/female, good/bad, happy/sad etc. However, in the centre of the graphic you can see a hole, corridor or simply a void, which is itself indicative of the kind of event horizon of which I speak. To awaken I found I had to jump into this unfathomable mystery feet first. Leaping before I looked, so to speak. It was like coming across the edge of an inaccurately drawn medieval map, conceived by a poor cartographer. Not much more could be known to my limited human psyche beyond the periphery of the map's border than—*There Be Dragons!*

The End of the Beginning

During meditation, a real physical itch may arise that desperately requires your attention. You realize it is simply a ploy, instigated by the powerful mind, to get you off the matter at hand. Consequently you resist the growing urge to scratch until finally it becomes unbearable, and you relent and scratch the damn thing. But what if you couldn't? What if instead of being a localized trivial irritation, the annoyance was located deep down in the pit of your stomach or embedded somewhere in your psyche? What then?

That was how the reality question presented itself to me. The itch that could never be scratched. I knew something was off—not quite tickety-boo—somewhere in the spiritual department, but, wherever I looked, I could never seem to locate the source of the irritation. Furthermore it became increasingly evident that it would take more than a few aspirins and some bed rest to relieve this malady if it were ever identified. After all, what I am talking about here was some kind of divine discontent, an undiagnosed spiritual *dis-ease* that would surely require treatment of the highest order.

What follows is in essence a chronological description of some of the more metaphysically salient points in my life. Certain episodes drawn from the past serve as a preface of sorts to the spiritual pilgrimage I eventually undertook to discover the ultimate nature of reality. While describing the preparation for this quest I occasionally interrupt the narrative by interjecting a spiritually edifying anecdote. These vignettes are mostly drawn from the two decades that preceded the start of the quest, which itself occurred while I was in my mid-forties. Some of the anecdotes are travelogues which serve to illustrate my urge to merge with the Truth, though at the time it was not readily apparent to me they included a spiritual component. When I was embroiled in the thick of it, mired up to my earlobes in the muck of sound and fury, I was pretty much oblivious to the workings of Spirit. It was largely due to hindsight that things later became clear enough to offer up spiritual editorializing in the telling of the story. Though, as you are about to learn, I always did have a yearning to discover the quintessential mystery of all mysteries.

Advancing through my twenties, I increasingly discerned, not so much conceptually but rather intuitively, that there is *more to the game* than meets the eye. But I never dared express this musing overtly. Not to anyone. Particularly not to myself. The set-up seemed designed to keep us firmly identified with illusion. The idea that consensual reality is merely a dream state echoed throughout the ages. More than 2,000 years ago the great Taoist sage, Chuang Tzu, wrote, "Only when they have awakened do they begin to know that it was a dream. By and by comes the great awakening, and then we shall know that it has all been a great dream."

Edgar Alan Poe seemed to be pondering the same idea when he penned,

> Is all that we see or seem,
> But a dream within a dream?

Or Lewis Carroll, when he wrote:

> In a Wonderland they lie,
> Dreaming as the days go by,
> Dreaming as the summers die;
> Ever drifting down the stream—
> Lingering in the golden gleam—
> Life, what is it but a dream?

How about John Keats who seemed to be taking a page right out of a Buddhist scripture:

> Can death be sleep, when life is but a dream,
> And scenes of bliss pass as a phantom by?

The End of the Beginning

The transient pleasures as a vision seem,
And yet we think the greatest pain's to die.
How strange it is that man on earth should roam,
And lead a life of woe, but not forsake
His rugged path; nor dare he view alone
His future doom which is but to awake.

American satirist Mark Twain, during his twilight years, was exploring the issue of the duality of self, namely what he considered to be the *Waking Self* and the *Dream Self*, when he wrote in *The Mysterious Stranger*, "there is no God, no universe, no human race, no earthly life, no heaven, no hell. It is all a dream—a grotesque and foolish dream. Nothing exists but you. And you are but a thought."

Some two hundred years later contemporary American satirist, Bill Hicks, examined similar territory, while speaking on the topic of death:

Today, a young man on acid realized that all matter is merely energy condensed to a slow vibration— that we are all one consciousness experiencing itself subjectively.
There's no such thing as death, life is only a dream, and we're the imagination of ourselves.

Examples started popping up everywhere once I started looking for them. Let's conclude with that familiar childhood ditty:

Row, row, row your boat
Gently down the stream.
Merrily, merrily, merrily, merrily,
Life is but a dream.

I think deep down most people intuit that the ultimate nature of reality is more than a mere canine and equine show. We are just usually not motivated, or aware enough, to pursue this vague feeling to a greater level of clarity. Was the human condition as meaningless and inconsequential as Shakespeare painted it in *Macbeth:*

9

A Fleeting Improvised Man

> Life's but a walking shadow, a poor player,
> That struts and frets his hour upon the stage,
> And then is heard no more. It is a tale
> Told by an idiot, full of sound and fury,
> Signifying nothing.
> M ... Act 5, scene 5, 19–28

I reflected upon those words deeply as a high school student and hoped that the dreary prognosis they offered was not actually the case. For the most part though, reality seemed to prove the Bard correct. Admittedly novel experiences, be they travel, the acquisition of new skill sets, creative endeavours or sensual pleasures. temporarily mitigated the banality of it all, but to a great degree life seemingly reflected the title of that great Canadian board game, Trivial Pursuit.

Yet in Shakespeare's description lies a clue to our salvation, if we only pay attention to the allusion he is making. Whom, or what (if anything), is animating this *walking shadow* of which he spoke? Must it be that we perpetually confuse this hazy, phantasmagoric representation of reality for the real thing? Precisely what is the nature of this walking shadow? Perhaps we should take a page out of distinguished German jurist Daniel Paul Schreber's biography *Memoirs of my Nervous Illness* for a moment and consider his *fleeting improvised men* concept.

Schreber's book was published around the turn of the last century and influenced the work of several eminent psychiatrists, Freud among others. Schreber's account chronicles the strange world that opened up to him due to his increasingly severe bouts of schizophrenia. Characters, known as *fleeting improvised men*, appeared with increasing regularity in his psychosis. They were seen as transient figures of human shape, which slowly dissolved after a short period of existence.

While appearing entirely *real* to him, these figures were eventually deemed to be mere *dream characters* by Schreber. As a result, he realized them incapable of interacting with reality in any significant way. While these beings were clearly the product of a deluded mind, they fit quite nicely into Shakespeare's analogy. For, by wider abstraction, we are all in fact fleeting improvised men. By my own direct experience, I have found the veracity of this observation to be entirely accurate. It is quite possible to discern this for yourself. If one embraces a spirit of total honesty and a mindset that delusion will be no longer accepted, as Schreber did when he realized the incorporeal nature of his fleeting improvised men, fruit will surely be borne. Through well considered observation, you will certainly find that what you take yourself to be is in reality, Shakespeare's *shadow actor*, or Schreber's *fleeting improvised man*. Of this you can be sure. Little did Schreber realize that, when viewed from the position of absolute truth, there was no great distinction to be made between himself and the illusory phantoms he perceived in his psychosis. To quote Shakespeare again, "We are all such stuff as dreams are made of." But once again I ask, what is it that animates the fleeting improvised man? When the persona (derived from the Latin for a kind of mask made to resonate with the voice of the actor) is revealed for the fiction it is, when the actor has been unmasked, what remains? To adequately answer that question will take the remainder of my story.

In a sense, I can pinpoint the moment in my life when the *shadow* first began to *dissipate*, like a mountain fog being stabbed by the morn's first rays. It was not much of a dissolution at first, but in retrospect seems to be the point where Humpty Dumpty, not yet inclined to tumble, became at least slightly unsettled. It would be a couple more decades before that thin-shelled, hollow character actually took his earth-shattering, whopping, *great fall*.

In my late 20s, I found myself doing the unspeakable. Literally, that which must never be uttered was expressed openly for the first time. At first glance the following incident may appear rather insignificant, but I found the ramifications quite profound and forever after unable to ignore at some level of my being. It occurred during a philosophical discussion, the typical kind of diatribe that my mother and I engaged in from time to time. This one became rather more heated than usual, with each of us holding strongly opposing viewpoints on some contentious mystical issue. Perhaps something originating from *Seth Speaks*, *The Baghavad Gita* or maybe some material from Edgar Cayce. Whatever the source, each of us held firm to our contrary position. Finally my mother, in desperation, played her trump card. She always had a full deck upon which to draw but this particular card had never been uncovered before. Indeed I was not even aware of its existence. She had had the temerity to exclaim in a rather dismissive haughty manner that the whole debate was of no real consequence because, as she put it, "I'm not actually sure you really even exist."

A Fleeting Improvised Man

I was flabbergasted and also more than slightly pissed off. It's very curious how the ego reacts to such an honest statement of fact. Here *ego* means the *me centre* or identification with self, not *egotism*. I remember thinking to myself something along the lines of, "Well I never … I mean really … who the hell does she thinks she is anyhow?" Let me tell you my ego was smarting from her low blow. I have since come to see that the highest point of contention that the ego can be presented with is the fact that it does not actually exist. At least not in any semblance to the way it believes it does. It constantly expends huge amounts of energy to prop up the hollow fiction that it is. Taken off guard, and completely out of my league, all I could counter with was a simplistically trite, "Oh yeah? Well I don't think you exist either!" I must admit that there was a certain stridency to my delivery. My tone, along with the directness of the message, infuriated my mother, such that she accusingly hollered back, "No you don't exist!" And so it went back and forth, for a few more rounds, until I stomped off in a huff.

So there it was, the dirty little secret had somehow finally slipped out—the emperor was reputed to be naked! It was quite a shock. From this point on, that admission would often arise during my mystical journey to jab me in the ribs. Once something of that magnitude is revealed, it can never quite be put back in its place. You can pretend you never heard it, but it is not possible to uncognize it. Something had been recognized somewhere deep down in my psyche. Nebulous at first, its nature would grow ever clearer with the passage of time. I could have saved myself a lot of bother if I had considered what my mother had said more carefully. If I had it to do over again, knowing what I do now, I realize we should have been directing the raised voices backwards, for in truth, it was actually our very selves that did not exist. How cool would that have been?

It would have been loads of fun to bandy back and forth, "I don't exist," as the ego self-destructed; its speedy demise occurring in a flurry of good-natured truth telling. Perhaps disappearing with the exclamation, "I'm melting!" much like the Wicked Witch of the West did as she quickly disappeared in *The Wizard of Oz*. If you recall, she met her demise when Dorothy accidentally spilled some water on her. One wonders how the hell she could have avoided that fate for so long. Didn't the poor woman ever bathe or scrub potatoes?

The End of the Beginning

A guru might similarly ponder a seeker's ability to so cleverly evade the truth for decade upon decade, lifetime upon lifetime. Regretfully, I think it is safe to say that egos rarely, if ever, cease to exist in the speedy fashion that Dorothy's nemesis did. Typically they resist coming to their senses until the bitter end—clawing and scratching all the way. Giving up from extreme fatigue, if nothing else. Or else disappearing, much like in the case of Eckhart Tolle, when one experiences prolonged, overwhelming suffering, which leads to utter despair and finally the dissolution of the ego. This *flipping-on* of the enlightenment switch may be permanent, or an individual may once again start to identify with the egoic state of being when the crisis has passed. This back and forth seesawing of, *I got it—I lost it—I got it*—can go on for some time.

Given time, I began to sense with ever greater surety that my mother was indeed on to something. But not surprisingly, I managed to pervert her message in one critical way. Rather than scrutinizing the specific nature of my own being, by taking a long hard look to confirm if I indeed did not exist as she stated, I instead I concentrated on the entirety of reality in general. was fundamentally *fake* in kind of misrepresentation like what occurred with Vuitton Bags and Rolexes alley black markets of Seoul, I had the impression that it some regard. That some was going on. Very much the cheaply priced Louis I used to spot in the back- South Korea.

Perhaps life was like an unimaginably super-sophisticated, virtual reality generator, and for some reason I had elected to engage in it. Like a video game box set which had the title *Reality 1.0* emblazoned on the DVD dust jacket. That would imply that everything was a simulation except, of course, for me. After all, it was quite obvious who was at the controls, I assured myself. Maybe this artifice was just a little R&R distraction I was enjoying as an intergalactic traveller aboard some spaceship's holodeck, as the *Star Trek* series would have it. Perhaps it was some kind of test, like running the gauntlet, which I needed to pass in order to progress up the karmic ladder.

There seemed to be some goal or purpose to this game, but its exact nature eluded me. There was a sense of an *I* that had pitted itself against this game and was seeking some kind of favourable outcome. It was pretty easy to buy into the premise that all objective reality was illusion. Never for a second did it follow that I must be incorporeal as well. I attribute this inconsistency purely to personal delusion. You can believe a lot of things in this life but entertaining the notion that you do not actually exist is apparently not one of them. Some years later, while I continued down this *spiritual cul-de-sac*, it occurred to me to test out the *all is illusion* hypothesis with a little practical experimentation.

I had hoped that the immediate outcome to the experiment would have been akin to throwing a monkey wrench into the reality generator. Something similar to a master proffering a Zen koan, as in *what is the sound of one hand clapping,* to a monk. The anticipated result of such koan practice being that sooner or later all hell would break loose in the student's mind. Like the mythical sci-fi robot that starts to emit smoke from its head as it fries its internal logic circuit board when given a problem that has no logical solution.

To this end, one day I approached my wife, and in all sincerity, simply asked whether or not *she was actually real.* In retrospect I see the absurd humour of such a query. At the time I hoped that she would somehow be obliged to tip her hat and slyly admit, "Well, yes honey, we are all just jerking your chain, because, as you so correctly surmised, none of this is actually real." Unfortunately neither admissions of that nature nor general system crashes were forthcoming that day. I never dared repeat that particular experiment again, because, as anyone would expect, it elicited a rather terse reaction from my partner. Something along the lines of, "You're kidding me right ...? Oh come on get serious .... What's the joke?" When pressed further, she dryly commented that, well yes, she did indeed exist, and if I required tangible proof she was more than happy to prove it by giving my ass a good kicking. You can't fault a guy for trying ....

A lot of my time and effort was spent exploring non-mainstream viewpoints of reality. Books on cutting-edge science, or those of a mystical, esoteric, philosophical or New Age slant, attracted my attention. Also alternative sources of news and information were consulted for differing viewpoints than those typically offered in traditional media outlets. Such issues involving military, political and corporate wielding of power were of prime interest. Always in the back of my mind was the burning question—just who or what was actually guiding human affairs? I was not drawn to mystical contemplation alone. Understanding the actual day-to-day realities of how power and influence were created, shared and ultimately wielded was equally of interest.

The End of the Beginning

Freedom was one of the things that I valued most, so I guess I wanted to figure out where my liberties were being challenged, eroded or completely curtailed. Of even greater importance was truth. Yet they are intrinsically related aren't they? Consider the Biblical quote, "And ye shall know the truth, and the truth shall make you free" (John 8:32), for a reminder of this.

Once I broached this subject and carried out even a cursory examination of the material, it was clearly evident that the world was a far different place than it appeared on the surface. I was compelled to get to the bottom of the mass manipulation and subterfuge that was clearly going on. I wanted the truth—good, bad or indifferent. I followed thousands of leads, never caring where they sent me as long as I felt they were helping divulge the truth.

In that regard, I found out that politicians were little more than elected figureheads. They appeared to be essentially puppets of special interest groups or groups beholden to fantastically powerful individuals. The military and corporations similarly misrepresented reality to suit their own idiosyncratic needs. Public relations shills were constantly at work guiding the masses' perceptions in whatever direction the powers-that-be desired. But just what was it that these people were working so hard to obscure and distort?

Understanding matters related to the global octopus of power brokers, now commonly referred to as the *Illuminati*, was, like their namesake, certainly illuminating. I sought out non-mainstream information sources, like the once very popular Art Bell talk show or Jeff Rense's long-running talk show and Internet presence.

The subject matter these alternative forums explored was eclectic and worthy of my consideration. Some of it was too *far out* or *fringy* for my tastes, but lots of great nuggets could be discovered. Discovering how the power brokers operated was a very eye-opening endeavour. I learned to discern the difference between a wacky conspiracy theorist and a sober-minded conspiracy researcher. Slowly the puzzle pieces began to fall into place. The news was rather bleak. Dark forces appeared to be at work and certainly the interests of common folk were not forefront. Milton Friedman, one of the most highly influential economists, political commentators and defenders of capitalism of the last century, stated that the world was run by individuals pursuing their separate interests and that greed was God—oops—I meant good.

He further informed us that the world was primarily run by economic self-interest and that this was a fine thing indeed. Judging by the current state of world affairs I beg to differ. Society has been running in this fashion since the power structure of egalitarian tribalism was abandoned in favour of an institutionalized, self-serving, cultural hegemony. Power continually accrues to the rich and the influential while the masses suffer disenfranchisement. Nothing new here folks. Just go to any alternative news source (you know, the places that report what is actually going on), and one can always find something along the following headline picked up from "Progressive Radio Network" dated June 18, 2010:"Oval Office Duplicity—Cover For Corporate Criminality." Or occasionally even the *lame-stream* press, like the *British Telegraph*, which ran the following headline dated June 26, 2010, "Canada's chief spy: foreign powers control country's politicians."

Throughout the ages power brokering has varied in degrees but not kind. The American writer, Robert Anton Wilson, succinctly summed it all up in a talk he gave a few years back, entitled, "The Universe Contains a Maybe," when he said of the powers that be, "We all know the bastards are lying to us!"

The power brokers have become very sophisticated in their ability to manipulate public perceptions in their bid to obscure their true motives. Though things are not very different now than from the times of Machiavelli, as portrayed in *The Prince*, written in 1513. This political primer examines the acquisition, perpetuation and wielding of political power as a means to acquire or maintain the throne. The ideas presented in that treatise are still as relevant today as ever. However, one must largely substitute corporate power for political hegemony if one is to better understand where influence truly lies today. We do indeed live in the age of the all- powerful *Corporatocracy*.

What I am referring to here are non-governmental organizations. Those private affiliations that actually run the show for the most part. These may be in the guise of American think tanks like Project for the New American Century (promulgating greater American hegemony through militarism in the Middle East, among other things) or other organizations like The Council on Foreign Relations or the Trilateral Commission. On the other hand they may be more global in nature like the Club of Rome or The Bilderberg Group. Regardless of their origin or sphere of influence, I was startled to find how much backroom manipulation was actually going on by these boys (indeed it seems to be a domain more suited to the male psyche) and how far they were willing to go to realize their vision of a *New World Order* (of which President Bush, Sr. was the first to speak openly). We are brought up to believe that we live in a democracy, but I found that this was not really the case at all.

Sure there is a semblance of choice but step out of line and you better watch out. Take the American Democratic and Republican parties for instance—different puppets, same puppet master. Recall Chinese Premier Deng Xiaoping's famous saying, "It doesn't matter if a cat is black or white so long as it catches mice." If you offered the illusion of choice you could keep the sheeple relatively contented.

It seemed that power had accrued to a very few organizations, corporations and families. They were keen on keeping it and were actually the ones calling the shots, for the most part. We, on the other hand, were nothing but "useless eaters" (ascribed to Henry Kissinger as his description of humanity in general). Or "landless peasant fucks," as I have described by an Internet in a nutshell, is what I precludes me from going you will. Doing this kind of to anyone with an open mind, heard the British populace media commentator. That, found. Space and interest any further. Make of it what research will demonstrate and the cognitive ability to adequately analyze the information presented, the simple fact that the world is not at all as it may appear from just a cursory glance of today's top newspaper *headlies*.

Growing up on a beef farm, I grew accustomed to the yearly slaughter of a steer to help stock the family's larder. This unavoidable ritual was a grim reality of farm life. While never being a pleasant undertaking, that experience was surely preferable to the *sacred cows* I found falling by the wayside during my continuing research. Things I held onto as pretty much fact turned out to be not quite so. The peak oil scare turned out to be way overstated. The supply of oil was being artificially controlled and was actually in far greater supply than was officially claimed. Man-made *global warming* was really *climate change* and it was debatable as to how much of it was actually due to mankind's influence. The list grew such that I found I could put faith in very little. Duplicity abounded everywhere, if only one cared to look. There seemed to be no place where I could hang my hat and call it a day. Eventually this avenue of investigation started to feel pointless. Where did it all ultimately lead? Could anything be clearly deduced? If so, was it really important? This kind of research seemed merely to point to symptoms of some greater malaise. Any healer knows that once the symptoms have been identified, it is to the core illness that the doctor must attend. What the heck was going on here? Just what kind of *illness* was humanity suffering from?

Perfect Storm

Unbeknownst to me at the time, a *perfect spiritual storm* had begun to foment. Slowly but surely all the key factors were dropping into place. It created conditions such that I would eventually be compelled to flee my surroundings and seek *refuge*. This particular refuge would eventually take the form of a Buddhist retreat centre where meditation was taught and *dharma* shared. Dharma (the teachings) being one of the three *jewels* one accepts, or *takes refuge in*, when seriously taking up the path of Buddhism. The other two are the Buddha and the *sangha* (spiritual community).

In some sense, the impetus for setting out on my spiritual journey began several years before I was moved to do so. One day a thought popped into my head quite out of the blue. I was out working in the vegetable garden when this rather odd question suddenly formulated itself quite unrelated to anything I was thinking about at the time. It simply asked, "If you wanted to become enlightened, would you actually give up all your wants and desires to do so?" After a moment I took this question to mean, *would you exchange all of your material possessions (contents of my humble farm home) for enlightenment?*

This took me completely by surprise. Nothing like this had ever occurred to me before. I had no idea where it came from. It seemed to allude to the Buddhist idea of spiritual awakening, a topic I knew virtually nothing about. I certainly had not been doing any kind of recent spiritual research related to this area that might help explain the origin of this odd question.

I laid down my hoe, brought the brim of my cap down to cut out the harsh noon-day sun and pondered just what was being asked of me. The tone of the question was serious and seemed to desire a thoughtful response, but I was confused.

I remember initially thinking, *where the heck did that notion come from, I never said I wanted to be enlightened in the first place.* I didn't really even know what the term meant. Not much beyond the stereotypically silly notions that once enlightenment arose, it provided one access to cosmic consciousness and never-ending bliss, while at the same time making the avatar omniscient, morally superior and infallible. Somewhere along the way I developed a notion that in order to become enlightened all one had to do was *give up all wants and desires.* That was essentially all I knew about the subject and, of course, it turned out to be completely erroneous. Fundamentally the question seemed to be addressing materialism and its relationship to enlightenment and my possible desire to engage in some kind of spiritual practice.

In a conventional sense, I am pretty much a *failed* materialist at heart. Despite the constant media bombardment to consume, I don't buy into it. I am loath to purchase brand-name goods of any sort and by preference most of my clothing is pre-owned. I found the happiness that material things brought me to be fleeting at best. I never entered into the status game of identifying myself with my acquisitions. I recognized long ago that I was much more than the sum total of all the goods I managed to accumulate. A car was no more than a mode of transport. Yet I did indeed acquire things.

These possessions were predominantly objects of creative or artistic expression and beauty. Things wrought by my own hand or else collected here and there during my travels. The majority being art objects and curios picked up during my trips and residency in Asia. None were of great value, yet these objects brought some measure of wonder and joy to my soul.

Every wall and free space of the small cabin was jam-packed with the stuff. Paintings and other graphic art forms were liberally sprinkled everywhere. Chinese landscapes, Japanese ink blocks, Korean mother-of-pearl inlays, Thai silk paintings, Tibetan thangka and Burmese sequin-studded tapestries adorned almost all available wall space. Antique Asian furniture was scattered about and display shelves and cases were packed with such things as teak carvings, lacquer ware, ceramics and a collection of Japanese dolls. The substantial Buddha collection stands out in my mind for its serene beauty and ability to encapsulate the exoticism of the Far East. I was not a Buddhist, nor knew anything about the religion. Perhaps I collected these in anticipation of my spiritual journey yet to come or from those long past. This urge to acquire beautiful things that brought joy to my heart was actually a bit of an obsession.

My CD and book collection was highly treasured as well. On top of all this stuff were the things that I had created over the years, like videos, photos, woodworking projects, screen plays etc. That then is a quick catalogue of the kind of materialism that *possessed* me. These things did indeed reflect my *wants and desires*. Was I really a closet materialist? I think the question that was posed to me proved that I was. Would it be possible to willingly exchange all of my treasures for enlightenment? The very fact that I didn't say, "Hell yeah!" immediately, spoke volumes. Yet a definite, "No," was not forthcoming either. Rare was the occasion that I was at a loss for a quick opinion.

To this day I have no idea what generated that question. Perhaps it was a case of precognition or maybe it bubbled up from my subconscious. Maybe it didn't originate from me at all. I considered the question for a while but had no serious inclination to entertain it. It simply drifted away into the ether unanswered. Though if pressed for a reply, gun to head as it were, I expect the answer would have been "No." After all, I did not have a clue what enlightenment meant. I had never even considered that a possibility for myself. In fact quite the opposite was the case.

I reckoned I had way too much shit to work out in this lifetime to ever be rewarded with that *special state*, known as *enlightenment*. In reality it turns out it is neither special, nor a state. It's something that has always existed; you just have never had occasion to notice it before. This illustrates my utter ignorance of the subject at the time. Trade all of my treasures for some kind of unarticulated, nebulous, airy fairy promise of future salvation—not bloody likely. But I guess leaving the barn door slightly ajar was significant. I certainly hadn't dismissed the whole notion of enlightenment outright. That would prove important later on. Leaving the implications of this question for now, let us fast forward to approximately a year later. Things were not looking entirely rosy.

I had spent several years employed as a corrections officer. This occupation proved to be quite stressful. Prisons are not inherently joyful places to be for any length of time. To make matters worse, I developed a severely debilitating case of sciatica during this time. I had suffered from a lower back problem for years but sciatica was a whole new level of pain. No amount of medication could mitigate the pain enough to be bearable. I just had to learn to live with it. I have always been quite stoic in nature, and I think my years of martial arts training were helpful in this regard.

After about eight months, the sciatica stabilized somewhat. Things were looking up. I had just completed the training required to become a parole officer. I was being transferred to a new institution where, in all likelihood, I would never have to walk a prison range nor count another prisoner again. My new digs would be an office with university grads for peers. How wonderful! Life though seemed to have other plans ....

Behind the scenes the spiritual storm had been gathering strength and meteorological forecasting had it headed my way — fast. Though like those really destructive hurricanes of the past, its exact speed, ferocity and arrival date were not completely apparent. There I was, in the serene eye of the storm, quite oblivious to it all. It would take several more years before I suffered the complete brunt of its ferocity. As the back pain continued to diminish, an even more debilitating disease struck.

Just as I was literally about to sign the paperwork assigning me to a new correctional institution, I was diagnosed with a career-ending medical problem. It turned out to be a rare eye disease that would rob me of my vision and livelihood. Had the paperwork been signed, the Canadian government would have been obligated to accommodate me for the rest of my working career. I missed that opportunity by about a week. The timing couldn't have been worse. The disease was chronic and irreversible.

It seems that, from mucking out the chicken coop as a youngster, I picked up a rather malevolent pathogen, a fungus found in bird or bat droppings. In most cases it creates minor flu-like symptoms. In something like 3-5 percent of all cases, secondary symptoms strike decades later, leading to a profound vision loss. As a kid, I went through a year of a chronic hacking cough. It eventually subsided without treatment. I didn't realize at the time what the problem was. Now it was all quite clear. It is amazing how things can change in an instant.

Perfect Storm

Struck down in my prime with no forewarning at all. Buddha always stressed the impermanent nature of all things. It is instances like these that really drive that concept home. There I was, still suffering from back pain with the added burden of failing eyesight and no job, and then things took a turn for the worse.

I started to get laser treatments to slow down my vision loss. Within half a year from the first treatment my wife and I split up. This was a huge blow. We had been running a farm venture together as a sideline business, so of course that was no longer possible. I was left with bank payments, a modest disability income, my cottage and little else. Yet I was surprisingly unperturbed by all of this. As I recall, I did have a short-lived, minor bout of depression. That was the first and last occurrence of such a state. I didn't seem to have a natural affinity for hanging out there long. Frustration and stress were obviously present. Suffering such a profound and rapid change in my circumstances certainly elevated cortisol levels to new heights, let me tell you. My response, though, was to treat the experience like any another challenge life had thrown at me. I kept things in perspective and stayed positive. I avoided falling victim to lamenting my bad luck or grovelling in self-pity. I am not a complainer by nature. I saw victimhood as a lifestyle choice.

As my spiritual guide, American Zen/Advaita teacher Adyashanti, has pointed out many times, "There may be pain, but suffering is always optional." Certainly my life had been drastically changed. It sucked, but what could I do? Things were the way things were. Nothing would change that fact so getting upset about it was rather futile. Resistance to reality only made it worse. It was around this time that, once again, a question came to me, shot like a lightning bolt out of the mysterious dark ether.

The same question as previously posed arose once again. I recognized it as that common little voice in the back of all our heads, but it was a little more direct and pointed. It again wondered if I would be willing to give up all my material possessions contained in my humble cottage in exchange for enlightenment. Geez what was up with this questioning presence and why the same asinine question again, I wondered? Again I demurred from directly addressing the question. Enlightenment was about the furthest thing from my mind at that point.

With my wife's departure I found myself almost entirely alone. No close family members remained in my life and friends were few and far between. There was little for me to actually do due to the limits resulting from my disability. The future looked quite grim, but it turned out that there was even farther to fall. You never truly plumb the bottom of the barrel until the jackboot presses firmly on the side of your neck, forcing you to scrape the bottom clean with the tip of your tongue. At the time, I would have doubted the possibility that there was any farther to fall. When you get to the point where you believe, *well, surely there is no way but up now,* be advised to take into account the *wiggle factor*. There's always that little bit of unaccounted wiggle room left. Just enough space to allow you to continue to deny reality. It was just a matter of time before that other shoe dropped. And drop it did, with a most resounding thud. Yep … my damn cottage burned down to the ground.

I could see it coming a mile away—literally. That is about how far away I was when I first noticed the rising smoke plume. Driving closer, the ascending smoke became much more impressive at the half-mile mark. I turned to the driver and remarked, "Look, that's my house on fire."

After noting the smoke herself she said, "No, it can't be." She thought I was kidding. I assured her I wasn't. She said, "How can you be sure?" There were several buildings on the farm it could have been, but I knew which one was aflame. Any dummy could recognize when the other shoe had fallen.

Arriving at the scene I got out of the car and the first thing I did was go over to her side and say, "Hey why don't you take my picture?"

Looking down at the camera on the seat beside her she turned and said haltingly, "Whaaat … what are you talking about?"

I said, "Yeah, go ahead and take it."

She looked at me in confusion.

"Don't you get it?" I said, "This is the face of a guy who has just lost everything."

I said this with a sense of levity and this confused her even more. In fact, at that moment I found the whole situation quite surreal and in some ways pretty darn funny. I have never seen the resultant snapshot, but I bet I have a pretty big goofy grin plastered across my face.

Like tears in the rain, not a trace remained of my prized possessions, save for the memories. I can't say that I was that taken aback. I had gone through so much; I just didn't have any extra energy to waste on the usual histrionics. Wailing and gnashing my teeth never occurred to me. Once again, what purpose would it serve? The fire department must have thought my lack of emotion odd, particularly as I had no insurance.

This was not the first residential fire I had experienced. When I was a youngster, the family farmstead was partially destroyed by fire. Then there was the conflagration I survived in Japan that left me with second and third degree burns to about 25 percent of my body.

At this point I bet some of you are inclined to think, My what lousy luck this guy has had. He must have accrued some pretty terrible karma to deserve all of this crap. I assure you quite the opposite is true.

Perhaps not immediately, but certainly in retrospect, I have recognized these experiences to be highly rewarding opportunities indeed. It may sound cliché but it is true—we grow from experiencing life's adversities. Using a little farm analogy here, shit is a repulsive thing if viewed as a smelly, repugnant waste product. Looked at another way, it makes terrific fertilizer that helps sustain billions of people and can even be used to run your car. Some people recognize this fact. Where do you think the term, *that's good shit*, arose from?

Ram Dass, the American spiritual writer, wrote a whole book devoted to this idea called *Grist for the Mill*. This title refers to the more difficult aspects of life and how it could be seen as a kind of curriculum or viewed as karmic yoga. I certainly came to appreciate whatever life had to offer up, because I learned through experience that at any moment everything could disappear in a flash. *We don't know what we've got till it's gone,* as we hear in the familiar Joni Mitchell refrain. It is through life's most difficult challenges that one becomes grateful for small mercies and the simpler things in life. What doesn't kill you makes you wiser. It's all grist for the mill.

A week or so after the fire, once the smoke had cleared so to speak, I remember thinking, "Well I'll be darned, losing everything really changes nothing at all." I couldn't see any way that I fundamentally differed presently as compared to before the fire. It seemed like *I*, the core aspect of DJ, had lost absolutely nothing at all. Apparently losing so much—my spouse, my health and my wealth—had not diminished *me* in the least. "What could this possibly mean?" I wondered. I was mystified.

A Fleeting Improvised Man

Later, though, I learned that, when seen from the viewpoint of our true nature, there is nothing at all that can possibly be lost. How can you lose anything when everything is one; when you are in fact everything? What is there to be diminished? As the basic scientific principle goes, *Matter can be neither created nor destroyed, just changed from one form to another.*

Of course, the answer to the question that posed itself to me several times previously no longer needed to be considered. I hadn't consciously chosen to shed all of my possessions, a simple woodstove accident took care of that, but nonetheless they were gone. It wasn't so bad. Not at all like what I imagined. In fact I eventually came to see it as a kind of blessing. How free my life had become. Unencumbered by almost everything one conventionally valued, it was stripped down to its simplest nature. If nothing else, with the cottage now gone, I was afforded an unobstructed view across a wide verdant meadow of the glorious morning sunrise. How fortunate I was!

Upon hearing of the consequences of the fire my friend, who once described me as the only guy he knew who would be happy to live in a fox hole, turned his attention towards the weird question that posed itself to me several times. He said, "But don't you see, it's come to pass. For the most part your attachments, wants and desires have been obliterated. You have nothing else left to lose! What is holding you back now from seeking enlightenment as the question suggested?"

What a ridiculous line of reasoning. And what nerve ... how dare he suggest that I had nothing at all left to lose? Surely this could not be true. Of course I had things, I assured myself. My ego was certainly in denial over this reality check. When I honestly looked at it though, I could see he was correct. There was no way that I could continue to deny the fact that I didn't have a job, home, good health, possessions, a family or much of anything else at all.

With that the spiritual storm finally struck home. Its full fury was upon me. There was no longer any wiggle room left for denial. Though I didn't immediately act, or even know I was going to act, it was too late—I was hooked. It was now only a matter of time before I set out on a spiritual quest.

Preparation

For some reason I decided to get into the best shape of my life. I don't mean lose a few pounds or firm up the old biceps a bit. Since high school I had sporadically weight-trained. Now I intended to get serious about it. Where the impetus originated I was not sure. The motivation to transform my body was very strong. I dedicated the next two years to pursuing a strength and conditioning regimen. I learned everything I could about the philosophy, science and practice of gaining muscle and losing fat. I approached this enterprise as I did my future call to enlightenment. I checked out common wisdom and if it didn't jibe with my own inner intuition and inclination, I ignored it. For example my goal was to lose weight and gain muscle mass at the same time. Many experts advised this was impossible. You could never gain muscle while losing weight. First lose the weight then work on the muscle by lifting heavy weights and eating well. I reckoned this was nonsense and proved this was so.

I undertook a routine that completely exhausted me every day. Sunday was the only day of rest since at least one full recuperation day was required per week. If I could have cut it out, I would have. To lose the weight, a severe diet was imposed. Breakfast was just tea. A soya shake for lunch and high-protein, low-fat, low-carb dinner finished off the day. I repeated this every day of the week but Sunday when I enjoyed a carbohydrate-rich dinner. I suffered constant headaches for the first few months due to the poor diet and gruelling daily workout. Feeling lousy was a great aid for appetite suppression.

I persevered with the fifteen hours per week fitness regimen, lift after lift, set after set, hour after hour, day after day and week after week; working through the ever constant pain. Bedtime was a welcome respite from the discomfort and fatigue. By the end of seven weeks of this gruelling punishment, I was utterly exhausted. I learned that it was necessary to schedule a week of recuperation every eighth week. If not, I would become a complete physical wreck, which had been the original outcome of pushing myself too hard in the beginning.

Two years on I had lost seventy pounds of fat and gained back about twenty in muscle. I could now bicep curl over 100 pounds on the straight bar. The old warrior was back in fighting shape once again. My strength improved and aerobic fitness substantially increased. What a mental and physical tonic this exercise proved to be. My mind became clearer and uplifted, while chronic aches and pains were reduced substantially. The back pain lessened, and my knee pain went away entirely. On the down side I developed a very painful case of tendinitis in my forearms due to very heavy bicep curls.

So why have I described this? What could weight training have to do with enlightenment? I wanted to give you an idea of what kind of physical preparation I underwent prior to setting out on my journey. First get the body in shape, then the mind will follow. I also want you to understand something else. The fact is that the years I dedicated to physical fitness didn't come close to the level of fortitude, dedication and perseverance I found necessary to make headway spiritually. As they say, "You should desire enlightenment as intensely as a drowning man wants air." My first two weeks spent on a cushion in formal silent meditation were by far the single most difficult thing I ever did in my life!

While getting in shape, the thought of a taking a trip occasionally came to mind, but it was not clear where, or even if, I would go. I had always been drawn to adventure travel but had not gone anywhere for ten years or so. My eye disease precluded any sort of future travel of this nature. I think during this period I gave a cursory thought to going to some kind of spiritual venue like a retreat centre. Buddhism intrigued me. Occasionally I would get on the Internet and see what was available in Canada. But that option was only one of several possibilities I considered. I once spotted an advertisement for a small retreat centre that was fairly new and situated in a picturesque natural setting near the ocean. Something about it resonated for me. Nothing, though, was clearly apparent in my mind. At the same time that I was devoting much time to fitness, a new interest developed around acquiring survival skills. For awhile it was a real passion.

Living on a farm necessarily required a certain understanding of rustic life skills and the ability to be self-reliant. You wouldn't believe the wonders I could work with a little black wire, duct tape and some hose clamps. Money was always short so frugality and self-sufficiency were a part of life. The Y2K scare caused me to consider more deeply the possibility of making do with only the barest of essentials over a long time-span. How would society fare if thrown back to a less technologically advanced age? This new interest of mine differed in that it only focused on the lone individual's need for short-term survival.

My new interest involved learning the skills required to extricate yourself from immediate, short-term, life-threatening situations; for example, suddenly finding yourself unexpectedly stranded in the Canadian wilderness, with no provisions to speak of. The desert or jungle were equally challenging environments to consider. Just how did one make fire by primitive means? How about other essentials like finding shelter or procuring water or food? There was a tremendous amount to learn in this area. Eventually I felt there was at least the possibility that I could survive in the woods with little more than a knife. It was a fascinating field of research, as was the related field of ultra lightweight backpacking.

I learned that huge gains in compact lightweight camping/hiking equipment had been made since I was a kid, but more importantly, there was a new ethos that delighted me. Ultra lightweight backpacking had come into its own. If one desired to commune with nature, this was a much more natural method to use. One worked with, rather than against, the wilderness. It required a mindset that embraced the notion that less was more. Creature comforts were foregone to get the pack weight down to around an astonishingly light ten pounds, excluding food and water. That was an amazing figure!

Surprisingly, I found the time I spent acquiring survival skills a helpful aid to spiritual awakening. At first glance they seem quite unrelated don't they? Actually that broaches a key concept involving the ego and its preoccupation with issues of its survival.

It seems humans are motivated by two main drives—the drive to feel safe and secure and the drive to enjoy oneself. What propels humanity forward is not much more complicated than that. From those two primary drives spring forth all other subsequent ones. But there is a problem here and it is one of limits. The human condition seems incapable of ever finding any.

Humanity exists in a perpetually unsatiated state. How many among us can claim that we have experienced a sufficient level of security and enjoyment such that it mitigated the chronic feelings of displeasure, discontentment and dissatisfaction we all have endured throughout the entirely of our lives. Sure there are brief moments of fleeting ease, but soon a new desire arises and we're off to the races once again. The human condition seems to be such that all of us are inexorably driven to seek just a wee bit more. The reality of this situation is really quite insane. It brings to mind Mr. Creosote, a satirical character in Monty Python's movie, *Monty Python's The Meaning of Life*. This truly larger-than-life figure is presented as a tremendously obese man with an obscenely compulsive eating disorder. In fact, he is incapable of stopping himself. His demise comes when he elects to consume just one final after dinner mint which causes him to promptly explode. It's all terribly amusing in characteristic Monty Python fashion. Buddhist psychology might very well describe Mr. Creosote as a *hungry ghost*. That is the mythological creature that sported withered limbs and a grossly bloated belly, perpetually gripped by unfulfilled cravings and insatiable demands. Of course, by wider abstraction, so are we all.

It seems that no matter how much care and effort is expended in favourably securing one's situation, fear and doubt remain. A perpetually vulnerable feeling is the norm. The issue of genetic survival, that is, survival of the species as a whole, is perhaps foremost. These concerns are largely subconscious.

Similarly, there are personal and familial needs which one must constantly attend to. By further extrapolation you could also include the welfare of one's homeland. Despite whatever advantage one accrues in any of these areas, ultimately it is always found lacking. And if it is not, the mind will simply invent problems to give you something else to fixate upon.

Thus endless thoughts arise such as: I never get enough sex, we are a persecuted minority, my country is being threatened by an external enemy, my job is not prestigious enough or too tenuous, the neighbourhood is dangerous, my bank account is not large enough, my health is poor, she/he doesn't really love/understand me, to cite but a few. I am sure you can add several dozen of your own. Given a moment to reflect, I think most will recognize that the drive to improve one's lot in life is insatiable. It's a plain fact that the day will never come when you finally say, "Yes I see it, I finally have enough, I can now relax as I feel completely safe, secure and happy. There's nothing left that needs doing." It just ain't gonna happen folks. Never. Isn't that bizarre? So how does all this relate to my foray into the survival field?

Simply put, I think learning to live on very little enabled me to pretty much determine what the limits of human survival are. I mean, being able to actually determine, in a practical, experiential manner, just how little is required to actually keep the old heart ticking, with enough comfort to avoid feeling totally miserable. This kind of investigation will reveal quantifiable limits. Rather than trying to determine when enough is enough (which is impossible) I found out when too little is too little. It's interesting to discover how few resources one truly needs to furnish the basic necessities of life. It seemed that once the core of my being became aware of that fact, it relaxed a bit and fear and stress went way down. With less striving and an acceptance of things as they were, I found life rather sweet with or without all the creature comforts at hand. Things pretty much took care of themselves given half the chance. Instead of constantly expending huge amounts of energy striving to avoid danger and discomfort, I found myself much more open to everything existence had to offer. The good, the bad and the indifferent. As Henry David Thoreau, noted American author and transcendentalist wrote, "When a dog runs at you, whistle for him."

Acceptance includes the Buddha's admonishment that we must wholeheartedly embrace the fact that everything is impermanent. Having your mortality confronted works wonders with fear and freedom which, of course, are mirror opposites of one another. As any true warrior can attest, absolute fearlessness begets absolute freedom. Using several vignettes from my own life, I now hope to demonstrate the rather liberating qualities of confronting one's own mortality, up close and personal, as it were.

Life Revealing Itself

Along the path to discovering the truth of Buddha's words, "All conditioned things are impermanent," I experienced several skirmishes with death. For example, I fell through a half-frozen river as a child. This scared the heck out of my grandmother. She brought me inside and got some hot chocolate inside me. After recuperating for awhile she asked me how I was doing. I told her there was no longer any need for concern as I felt fine. She said that was wonderful. She was so pleased that I had made such a speedy recovery that she wrapped her arms around me in a comforting big hug. Aren't grandmothers just the best ever? Once I had made a full recovery she then spent the next fifteen minutes taking a strip off of my hide, reminding me over and over how she had quite clearly warned me not to venture out onto the half-frozen body of water, how my behaviour was totally unacceptable and how she was now reticent to take me anywhere ever again. Aren't grandmothers just the biggest bitches ever?

I guess my proclivity for risk-taking had already emerged by then. Years later it was *déjà vu all over again* as I and my snowmobile went crashing through a half-frozen pond. My full body snowmobile suit quickly filled with icy water, like a kid preparing a balloon water bomb. Surviving several different house fires also comes to mind. I once had a race with a huge crashing maple tree I had just felled with a chainsaw. I found out they fall remarkably fast—especially if you are underneath one trying to outrun it. Furthermore I found that given the proper motivation, even husky men can be pretty fleet of foot. It was a near photo finish with DJ finishing by a toe. The huge crown of the sixty-foot behemoth brushed my ankles in the last moments, as I made a final desperate sprawling dive to safety. Sprawling is also an apt description of my body on another occasion when it was blown backwards from a gas explosion. In that case most of my eyebrows were removed, but, other than that, I was none the worse for wear.

There were more harrowing brushes, like experiencing a serious car crash that totalled the vehicle and could have resulted in the deaths of several people. I was a passenger in the front seat of a station wagon that was completely filled with farm produce ready for market. There was also a driver and another passenger. We got out early just before sunrise on a fog enshrouded highway and the tire blew at full highway speed. The car careened and spun wildly around then seemed like it was about to tumble down a steep embankment. Fortunately it was instead restrained by a roadside steel cable barrier. The car slid along the cable, snapping off posts as it went. In so doing, the cable rose higher and higher. Much like a wire sawblade or huge garrotte, it eventually started to slice into the windshield, almost decapitating the driver in the process. The wrecked car finally ended up back on the highway, completely impeding the flow of traffic, as it was now perpendicular to the highway. I was not injured so yelled for the occupants to flee the vehicle while they had the chance, but they were immobilized with shock. Sensing an imminent catastrophe I dashed out of the car and ran down the highway far enough to flag down an oncoming transport truck. Alerted, the driver managed to slam on the air brakes and stop just in the nick of time, with barely enough space for me to slip between the truck's front grill and the driver's door of the demolished car. Lucky thing, as the driver was still there behind the wheel, gripped with fear.

Later, when I had a moment to congratulate the truck driver, I asked him how in God's name he had managed to see me through the thick fog. He stated that he didn't actually *see me*, which was not surprising given the fact that the sun had only just risen and the fog was as thick as oatmeal porridge. Instead he said that something caught his attention, he wasn't sure what (perhaps my frantically waving arms), and peering through the miasma he reckoned something was just *not quite right* and he needed to stop. He said he was rather shocked to find himself coming to a halt in front of a car. He lit several flares and the danger passed. It was amazing that, while the car was a write-off, no one was injured. I remember having a strange sort of out-of-body experience while the car was crashing around. Time definitely slowed down and there was a sense of calmness and peace. It was like I was a witness to everything that was going on, but it wasn't really happening to me. Once the car came to rest, I knew instantly what had to be done. There was a strong sense of clarity and calmness to the whole drama.

No less serious in potential danger was the time I ended up on a mountain top, in freezing weather, wearing only a light windbreaker, t-shirt, shorts and running shoes. To make it even more dire, I had to survive the entire night up there without any kind of shelter or sleeping bag. I really wonder how I managed to get myself into such predicaments. This certainly was one of the more asinine ones. I can assure you that that kind of experience really clarified what was truly important. While sitting on that dark, barren, windswept mountain top staving off hypothermia and suffering from dehydration, all I could think of all night was how wonderful it would be to be back home in bed, snuggled up with a nice comforter and a cup of hot chocolate. It's wonderful how these experiences bring what is truly important to the fore.

There was also the time I elected to cross the wild interior portion of a tropical Japanese island on foot. When I lived in Japan (primarily for film and martial arts purposes), I preferred to holiday as far away from Tokyo as possible. My spirit was lifted greatly whenever I left this huge sprawling centre. The beauty of Japan's traditional architecture and its natural landscapes was varied and charming. Japanese folk seemed to be much more welcoming and soulful the farther away from Tokyo I managed to get. It was this kind of refreshing tonic that I sought whenever possible.

The first such opportunity presented itself after I had been cooped up in Tokyo for eight intolerable months after first leaving the farm. During that time I saw no greenery to speak of. Can you imagine the toll this took on the psyche of someone accustomed to awakening to the sound of songbirds and the smell of freshly mown hay? Finally I had a chance to escape so I boarded a train to the countryside.

For the longest time, the train moved through bleak industrial wastelands and suburbs consisting of generic grey concrete apartment complexes. I was astonished at the vast expanses of this *zoo*. Then a smattering of open land mixed with less congested housing finally gave way to the countryside. Soon I was dazzled with the most intense emerald green colour I had ever beheld. A view of charming rice paddies presented itself through the window with a pleasant mountain vista serving as backdrop. I almost wept with joy. What a feast for my famished eyes.

I turned to the young American soldier seated beside me and asked him his impression of the wonder spread out before us. He saw only common agricultural land, with low nondescript hills in the background. Nothing special, he assured me. He'd seen it all a million times before. As for me, well I sat there spellbound, transfigured by something much greater than what my mere senses were registering. Call it what you will—Gaia, Spirit or the recognition of the Divine. Magnificence was beaming forth and the effect was sheer delight and wonder. By God, I was experiencing *Cezanne's carrot*! The painter had spoken of such a possibility, and here it was manifested before my very eyes.

Cezanne was specifically referring to perceiving things directly, not filtered by Vaseline coated lenses of conditioning, as though *through a glass darkly* as the Bible puts it. He admonished us to "Get to the heart of what is before you! The day is coming when a single carrot, freshly observed, will set off a revolution."

What he spoke of was not simply the superficial feelings that were commonly evoked when you saw a particularly beautiful sunset, a lovely mountain vista, a favourite rose or even a fetching man or woman. Rather, it was the pure essence that lies behind all of these things. Cezanne stressed that it didn't matter what you apprehended, as long as it was freshly observed, as though through a newborn's eyes; everything from the lowliest vegetable to a common agrarian rice field was equally imbued with the same marvellous quality. Cezanne pointedly referred to *the mystery* as the *heart* of the matter. Others call it Truth, or Reality. Seeing things as they really were. William Blake's poetic comment is equally relevant:

> To see a World in a Grain of Sand
> And a Heaven in a Wild Flower,
> Hold Infinity in the palm of your hand
> And Eternity in an hour.

The effect of this realization, if experienced deeply enough, can indeed be revolutionary. Depending on the quality of the experience, it may sometimes lead to the dissolution of long-held, conditioned beliefs, shatter paradigms and help ease one down the path to enlightenment. Though to be clear, what I experienced at that point was a mere foretaste of what Cezanne was alluding to. This could be termed a very minor awakening experience, not to be confused with being absolute Reality itself. Nevertheless it was a wonderful moment that I still hold near and dear to my heart. After all, it is always noteworthy when reality decides to peek out from under the obscuring veil of delusion—if only for a second.

My first prolonged holiday while in Japan was to an island known as Japan's *last frontier.* It carried that moniker for good reason. Fewer than 2,000 people inhabited it. It lacked an airstrip and the population was serviced by a partial ring road. About 80 percent of the land was state-protected jungle. You get the idea, a very pristine and undeveloped outpost of the former Ryukyu kingdom. This place was as far away from Tokyo as you could possibly get. In fact it was closer to China than to the main island.

I had heard a vague reference about the possibility of walking across the island from one shore to the other via a little-used trail. I could not confirm any details of this route while in Tokyo. Where it began, the condition of the trail and exactly how long the trip would take were a mystery. Nevertheless, I elected to travel to this little outpost via several ferries.

Once I arrived, I stayed at a youth hostel on the island and spent my time intelligence gathering. I still knew nothing of this supposed island trail. I could not figure out if the problems were a language barrier or something more serious, but a staff member I approached was completely mute on the topic of this trail. A few others I asked were equally unhelpful. Undaunted, I made plans to depart after I managed to find out where the trailhead began. Apparently a tour boat operator offered boat trips out to a waterfall that also served as the trailhead. That information was the bare minimum I needed to proceed.

When I asked the youth hostel manager if he would kindly look after my main backpack since I intended to travel with minimal gear, he refused. I rephrased the request given the possible Japanese/English language problem. Still he said it was not possible for the youth hostel to take responsibility for my bag. How odd I thought. Very unlike the Japanese penchant for politeness. Pushed for an explanation, he informed me it was very dangerous to undertake such an extreme trip, that in all likelihood I would end up dead and he wanted no part of it. He assured me that the terrain was very rugged, the path poorly marked and maintained. I could easily go astray. He explained further that if the famed wildcat, native only to this and several nearby islands, didn't get me then surely the extremely poisonous habu snake would. The jungle was full of danger, and he considered it foolhardy to consider such an undertaking. He stated forcefully that people had died trying to do so. I thought this was surely an overstatement. Subsequently I learned that, during WWII, several hundred Japanese civilians had been forced to relocate to the island and many had perished due to tropical diseases and bad water, among other reasons. For some reason this was just the kind of place I wanted to experience. In his poor English he just kept repeating, "You get hurt, you die, you get hurt," and then for emphasis in Japanese, *Hyaku pasento*. (100 percent) *Dame!* (impossible) It wasn't this sentiment that concerned me so much as all the extra gear I would be forced to lug around on my back if this guy remained intransigent about not taking my extra stuff. He never did reconsider, so in the end I had to haul about thirty extra pounds of gear around. Oh well, just an extra challenge to add to the mix. If that wasn't enough, an even further possible hindrance would be foisted upon me, which I was completely oblivious to until literally moments before setting foot upon the trailhead.

I should have been alerted that something was amiss when a strange character kept showing up at my door as I was packing. A van was to arrive mid-morning to take me to a boat and then on to the trailhead so I did not appreciate, nor understand, why this guy kept pestering me. Every so often he would appear with a question, which was unintelligible as he spoke little English, or to show some of his gear or a piece of clothing, etc. I was completely stumped as to his purpose. I just wanted to be left alone to finish my packing.

I had a similar interchange with this fellow the evening before, as a group of young Japanese hostellers and I sat around socializing. I explained the nature of my journey, and the fact that it would begin the following morning, to the one guy who could actually comprehend what I was saying. The group seemed interested as he translated my plan. From that point forward they mostly spoke Japanese and I sometimes nodded as if I could keep up with their conversation. For the most part I was oblivious to what they were talking about. It was apparent though that one guy was particularly interested and it turned out this was the same fellow who visited me in the morning. I thought he must be wishing me well, nothing more. I was further touched that he had elected to accompany me in the van and then the boat in order to bid me farewell. So I felt great shock and incredulity when, upon reaching the trailhead, he stepped out beside me. I asked what was up and someone explained to me that the previous night, apparently we had discussed the trip, and I consented to allow him to accompany me. Holy crap, how did that one escape me?

So that was what all the intrigue had been about. One thing that was perfectly clear was the fact that this chap was suffering from some kind of mental illness. He had a nervous tic and would occasionally blurt words out uncontrollably. His overall demeanour demonstrated an unsettled mind at work. I guess the *cosmic giggle* was up to its old tricks again.

After I learned his name, Mr. Keishi, and confirmed that he intended to accompany me for the whole trip, I simply accepted the situation, and off we went. He was of average height for a Japanese male and appeared to be in his early 30s. He stated that until recently he had been employed as a staff member at a hotel. His complexion was poor, hairline receding, but most pronounced was his skeletal frame. He was almost as thin as the chopsticks he carried in his pack. These he required for his instant ramen noodles—practically the only thing he consumed during the entire trip.

It is with a sense of irony that I now reflect upon the content of writer Joseph Conrad's novel, *Heart of Darkness*, and film director Francis Ford Coppola's later retelling in *Apocalypse Now* and compare those tales to my own trip down the river. There I was about to step into the bowels of the primordial jungle, just like the book and film's main protagonist did, but rather than eventually discover the mentally deranged Kurtz, which I recall occurred quite late in the movie, I was to start the adventure with him by my very side. That made for an interesting plot twist indeed!

True to the manager's words, it turned out to be a rather difficult trekking environment. Tangled, dense undergrowth obscured the poorly marked trail. Large blood-sucking leeches continually fixed themselves to exposed patches of skin and somehow, from time to time, even managed to slide down to one's nether regions. I attempted to remedy that problem by further cinching my pack belt around my waist. These critters were often difficult to remove, except with a companion's aid. The ticks were equally pesky. Every time I got near a tree trunk I risked having the buggers alight on me. If allowed to get a firm hold they would swell up to a thumb-tack-size, purple bag of blood. Then there was the heat and humidity to contend with. Lack of suitable water was also a worry. But the worst things were the rough terrain and poorly marked trails. There was always the dread of getting lost. We didn't have a compass or map, so constant vigilance was imperative. Mr. Keishi kept one eye open for trail markers while the other he set to alert us to the presence of the infamous wildcat. One of my eyes was on the lookout for the habu snake, while the other was exclusively reserved to detect any worrisome behaviour Mr. Keishi might be displaying.

Mr. Keishi was not reacting well to all the stress. As we ventured deeper and deeper into the thick of the jungle with scrapes, welts, itchy sweat-saturated clothing and simple fatigue taking their toll, Mr. Keishi's mental condition deteriorated concomitantly. His nervous ticks became ever more pronounced, his outbursts more frequent and much louder. As we covered more and more miles, he started to have brief conversations with himself, and I feared a full-blown psychotic episode was just around the corner. From time to time he would ask in broken English, "*Sumimasen* (excuse me) DJ san, when we havu funny?" I would always reply, "Now Mr. Keishi, we are having fun now!" A quizzical look would appear on his face as he carefully considered my response. Though he was polite about it, I wondered if he actually believed me.

We managed to clear a small area in the jungle for my tent and made camp, just as the sun set. We ate some cold food and fell into bed, relatively unscathed from the first day's trek. "A small victory," I thought. My tent, though small, would have to suffice for the both of us. Mr. Keishi slept on newspapers he had brought for just such a purpose and pulled a thin blanket around his chin. I felt sorry for him as the lack of padding below his skeletal frame would surely cause an uncomfortable night's sleep.

Though I tried to ignore his odd behaviour, the bizarre vocalizations were particularly distracting. There was no respite even in my dreams. Scenes inspired from the POW movie, *Merry Christmas Mr. Lawrence*, danced in my head, but in this case the sadistic Japanese guard was none other than Mr. Keishi, bent on revenge. After awaking from this fright, I spent the rest of the night with one eye firmly placed on Mr. Keishi's slumbering torso. I wasn't about to succumb to any number of horrors a crazed samurai bellhop could commit. After all he did have a rather pointy pair of chopsticks at his disposal, didn't he? Just the perfect tool for flinging cold noodles my way.

With dawn, I realized what an idiot I had been. Mr. Keishi was as harmless as a Zen monk. He had been the perfect gentleman all night long. Amazingly, he awoke with a cheery *"Ohayo gozaimasu,"* (good morning). He looked visibly refreshed from a sound night's slumber and seemed much calmer. His relaxed manner held for the remainder of the trip. Consequently Mr. Keishi turned out to be a most able trekking companion. Sure he was crazy, but entirely harmless. Having a fellow adventurer for companionship was welcome. I certainly never feared for my safety again, at least not at the hands of Mr. Keishi. But the landscape, well, that proved to be something that demanded a high level of respect.

One mountain particularly stands out in this regard. We had no idea that this challenging feature was upon us until we were virtually smack-dab in the middle of it. The trek started out well enough as we slowly trudged up an increasing grade. At first it was slight and then gradually became greater and greater. The vegetation changed as we left the jungle canopy. Rock outcroppings appeared with greater frequency. I thought it quite odd that we would have to hike up such a steep slope as the previous jungle terrain had been relatively flat. What I found odder still was that scattered here and there amongst the rocks were rotting and rusting bits of flotsam and jetsam. Just what was going on here I wondered? Not enough refuse to be indicative of an air disaster. Upon closer inspection I realized the truth of the matter.

It seemed as if some great tsunami had suddenly engulfed a Japanese Boy Scout troop and scattered in its wake bits of decaying camping detritus. Such things as clothing, ramen noodle packs, comic books, drink boxes as well as assorted camping gear, such as spare fuel canisters, the odd umbrella or two and even a collapsible fishing rod were strewn about willy nilly. Standing before us was a small mountain, looming as large as Godzilla. Was ridding themselves of these articles a bid by hikers to appease the behemoth blocking their way or rather just a strategy to lighten their loads? The blight on the landscape had accumulated over many years. I reckoned at least 100 trekkers had traversed this peak. There was enough refuse scattered about to stand as silent testament to a group of fairly anxious hikers. Apparently some were desperate enough to lighten their loads as much as possible.

It really was quite a chore hoisting myself and forty pounds of gear up what was turning out to be a genuine alpine slope. Then I spotted a sheer cliff face about 200 yards in the distance. There was no track or other seeming way around it. Apparently hikers had climbed straight up it since I noted more bits and pieces of gear left at the bottom of the vertical cliff as hikers had apparently made one last desperate attempt to lighten their load. Man, I couldn't believe my eyes. This thing was almost straight up and there were no ropes or climbing aids of any sort to be seen. Removing my sweat-soaked bag from my back, I sat down to reflect upon the situation. It made absolutely no sense. Why be forced to climb such a treacherous precipice when the rest of the jungle plateau was freely available below? For God's sake, we had the whole interior of the island to play in—what kind of idiot had decided to run a trail straight up a mountain, I wondered?

The path was fairly well trodden. It certainly *appeared* that this was the correct route to take. Yet, glancing once again at that looming cliff face in the distance, I just couldn't move myself to accept it as fact.

At this point I made a decision that I doubt few Japanese hikers made. I elected to turn around and go back down. Mr. Keishi protested. I tried to give him my reason for back-tracking, but he was not entirely convinced. Most Japanese adhere to group-think and, just like the incorrect but often-quoted lemming behaviour, he was pretty insistent upon *throwing himself over the cliff*. In the end though, he relented and made his way down with me. Ever the follower that man would remain.

This same kind of scenario has played out countless times in survival situations. When hikers start to feel unsure of the way, invariably they proceed further down the wrong track, rather than just return from whence they came. Once people have seemingly poured so much into the endeavour, expended such large amounts of energy to make it as far as they have—in our case slogging it up through the mountain brush for a couple of hours—there is a strong disinclination to admit you have erred and backtrack. If you just remove your emotional attachment, force yourself to turn around 180 degrees and take that first step backwards, chances are all will turn out in your favour. This analogy works for spiritual matters as well. At some point a *sinner* (simply one who has *missed the mark* as an archer would) will have to repent (*turn away from*). Failing to make this shift will only lead you further down the path of delusion, which in turn makes it only that much more difficult to eventually find your way *Home*.

In our case, hoofing it back down the mountain led to an overlooked fork in the path. Most had clearly taken the more trodden path upwards to the mountain as we had originally done ourselves, but when I looked carefully there was a faint impression of a trail that led elsewhere. It was exceptionally easy to overlook as we had done in the first place. This turned out to be the correct path. From this point on we never failed to find our way. I still wonder what happened to all those who elected to climb that sheer cliff face. Robert Frost's memorable lines from the poem, "The Road Not Taken," echo in my mind:

> Two roads diverged in a wood, and I—
> I took the one less traveled by,
> And that has made all the difference.

In the end, Mr. Keishi and I did make it across the island not too much worse for wear. The trip started with a surprise and fittingly ended so. One moment we were in dense jungle and the next we literally found ourselves stumbling into someone's backyard. An elderly woman was hanging up her laundry. We found ourselves surrounded by aromatic tropical flowers, an open grass yard and a bright blue sky. There we were, suddenly transported from the dark confines of the steaming tropics to a modern suburban setting, in about the time it takes to finish off a sushi roll. Turning to us, she politely inquired about what we were up to. This immaculately made up housewife, who had probably never ventured any farther into the great unknown than the confines of her own back yard, held her composure well. It was as if it were quite usual for her to behold two unshaven, bedraggled strangers suddenly popping out of the jungle for a chat and a spot of tea. Mr. Keishi explained our situation to her and then, turning in my direction, he bowed, grabbed my hand and with a huge beaming grin, in fact probably the greatest display of happiness I ever saw come over him, announced in his best English, "Oh, yesa we havu funni. Beri biga funni. Eberi daya, funni, funni, funni!"

This kind of *travel* invariably has turned out to be very rewarding for me. While appearing foolhardy and dangerous to some, experiences of this nature were not at all about a death wish but rather quite the opposite. By pushing the envelope, taking risks and seeking the peak experience, I always felt more alive than ever. These adventures were apt to put things into perspective quite quickly. By removing normal daily routine and reducing things to a simpler, more basic level, the fullness of life had a much better chance of shining through.

The wonder and simple charm of existence was there. All I had to do was remove myself from habitual routine and environment to allow awareness the opportunity to experience the *shock of the new*, as it were. And speaking of novel environments, what better place to glimpse *Reality* than on a trip to the moon?

Indeed, when Apollo 14 astronaut Dr. Edgar Mitchell was transported to this shockingly alien world and back, he experienced a life-changing spiritual realization. Upon his return journey, while seeing the sight of the earth rising up over the lunar horizon, a kind of *samadhi* or unity experience was induced. Since that time he has devoted himself to the exploration of consciousness and human potential.

Uprooting oneself is a common technique employed by mystics since time immemorial. I'm not necessarily recommending extreme travel, the peak experience or becoming a wandering ascetic as a means to spiritual awakening. I'm just saying I seemed to have been drawn in that direction. These kinds of experiences are in fact completely unnecessary when it comes to revealing *Spirit*. For in truth, it is absolutely everywhere, in everything, right here and now. Indeed it is all there is. When you are trapped in illusion, though, it is most difficult to perceive this reality. Sometimes experiences that remove you from your comfort zone may help to momentarily push aside the veil which normally obscures the Truth from being revealed. Perhaps a few more travelogues might help illustrate what I am talking about. A further theme revolving around the concept of impermanence and mortality will be introduced as well.

Fields of Flowers and Killing

The setting was South-East Asia about a year after the story just recounted. This was my first foray into Thailand. I was looking for the opportunity to get off the tourist track and have a real adventure or two. I decided to rent a motorcycle and head off into the nefarious Golden Triangle. It was a huge, sparsely inhabited, mountainous area bordered by Burma, Laos and Thailand. This area was one of the most important opium-producing regions of the world, at that time. What gave it its unsavoury reputation was the fact that it was inhabited by drug smugglers, arms dealers and other assorted outlaws and was an area of interest to U.S. drug enforcement officials. But for the most part, it was made up of ordinary indigenous country folk simply trying to eke out an existence. Definitely considered closed to outsiders, as the potential for misadventure, violence and even worse was a distinct possibility.

It was with this sense of things in mind that I invited a French nurse to accompany me on the back of a rented 125cc Honda Enduro. It was never quite clear to me if my companion knew the reputation of the place we were about to enter. That this wild territory was truly off the beaten track would soon become apparent to her, if nothing else. We packed a couple of small bags with the barest of essentials. Using an old reference book acquired from a local used bookstore as a guide to locate the general area, I simply turned off the highway at some random point, found an unmarked, rough, terribly washed-out sandy trail to follow and headed out into the thick of it. What a great way to start an adventure. I had absolutely no idea where I was going, so I never had to worry about getting lost. Wherever I was, well ... that was where I found myself. Exactly where I should have been. In this way of moving through the world without thought of destination or intent, infinite possibility and freedom are the norm.

I should note that the nurse found the *flower fields* charming, though she was curious as to why this area was producing such quantities of only one particular variety. I gathered she didn't know the origin of the morphine painkiller she surely administered to her patients at work. Finally making it out of this exotic locale, my companion and I headed to another area several hundred miles away.

This village was only a point on the map and went largely unmentioned in tourist guide books. Getting to it was half the fun. Pavement gradually transformed into dirt road, then for many miles a trail that would barely pass as a logging road, until that gave way in turn to a washed-out path and finally nothing more than a creek bed. The last few miles were among the toughest I ever travelled on a motorcycle.

Somehow we managed to make it to this village with a fully operational motorcycle and nurse intact. Beaming, I pulled up onto the dirt road, which passed as Main Street, and therein the rear wheel promptly deflated. The timing was not too bad, I thought. Though making it back out by motorcycle proved impossible. I had brought no tools or repair supplies (in retrospect a ridiculous oversight). The village store had the only pump in the entire enclave and I desperately needed it. However, the store-owner would not part with it as it was used to inflate the local kids' soccer balls. Therefore there was no chance to make it back out on motorcycle. This village was incredibly remote, poor and located on the periphery of a civil war.

The clearing sat on the bank of a large river, across from which lay Burma. It was in the nearby Burmese territory that indigenous peoples were continuing their decade-long struggle for freedom and independence from the oppressive Burmese military regime. Added to this was the fact that illegal smuggling of all sorts was going on at this border area and you get a situation that invites interest from local security forces when outsiders show up. We had no idea what we had stumbled upon. After finishing a pleasant talk with Thai security, the Burmese counterpart had their opportunity to question us. I don't think they believed us when we explained we were just a couple of tourists trying to get a little off the beaten track. Surely we had other motives, they reasoned. Nobody would come to this Godforsaken place just for the hell of it. They preferred we high-tail it out of there immediately but the damaged motorcycle prevented this. There was intrigue about and it was better foreigners weren't privy to it.

This suspicious activity was revealed to us in several ways. We saw a partially clad corpse slowly float down the gently flowing river. This invited very little interest from the locals—though one mahout did nudge his working elephant out of the way to prevent a possible collision. Folks seemed far too preoccupied with matters of the living to pay any attention to the dead. They had obviously seen this same kind of incident played out before. Let the crocodiles or the next village worry about it, seemed to be their attitude.

We also observed illegal tropical hardwood smuggling. Elephants were used to move the logs from the river and shore to the holds of small barges. More circumspect smuggling, like weapons, precious minerals, drugs or people was going on as well. Amid all of this dubious activity, a covert invitation was issued to us to please come and visit a nearby refugee camp, located some miles upriver. Apparently someone had heard about our arrival and sent a representative to come get us. The invitation was issued on the assumption that we were undercover civil rights activists. After all why else would a couple of Westerners be in town? I am sure security thought this a distinct possibility as well. It was beginning to look like no-one ever came here for the pure joy of it, or as in our case, with no purpose whatsoever. We decided to decline the invitation to visit the camp.

Nope, we were just an adventurer and a nurse on holiday. She had come on holiday to experience the normal tourist fare Thailand had to offer but, in accidentally hooking up with me, ended up with something never seen in the glossy pages of a tourist brochure. I doubt very much she would ever have an occasion to travel like that again. But who knows. Once bitten, maybe she would one day set out on her own and make some kind of foray into the great unknown. As for me, I returned to Canada and one year later went back again to South-East Asia, this time to make a self-produced documentary. By this time the adventure bug had really taken hold. The world was my oyster, and I hoped to chronicle a few of its pearls on video.

Fields of Flowers and Killing

The idea was to follow the old Mandarin Road/French Colonial Highway that linked Thailand to the gateway to China, passing through Cambodia and Vietnam along the way. I realized this trip had only become possible a short time ago, since decades-long hostilities had only recently ceased. By 1994 it was once again possible to travel in Vietnam and Cambodia as an independent traveller. The UN had just left Cambodia after holding democratic elections there.

At that time Cambodia was one of the eight poorest nations in the world. Modernization had commenced, but it was still a largely impoverished, ungoverned, relatively dangerous place. Think of the freewheeling spirit of the American Wild West, combined with a banana republic open to every kind of unregulated graft and vice imaginable, and you'll get a picture of the place. So it was with some trepidation, but even greater anticipation, that I pulled up to the Thai-Cambodian border crossing on my motorcycle. Despite being reassured by a Cambodian embassy official in Bangkok that it would be okay to enter via motorcycle, the border official standing in front of me did not concur. He was not prepared to grant me an entry visa under any circumstances. Only air travel would do. What a disappointment! I tried my darndest, but the officials were intransigent. It seemed that my timing couldn't have been worse.

The recent verification that three kidnapped tourists had been murdered by the brutal Khmer Rouge really put a monkey wrench into my plan. Also the area that lay just beyond the border was still largely controlled by the Khmer Rouge and apparently these chaps didn't understand that Cambodia was now *democratized*. I didn't care a bit about all this. I just wanted to proceed with my documentary. I smelled adventure and was raring to go.

I left the crossing and holed up at a nearby guesthouse for a few days, trying to figure out how I could best proceed. I tried bribery and everything else I could think of but in the end I had to backtrack. It was quite a testament to the level of danger when some of the most corrupt officials on the face of planet were too cautious to accept a bribe. Very serious security problems must have been going on at the time. Indeed, after flying to Phnom Penh, a travel advisory was issued advising tourists not to enter. The fallout from the discovery of the bodies of the murdered backpackers was immense. The story goes that they had tried to travel on a local train to a coastal town and had been intercepted along the way. The three tourists were held pending a ransom demand, and when that was not forthcoming quickly enough they were murdered.

There were other Khmer Rouge problems as well. Reports said sporadic ethnic cleansing of citizens of Vietnamese heritage was still going on in outlying areas. Large areas of the country were still unsecured, including a wide swath around the tourist attraction of Angkor Wat. In fact when I lodged in the nearby town, most nights I heard shelling and sporadic gunfire coming from the outskirts. The touristic site of Angkor Wat gave way to soldiers at night. They would set up temporary machine gun emplacements and lay mines each evening around the UNESCO world heritage site to prevent its occupation by the belligerent rebels. By early morning, before the first tourists started to arrive, all traces would be removed. Good morning Cambodia!

It was in this kind of atmosphere that I hatched a plan to go to Sihanoukville, the same coastal resort that the three kidnapped backpackers had intended to reach. The recent discovery of their remains had cur- tailed any interest in this destination from the few tourists who still remained in Cambodia. I decided to reach this town using the very same train that the backpackers had been snatched from a year before. This particular train had an interesting reputation.

The two front carriages were said to always be free to any and all who cared to board them as they were the ones that suffered the brunt of the exploding landmines placed on the tracks. When the foreign tourists were snatched from this train, thirteen Cambodians were also killed in the attack. It was with this in mind that I attempted to procure a ticket.

Not surprisingly all the train station ticketing agents refused to sell me passage. Bribes did not work. I attempted to get others, for example taxi drivers, to buy me a ticket but failed here as well. Man was I frustrated. First I was prevented from entering the country on motorcycle and now this foiling of my plans.

The newspapers got wind of what I was up to from a British Consul representative and that did not go over too well. The rep was extremely pissed off when he overheard me one evening bemoaning my frustrations to some fellow backpackers. I think I told my chums that I intended to just board the train and see if they would have the gumption to throw me off. Hearing this, the official walked up to my table and said I was a "bloody idiot" and Cambodia needed no more "fools like me causing trouble." He was quite right. I took the media coverage as a signal to cease and desist. The train adventure was put to rest but Sihanoukville still beckoned.

I ended up taking a shared cab instead. Seemingly that was the only way a tourist could get there in those days. The mid-size Japanese sedan held nine of us (normal capacity five). It was cheap, but so jam-packed that someone had to slam the door closed from the outside. Just like the white-gloved Japan Rail staff did each morning when stuffing Tokyo commuters into over-flowing compartments at peak rush hour. I was in the back seat with four more Cambodians. They complained that I was so large (certainly large compared to their slender figures) that I should pay double fare and free up some room. I told them to get stuffed. I sat by the door, which was extremely uncomfortable since my hip bone was wedged under the door handle for the entire trip.

The road was very poor. Each bump was magnified due to the pain in my hip. Along the way I noted signage indicating posted areas filled with landmines. From time to time we could observe land mine clearing teams actually engaged in their dangerous occupation. At the time, Cambodia was probably the most heavily mined country in the world. It was with great relief that we eventually arrived at our destination several hours later. I was finally liberated from the clutches of a cab ride that, in retrospect, seemed almost as dreadful as some scenario a crazed Khmer Rouge torturer would cook up.

Soon after arriving in the resort, I learned that one, out of a total contingent of two or three foreign English teachers, had recently been kidnapped from one of the very same cabs I had just arrived in. This teacher's fate was presently unknown. As a precaution, I told no one my return departure date and, when leaving town, only hopped a cab at the very last moment. I may have done things that *appeared* foolish but I was no fool.

There were things I elected not to do, places I declined to visit during my weeks in the former French colony, as intuition suggested otherwise. I certainly had no plans to shuffle off this mortal coil anytime soon. Somehow I knew the difference between a dangerous situation and something that would allow a wonderfully enriching experience to unfold. I can assure you that I felt it was never a case of *fools rushing in where angels fear to tread*. The idea was to fly *neither too close to the sea, nor the sun* as Icarus's father had advised. Icarus would have done well to follow those words. Instead his fate ended with self-immolation. A reality I intended not to emulate.

Death Shall Have No Dominion

Vietnam is a fascinating country; exotic, full of history and quite off the beaten track in the mid-nineties. It had only recently opened its borders to independent travellers. Lots of interesting experiences were to be found but unfortunately almost as much frustration, if one wished to travel on the cheap. I hooked up with a low-budget Swedish backpacker, and we spent several weeks together. We got along well and had a shared viewpoint regarding the people. We disliked how the Vietnamese were, by and large, only out to extract a buck from us. They didn't seem to appreciate the difference between a backpacker and a well-heeled tourist. We felt we were being exploited. In a trivial sense we were. I suspect that we manifested a certain amount of our own hardships along the way, due to our reactionary nature. I am sure the Vietnamese government would have suggested a year in a re-education camp to help clear up our *wrong views*. The following event, though, could hardly be blamed on our actions alone.

I suppose if we had kept our mouths entirely shut, none of the following would have occurred, but at that point the Vietnamese had a certain way of pushing our buttons and frankly we were a bit tired of it. Neither of us seemed inclined to shirk at the first sign of confrontation (my friend having served in the military).

Most small backwater towns were pretty serene in the late evening so our attention naturally focused on the spectacle of a group of people congregating in front of our cheap hotel one evening as we returned home. Getting closer we perceived the silhouettes of three or four

51

men standing beside a pedicab. They were all young, and, as things transpired, increasingly belligerent. One guy was perched on the bicycle rickshaw's seat, the other two or three standing beside him. When they noticed us approaching, they stopped talking and fixed us with an icy gaze. Getting closer one guy yelled something at us. By their appearance and manner it was quickly apparent that they were a tough lot out to stir up trouble no doubt. One guy, taller than the others, was wearing a kind of long, trench-coat-like jacket. He seemed to be the main rabble- rouser.

We stood our ground as this guy sent invectives our way, including a few choice English ones like, "fuck you" and "fuck America." I told my friend that was a good one, as neither of us was from the USA. We laughed and then told them what they could do with themselves. The bigger guy really didn't appreciate our comebacks and got even more riled up. At this point the manager, who was visibly worried, ushered us into the hotel and slid closed, and then locked, the accordion-style iron gate behind us. Emboldened by the knowledge that we were secure behind the impregnable barrier, we now let loose a series of the vilest insults and hand gestures we could muster. Through the heated yelling and mutual insults I decided to go for it and drop the A-Bomb. That would be A as in *ass*. I proceeded to drop my drawers and moon the ringleader. I thought this most humorous. Ah the innocence and stupidity of youth. Apparently he didn't appreciate the humour as much as I. What occurred next was totally unexpected. Unexpected and largely inexplicable.

It provoked something like a scene straight from a vintage John Woo Hong Kong action film or a montage from the *Matrix*. From beneath the confines of his long coat he pulled out a very impressive military type rifle. I was completely shocked. "How the hell did he just do that?" I wondered. My attention became exceedingly focused on the only thing that had any relevance at that moment. Just what the hell did he intend to do with that rifle. Time seemed to slow as he pulled it up to his shoulder. My eyes locked onto his. Very fleeting but there was a moment of recognition. I had experienced it before during martial arts tournaments. The moment just before the match started when both combatants simultaneously committed to bring everything they had to the battle at hand. To metaphorically *kill or be killed*.

But in this case, what I noted in his eyes had nothing at all to do with sport. The windows to his soul indicated a man who had just decided to murder me. There was no mistaking it. He pulled the trigger. The gun discharged with a loud retort and a single bullet slammed into my belly. I stumbled backwards grabbing my stomach and then folded over at the waist in shock. Tremendous pain shot through my lower torso. It was a unique sensation, a kind of pain I had never experienced before. A shockingly intense, searing agony, reminiscent of the sensation a serious burn evoked, only buried deep in my belly. Time slowed down, awareness grew. Without any superfluous mind chatter existing to interfere with the moment, my ability to concentrate improved dramatically. Adrenalin flooded my system. I struggled to come to grips with what had just happened. This was the point where things got very weird indeed.

It was like I became a third-party observer to two separate narratives that were unfolding simultaneously. Both stories were occurring to *me* yet at the same time something was also standing back quietly observing the unfolding drama. Imagine if you can, watching two separate tennis matches simultaneously on a split screen TV, while also being one of the competitors in both matches and you may get some idea of what I am talking about. Somehow I was experiencing two realities and neither, at the same time. In one I had been shot and was suffering the consequences of my wound and in the other I was standing there trying to figure out what had just happened. That story seemed to take hold of my attention.

I let go of my stomach and looked quickly outside to the pavement, then over at the Swedish guy, who was paying me no heed. He was looking at the Vietnamese gunman with a very quizzical expression on his face. I looked once more outside and was puzzled by what I saw. The ringleader was scrambling around on the ground searching for something. The rifle was by his side. This whole confusing episode lasted but a few moments. I couldn't figure out what the hell was going on. I still thought I was shot. Once I regained my composure enough to flee, I bolted up the stairs two at a time. Upon reaching the second floor I proceeded to lock myself into a bathroom. I pulled up my shirt to see the nature of my wound. It was not so clear to me at this point whether I had indeed been shot. There was no pain. With great relief I found that I had sustained no injury at all. Again and again I asked myself what the hell had just happened?

A Fleeting Improvised Man

I tried to make sense of it all but fell short. The loud discharge and sense of pain seemed real enough. Yet here I was unharmed. Had the shooter missed? What about the sense of two separate narratives? Later, when I crosschecked my experience with the Swede I was shocked to find he had experienced something completely different.

Our stories corresponded up to the point of the rifle being drawn. He said that the Vietnamese did indeed level the gun at me but it is here that our recollections radically diverge. He noted that the gun was a Vietnam War era American M16. He had recognized it due to his previous military training. I had no clue what it was, but its lethality was never in question. He said that after the guy levelled it at me he pulled the trigger, or at least it looked like he did, but then something baffling happened. He said that the bullet magazine dropped off the gun and fell to the ground, spilling bullets. Startled, the shooter then dropped down to the tarmac to frantically pick up the bullets.

He said that what occurred was impossible as it took some deliberate effort to engage the magazine release in order to remove the clip. He saw no such action. Furthermore for bullets to fall out manner they had. Of this of the startled gunman conclusion. This incident happened …. it was completely impossible of the magazine in the he was sure. The reaction demonstrated a similar couldn't have possibly

Years later I took weapons training on a similar gun and can personally attest to the accuracy of his conclusion. The magazine is securely held in place and can never be accidentally knocked off. Bullets are held in place by a strong spring-like mechanism. They can't just pop out after being clicked down into place. They have to be purposefully removed one by one by hand. I saw the Vietnamese guy on the ground doing what I now take to be picking up bullets, just as the Swede indicated. However I considered it, something impossible happened. If it were a hallucination or mutual psychosis, then it was the first occasion for both of us.

So what do I make of all of this? Something inexplicable happened to be sure. What exactly I can't say. Whatever happened seems pretty far removed from everyday reality. That being the case, perhaps we can turn to the world of quantum mechanics to provide a possible explanation. More specifically, the *many-worlds/many-universes* theory. Let me elaborate.

Death Shall Have No Dominion

It seems possible that I was consciously aware of the effects of quantum probability at play, of which the many-worlds theory is a case in point. The ramifications of this theory sound like something straight out of science fiction, yet many physicists, including the renowned Stephen Hawking, support the theory. It centres on the principal that outcomes to possible events cannot be predicted absolutely. Rather, a range of possible outcomes exist, each single outcome having a different probability of occurring. According to the many-worlds theory, each of these possible outcomes corresponds to the creation of a different universe. As a simple example, consider an event that has only two possible outcomes, each having a fifty/fifty chance of occurring. Like flipping a coin heads or tails for instance. Thus one universe now splits into two actual worlds, the *heads* universe and the *tails* universe. Soon another event comes along with various possible outcomes. The *heads* universe will be further split at this point. Likewise splitting will occur in the *tails* world as it experiences its own differing events with varying degrees of probability as to their final outcome. Eventually an infinite number of universes will exist.

Perhaps I witnessed the splitting off of reality as two different outcomes were produced. For an instant I was neither alive nor dead. It was like I briefly entered the *bardo* state as described by Tibetan Buddhists. This term describes an *intermediate state*—also translated as *transitional state* or *in-between state*. It brings to mind the famous quantum mechanics Schrödinger's cat thought-experiment. Here a cat is imagined to be placed in a box. This cat has a chance of being poisoned by some kind of apparatus. Until it is physically observed it is considered both alive and dead at the same time. It takes an observer to collapse the wave function and *fix* the cats state of being. Only at that point can the cat be deemed truly alive or dead. As long as no one looks in the box, the cat is caught in a kind of nether world—being both alive and dead and neither at the same time.

Maybe the scenario that unfolded in front of my eyes had two possible outcomes, and my travelling companion, or the assembled Vietnamese, by a mere act of observation, collapsed the wave function in such a way that I am here to report what happened. In the other scenario I was shot but I can only report that I was not murdered, since, obviously, *dead men tell no tales*. Perhaps this holds for all of my other *close calls* as well. Maybe when I fell through the frozen pond, one possible outcome was my death and a new world split off at that point—but once again I would not be here to report that particular outcome. My grandmother could, however, or at least one version of her could. That would take place in a world that, unfortunately, no longer contained little grandson DJ. Some would say that my theory holds no merit as quantum effects are only possible at the subatomic level. Therefore they are not applicable to everyday reality. Recently quantum phenomena have been experimentally verified at the molecular level. Thus they may hold all the way up to our macro level of reality. Conclusive proof awaits the outcome of further experimentation. Obviously one is generally oblivious to all these other possible realities. Perhaps, though, I had a momentary glimpse of the splitting-off process at work.

A thought experiment, centring on the concept of *quantum suicide*, has been proposed to carry this idea to its theoretical limit. Much like in Schrödinger's cat experiment, a device is imagined that may or may not cause a gun to discharge and a bullet to be fired at a man's head. Each time the subject pulls the trigger, there is a 50 percent chance of him meeting his demise. Astoundingly, he is never harmed. He keeps pulling the trigger but the gun never fires. After a million squeezes he comes to believe himself immortal. In fact he is not. What has actually transpired is quantum mechanics at work. After each pull of the trigger, there was a splitting off of worlds. In one case he died, in the other he didn't. It is extremely improbable, though theoretically possible, to pull the trigger a million times and have a favourable outcome. Though exceptionally unlikely, in this particular string of events he remained alive to note his good fortune and erroneously conclude that he must be immortal.

One more travel story is in order, though, unlike in the previous anecdote, where mortality unexpectedly confronted me on its terms, now I will recount the case where I voluntarily took *the bull by the horns* and willingly stared Death in the face.

Speaking about *taking the bull by the horns* I am reminded of another occasion when I did so—quite literally and intentionally as well. This occurred one hot summer day, down on the farm, when I was feeling a little bored. I had decided to *play* with the bull (a full-sized mature Hereford). He was a solitary animal so usually welcomed the attention. I playfully riled him up a bit as I pushed and prodded his massive body. I also grabbed his horns in order to try to force his head down. This he particularly disliked. From this point it usually became a playful version of a bullfight. He would half-heartedly whirl about while sending his head in my general direction. He had a full set of horns so I had to take care. On this day though I decided to annoy him more than usual. I guess I wanted to see what would happen if I really got him riled up. Not surprisingly, I then had one ornery, pissed-off bull to contend with. Go figure.

He ran far out into the middle of the field, paused, and then charged me at full speed. This was new. I was surprised at how fast a ton of beef could propel itself if so inspired. My first instinct was to get the hell out of there fast, while I still had a chance, but instead I held my ground. I had never experienced this kind of situation before. I remained motionless, as he bore down on me from a couple hundred feet away. I wondered how it would all play out in the next few seconds. It was an awesome experience to just relax into the moment. To be a participant in life having a validating moment. How wonderful it was to be alive. The sublime nature of reality being revealed in this ridiculous interplay of man and beast. evoked in me. Something unfolding to be quite about to happen was now The exhilaration produced uncontrived moment was

I recall the nervous giggles it in me found what was amusing. Whatever was entirely beyond *my* control. by this spontaneous, amazingly palpable. This was

what it meant to be alive and in the moment!

I watched as the bull got closer and closer. What a mystery all of this seemed. A moment later the distance closed and he slid to a halt a couple of inches away from my placid body. The bull, wheezing and panting from the strenuous exercise, looked me in the eye, and I returned his gaze. I patted his broad forehead then reached down and plucked some fresh grass for him to munch on. I think we both felt that that had been a rather invigorating experience. Well worth the effort indeed. I found that, when I chose to grab *Life* by the horns and confront my own mortality, it made for a pretty wild but rewarding ride.

We pick up the final travelogue as I made it through the Vietnamese border crossing. It was a huge relief to pass into sleepy, laid-back Laos after suffering all the trials and tribulations Vietnam had to offer. At the time, this socialist country was far more insular and much less touristic than is presently the case. In the early 1990s independent travellers were few and far between. Infrastructure was basic. Amenities few. The people though were friendlier and more sincere (akin to the Thais) than their Vietnamese neighbours. I really enjoyed the country's rustic charm. The historical French colonial architecture was quite splendid. When I arrived, a local claimed that Laos was exactly the same as it had been twenty years previously and in all likelihood would be the same twenty years hence. It was truly the land that time forgot. This sentiment was particularly apt when it came to describing the lives of the minority Hmong people.

Sometimes referred to as the *Hill Tribe People*, they are a fiercely independent race loosely scattered through a narrow band that extended from China, Thailand, Laos, Vietnam and Burma. They typically eked out an existence through hunting/gathering and subsistence level agriculture or small cottage industries. These simple folk were extremely poor, disadvantaged and, most unfortunately, they had supported the wrong side during the Vietnam War.

In Laos, the long tentacle of American imperialism, namely the CIA, initiated something now referred to as *the secret war* (still little known). They enlisted the aid of the desperate Hmong people to help carry it out. They fought against the communist-nationalist Pathet Lao, who eventually came to power in 1975. After the war was over, the Americans simply folded up shop, keeping few if any of their promises to aid their former comrades-in-arms. Visas were not issued nor aid extended. They simply abandoned the Hmong to their own fate. For years American authorities denied any involvement in Laos whatsoever. Of course the Hmong minority were singled out for severe retribution when the Pathet Lao came to power. Many were forced to flee to Thailand seeking political asylum, and eventually tens of thousands of refugees were resettled in the West. It is into the back country of these hard-done-by *Hill Tribe People* that we pick up the story.

I needed to get from the Laotian capital, Vientiane, to Luang Prabang. Until the communist takeover in 1975, Luang Prabang was the royal capital and seat of government of the Kingdom of Laos. The guide book stated emphatically that one could only reach it by air. Though there was a road of sorts connecting both centres, overland travel was not considered an option. The explanation being that to pass in this manner was way too dangerous an undertaking. Well, well, I thought, this area would certainly be off the beaten track. In fact it was quite probable that not a single Nike had ever trod this pristine thoroughfare before. It sounded like an adventure in the making for sure.

I was always very unenthusiastic about travelling by air when given other options. Travelling with the locals was always much more rewarding. Also, in this case, the distance was relatively short. That fact made the expensive fare hardly worth it. How dangerous could this section of Laos really be, I wondered?

The guide series I used for S.E. Asia was the bible for off-the-beaten-track, adventure-seeking backpackers. So it was with some surprise that I read that this area was completely verboten to Western tourists. The more I read about it, the more intrigued I became. No question about it, overland travel was out. I recall it said something like, *Only the foolish and foolhardy would attempt this journey.* This territory was Hmong country and lots of guerrilla activity persisted there. The book gave an example of a recent attack on a Russian exploratory crew as a case in point. I recall something about a jeep ambush and several deaths. Unlike the Khmer Rouge, the Hmong did not attack for ransom. No, what they desired was terror. Apparently few if any tourists had gone this way in many decades.

A totally irrational decision had been reached on my part. It certainly seemed to run totally contrary to the survival instinct, and many would view it as a rash and very stupid thing to do. I would have no argument with that conclusion. Of course a part of me was quite apprehensive about this decision, but I was getting used to such inclinations. If this journey was what the cosmos had in mind for me, I was game.

This time I would enter the *heart of darkness* on my own terms. It would be a fairly simple undertaking I surmised. I figured I would hop a bus to the last safe town. From there strike out on my own, grabbing whatever form of conveyance came my way. I could not be too picky. Hopefully another bus or even a local truck or car would present itself. I would surely pass under the radar before anyone noticed. In and out just like that. Or so I hoped. As always, things didn't quite turn out as planned.

Let me stress that I am not exaggerating or embellishing the level of danger involved here. I scanned the Internet for corroboration; a quick check showed the following murders occurred within a few months of my time there. Just a month before my visit I found a report which indicated that in December 1994, four local UN drug prevention officers were shot on this road and about ten days earlier, six Vietnamese construction workers were killed north of Kasi. Again near Kasi a French travel agent and four Laotian men were killed after their minibus was ambushed. That occurred a few months after I passed through and in the fall of the same year I found a cryptic reference: "In autumn 1995 three foreigners were killed." Finally I found the following *Asian Development Bank Review*, Volume 31, No. 2 report, written in 1999, quoting ADB manager Mr. Preben Nielsen, about his reminiscences of his time spent there. He says of the area:

> During construction, the road was off-limits to tourists as it was often attacked by members of a rebel political group. Nielsen says that he had to travel under heavily armed escort in the early days. In several incidents, six personnel of the Vietnamese contractor were killed by rebels. Today, the asphalt-surfaced highway is much easier to police and security is greatly improved.

I read that at least ten-twenty such deaths occurred per year at that time but the government chose to keep most of them unreported. From these reports the Kasi area appeared particularly dangerous.

The guide book made clear that a day bus trip from Vientiane was possible to a town about halfway to my goal. To go any farther was deemed too dangerous. The whole rest of the route was completely off limits. The Laotians used the term *route* rather than *road* to describe this particular thoroughfare. To do otherwise would have been disingenuous for this thin grey meandering slit did not resemble a highway in the least. At one time it must have been quite a nice French colonial motorway, but decades of war and neglect had turned it into a track suited for not much more than local water buffalo carts. The fact that modern vehicles managed to traverse it was an amazing testament to Japanese spring/shock absorber technology. After the point where the day bus turned around, the road was largely composed of rutted, pock-marked, loose sandy soil, interspersed here and there with large, shredded shards of antique asphalt. What a test of nerves it took to navigate it at anything approaching highway speeds. The Laotian government, in an effort to modernize and pacify this area, had tasked largely Vietnamese work crews to resurface the whole thing. I noted the official designation number for the *route*—the inauspicious number 13 of course. How appropriate.

I caught a late morning bus from the capital heading north. The four-to-five hour trip was uneventful. There were a couple of other Westerners on the bus but by the time I arrived at my destination, the only passengers remaining were locals. Few tourists must have sought lodging at my terminus. A local I befriended seemingly could not comprehend the fact that I wanted to spend the night in town. Try as I might, I could not get him to help me secure a bed. Or perhaps he had my best interests at heart and hoped I would leave town very soon. Maybe the problem was simply a communication gap caused by his lack of English. Up to that point I never met anyone who could really converse in it. So it was with some difficulty that I wandered around town seeking a room for the night.

On the main street I spied an open air café with a short queue of men waiting by the roadside. This was the line to secure a seat on local through traffic. Typically, in the Laotian countryside, one travelled by local vehicles, mostly truck, paying for the seat beside the driver. This truck queue was a relief as the reality of any other public transportation was completely unknown. This was how I would leave, I reckoned. I decided I would spend the night and depart the following morning, as there were only a few hours of light left.

It turned out that the café was part of a hotel of sorts. Apparently the only such establishment in town or at least the only one I could identify. I asked the manager for the room rate. It was way too high for my liking. I tried to negotiate, then cajole, but he would not budge. Clearly, another case of *rip-off the affluent tourist* was about to go down. This was disappointing. I thought I had left that mindset far behind in Vietnam.

This chap was particularly smug about it. An attitude he may have picked up from his former colonial masters. Up to now my experience of Laos had been as a backpacker's paradise. Prices were reasonable and not subject to partisanship. I must admit this guy was really annoying me. He knew he was the only game in town so I would have to capitulate in the end and pay what he asked. Wrong!

On this matter I was willing to stand on principal alone. Since he was unwilling to play fair I let him know that I would simply enter the line for a truck north. Shouldering my pack, I took my place in line. This made quite an impression upon him. I am sure he never expected this from a tourist. After a while of waiting, a rather small, very dilapidated jalopy of a local bus pulled up. Fantastic I thought. What a marvellous turn of affairs! Much better than a local truck because it was probably scheduled to travel a fair distance. If I were lucky, maybe all the way to Luang Prabang.

Grinning, I started to walk towards it to see if there was a spare seat. The driver indicated yes but before I could negotiate the ticket price, the hotel manager butted in. His words seemed to affect the formerly friendly bus driver, who now quoted a very high fare. Much higher than I expected it to be. I believed the manager had something to do with this. He looked far too satisfied when he saw my reaction to the inflated price. Well, right then and there, I decided to wipe that smug grin off his face. I grabbed my backpack and announced that I was walking. To hell with them all, I would set out on foot and see what transpired. That was the backpacker's credo. Or at least mine. When the fare was in doubt, hoof it out. I went to some ridiculous lengths in Vietnam to avoid being taken advantage of. The Swedish fellow, of whom I spoke previously, and I once walked over twenty miles of Vietnamese sea coast to avoid an overcharged $15 bus fare. I think the manager thought I was bluffing. Before I had a chance to reconsider what I was about to do, I made a quick exit.

Route 13 beckoned, but I have to admit it was with some trepidation that I headed north out of town. The more upscale modern red-tile-roofed dwellings I passed quickly petered out to humbler affairs roofed in palm fronds or pieces of rusty galvanized tin. These in turn made way to open paddy fields with a mountain not far away in the distance. It was towards this rise that I appeared to be headed. That was unexpected. I had no idea I would be moving through mountainous terrain. Then a thought occurred—*Hill Tribe People*. Soon it would be nightfall. It was at this point that I started to question what the hell I had just gotten myself into. I wasn't far out of town. Why not just turn around? Then I saw a small group of people up ahead walking the valley floor in the same direction as me.

That is when the fear set in. It would only be a matter of minutes before I caught up to them. Who were they, I wondered? What reaction would be evoked when they set eyes upon my decidedly well-fed Caucasian carcass? Odds were probably not good. I figured this time I had finally done it. If they didn't kill me on the spot, surely they would quickly get hold of some badass who would. As I gained on them, my fear increased to outright terror. My heart was pounding, and I began to feel quite sick, deep in the pit of my stomach. I had never been so frightened in my entire life. Then something very much unexpected happened. A not unfamiliar, though certainly infrequent *visitor* suddenly popped into consciousness.

I take it we all have visits from this intuitive type of background guiding presence from time to time. Usually quite subtle in nature, occasionally rising to the fore as occasion dictates. It seemed to spring forth from a source of wisdom not typically found in normal mental chatter. The last time I encountered it as clearly and stridently as this was some twelve years previously. Then, as at this moment, its message was accepted without reservation.

On that last occasion, it advised me that my ambition of becoming a millionaire was pure folly. A completely pointless and unrewarding endeavour it assured me. In short, a total waste of time. No, it said, you should and will seek another path. And so I did. My goal of becoming an extremely wealthy and powerful person dissolved at that moment and never reappeared. My dad used to say that I was the kid who, if you sent him to school with a buck, undoubtedly would return home with ten.

Then one day, during my second year at university while standing in the cafeteria line for a burger, something popped into my awareness and announced a whole new story was going to unfold. Weird thing was I believed it implicitly. No questions asked. I just kind of said, "Oh ok," shrugged and that was that. So here it was back again. What did it have for me this time? The message was short and extremely welcome. In a familiar and warm friendly manner it simply announced, "All is well my friend. All is well and will be well. Everything is proceeding as it should so just sit back and enjoy it while you may. Wise one out."

With that my outlook and attitude was completely transformed. One second I was terrified. The very next ecstatic and high on life. All it took was another thought, or more particularly another thought believed, to transform my reality completely. Yet what had actually changed? Our lives appear to be informed by concrete objective reality, but was that really the case or rather was it, as Mark Twain put it, Nothing exists but you. And you are but a thought."

The heartening message invigorated me and put a joyful skip into my step. I trotted forward like a horse that had just spotted an orchard full of windfall apples. Though carrying a heavy backpack on my shoulders, I quickly caught up to the group of strangers ahead. As I gained on them I noticed furtive glances cast my way. It became apparent that they were as scared of my presence as I had been of theirs. They probably wondered what was up with this guy who was so quickly gaining ground on them. Was I friend or foe?

We met and a huge mutual sigh of relief was expressed on both sides. Hands were shook, shoulders patted. They were locals who recognized me from our shared bus trip of a few hours ago. Apparently they had spent time in town and were now heading back to their homesteads. Nervous giggles were shared and hands shook once more as I bid them farewell. I proceeded with renewed optimism. The air smelled fresh and cool as the amber sun hung low on the horizon. Patches of green mixed with the brown stubble of the recently harvested paddy rice were now giving way to mountainous terrain. Life was grand! As I ascended the road up the mountain, taking in all the wonder that that particular patch of reality had to offer me, the following from Ecclesiastes 3:1 came to mind:

> There is a time for everything,
> and a season for every activity under heaven:
> a time to be born and a time to die,
> a time to plant and a time to uproot,
> a time to kill and a time to heal,
> a time to tear down and a time to build,
> a time to weep and a time to laugh,
> a time to mourn and a time to dance,
> a time to love and a time to hate,
> a time for war and a time for peace.

I relaxed into the moment. Now was indeed a time for dancing. The thrill of what was yet to come awaited me, like a rancher anticipating the arrival of a newborn foal. Most pressing at the moment though was the little matter of where I would bed down for the night.

Transport out of there was looking unlikely at that point. As I ascended farther up the mountain, and the sun began to set, I realized I would have to spend the night somewhere among the rocky crags. This uninhabited area would keep me safe from predators of any sort. I managed to crest the top as the last rays of sunshine disappeared. In the increasing darkness I spied a cave-like recess in a rock face. I decided I would retire here for the night. What a wonderful stroke of luck to find such a readymade shelter. Unfortunately, I was not prepared for the cold that would creep in as the night progressed. Anticipating an equatorial climate, I had made no provisions for cold weather. I now regretted foregoing the extra weight of sleeping bag and sweater in favour of a lighter pack. I only possessed a light nylon rain tarp and a thin jean jacket to keep the cold at bay. At that altitude, that kind of protection was insufficient. Naturally I ended up freezing my ass off the last half of the night.

There was just sufficient time to brush aside enough rocky debris to fashion a rough sleeping area on the cave floor before the starry firmament above revealed itself. The town below could be recognized in the twinkling of a few incandescent lights scattered about. They were comforting but appeared rather insignificant compared to the majesty overhead. Given the altitude and lack of light pollution, as well as the amazing 360 degree panorama this view afforded, it was by far the most spectacular night sky I had ever witnessed. The cosmos was manifested above in all its grandeur. I was totally alone up there on that craggy peak but not at all lonely. Then out of the silence a breeze momentarily picked up, and I thought I heard someone whisper my name. A moment later I recognized it again. Yes, my name being called out on the wind. The original name given long before my parents ever took pen to hospital birth certificate. That which can never be clearly spoken, yet can be recognized in everything … or rather as everything.

If you had told me upon arising from my comfortable guesthouse bed the morning that I set out, that I would be bedding down on a dung-covered, rock-strewn cave floor, perched high on the side of a mountain, in some nondescript part of South-East Asia that very evening, I would have thought you mad. Yet here I was, and I didn't even know where *here* was. How totally amazingly great was this! How rewarding life could become if one only paid it some attention every once in awhile. What normally passes for life is very much removed from the real McCoy.

My attention momentarily focused on my stomach as it churned and gurgled in protest due to the increasing hunger pangs I was suffering. That's life too. I didn't have any food or water with me. Once again I was enjoying the experience of reality reduced to its simplest requirements. Not the plethora of mostly trivial desires and senseless dramas that usually pass for our lives. I realized that the water problem must be somehow addressed fairly quickly the next day but for now it was not a worry. Propped up against the stone wall I noticed movement in the gloom. Or at least I thought I did. What was that I wondered? There it was again—something seemed to be flitting about. Some indefinable black presence was appearing here and there in front of me, as if by magic. I began to wonder if my senses were playing tricks on me.

As I was trying to make sense of what was going on, a dark object brushed my cheek. I shrieked out loud and fell back away from it, hitting my head on the rocky wall behind me. Then I saw another. Bats. I was being surrounded by bats! But these weren't like the garden variety, mouse-sized, friendly creatures I knew from back home. Nope, these were whopping big, tropical-sized monsters. Looking very much like some crazed Chihuahua had just sprouted wings. Yikes! I shouted and waved my arms about, hoping that they would hone in on me via echolocation. I was the interloper here. This was their place. Luckily, once they figured out what I was up to, they flitted off and left me in peace for the remainder of the night.

Peering below I glimpsed a single bright light. It was slowly moving away from town in my direction. Then it hit me—the bus. Surely this was the bus I had seen earlier. It had made a stopover and was now onward bound. That explains why we had never crossed paths as I made my way up the mountain. Perhaps that is why the manager of the café seemed so friendly with the driver. It must have always parked at his restaurant so that passengers could refresh themselves. Why I'll be darned. This is my ticket out of here, I thought!

I would simply stand in the middle of the road and flag it down as it passed. Elated, I started to pack quickly as there was no time to lose. I stuffed things into my bag and then hoisted it onto one shoulder. Moving as quickly as I could among the rocks, I started to jog toward the road then hesitated. A strong feeling came over me, accompanied by a thought. Perhaps it would be better to remain here for the night. "Why the hell would I do that?" I wanted to know. The bus was fast approaching. My window of opportunity out of there was rapidly disappearing. Another step towards the road and then it was clear to me. It was like Obi-wan Kenobi, of *Star Wars* fame, was standing right next to me, pulling one of his Jedi mind tricks. "Yes," I repeated to myself, "best to spend the night here." And with that the bus was upon me. I stepped back under the cover of a boulder and let it pass. The rumbling of its poorly tuned engine faded into the distance. All was silent once more. Once again I intuitively knew that I had reached the correct decision. Rationally, there was every reason to get my ass the hell out of that cold, desolate place and onto that bus. But something thought the better of that idea. And that something had a way better batting record than my impulsive chattering monkey-mind ever did.

I hunkered down for the duration and spent a rather uncomfortable night trying to get some shut eye. At around 3 a.m. it turned frigid and my back began to ache from my lumpy stone mattress. Well, at least I had the company of a full moon. The light it cast was strong enough to reveal grey, sharp-edged, low rocky outcroppings receding into the background, punctuated by the presence of several eroded monoliths jutting skyward. Its cheerful glow cast warmth over everything. My teeth may have been chattering but my heart was contented indeed. Dawn would arrive shortly, hearkening in a new day. What would it bring, I wondered as I nodded off once again to a few minutes of slumber.

I welcomed the heat brought by the rising sun. I was just as excited about the misty fog that had moved in. Its quality, probably due to the mixture of warm moist tropical air below rising to meet the cool alpine one above, was unique in my experience. Not the typically uniform, thick pea soup concoction I was used to seeing. Its effect on the landscape bordered on the surreal, creating a spectral, otherworldly atmosphere. The effect was like that sometimes portrayed in misty, classical Chinese watercolours. I had always thought that those ethereal mountain scenes had been mere exaggerated flights of fancy. Having occasion to stand in the middle of one proved that was not the case. Surely this was one of the reasons why Taoist sages sought the rarefied air of rugged mountain tops when they wished to be in communion with the Tao, the Spirit of all. Inspired, I brought out my video camera and began taping. That would be the last time the camera saw the light of day until I made it to my destination. Flashing such an ostentatious display of Western wealth around these parts would not be wise.

Once the fog had largely dissipated, I set off once again down Route 13, wearing the cheapest, flimsiest, thin-soled sandals imaginable. That fact alone would help make me appear much less like a rich foreigner, drug agent or any other desirable target of the Hmong's wrath. My old, faded green canvas alpine rucksack, stained by many years of use, was equally modest. It looked like something a local might conceivably cart farm produce around in. I was wearing shorts and a bright, almost fluorescently so, orange t-shirt. Originally I had picked out a fresher, tan coloured one to wear but something inspired me to dig to the bottom of my bag and change to a rather wrinkled, soiled, attention-getting orange one. Good thing I did too, as it probably saved my life.

Setting out, I hoped that some form of transportation, preferably of the long distance sort, would present itself as quickly as possible. Judging from the lack of traffic the previous day, I wondered what the likelihood of that would be. Within the course of an hour I had the good fortune to hear some kind of vehicle approach. Noisily sputtering up the road belching black greasy smoke from its small two-cycle engine came a tuk tuk (three-wheeled motorcycle taxi). To put it bluntly, it was a decrepit, potentially dangerous piece of shit. The fact that it was still cruising these back roads amazed me and was a testament to days gone by when things were built to last. Unperturbed, I elected to hop on board since it afforded me the opportunity to gain some ground quickly.

I seated myself next to a woman of about forty who was nicely attired in floral print Western-style dress and matching hat. Not the kind of outfit one typically expected to see in those parts. I wondered what she was doing out here but it would have to remain a mystery as communication proved impossible. Thankfully, it was an uneventful ride owing to the fact that it unfortunately ended far too quickly. I was really disappointed that we were both left at the side of the road after only a few miles. Despite my request and promise of money, the driver would proceed no further. No wonder. This was the infamous Kasi region, where I noted so many had been murdered in the past. Oh well, time for some more exercise ….

Death Shall Have No Dominion

Hilly terrain, covered by low mountain scrub with taller mountains receding into the distance, met my eye. "What is up with all these mountains?" I wondered. Most unexpected. The good news was there was no sign of the *Hill Tribe People* yet. By this time I was very hungry but even thirstier. I continued on and finally spotted some habitation. Peering into the distance, I could make out a few simple, shanty dwellings with rusty brown rooflines. "Ah, some kind of small village," I surmised, as only the well-off could afford to clad their hovels in galvanized metal. Really no more than five or six primitive wooden shacks in total. This was definitely a small Hmong enclave of sorts. Though I was quite anxious, my thoughts were mostly on acquiring food and drink at that point. If that village had a store, it was obvious from the signage I spotted that there was only one possible candidate. With that realization I took a deep breath and entered the belly of the beast.

Quickly scanning the room I noted two women and one man. The man was seated at a rough, plain, wooden table and the women, who must have worked there, were behind a counter of sorts. The male patron shot to his feet as I walked by him and almost overturned his chair in the process. Fortunately he appeared to be unarmed and not aggressive. He wore the basic blues of utilitarian workman's attire, was of dark complexion and had a well-wrinkled face, as if he had spent decades out under the harsh glare of the tropical sun.

It is certainly an understatement to declare that they were surprised to see me. Surely an alien from the Pleiades star system could not have elicited a greater response than my entrance. I have never seen Asians' eyes grow so large, nor so intently focused. They reacted as if a spirit had just walked in. A ghost straight from the pages of history had appeared in their midst. Thoughts of past misdeeds against them must have surely crossed their minds. From French colonialism, to the American intervention, to the present communist regime's persecution. I tried to make them understand my interest was solely in food and water.

After the initial shock wore off we all stood there silently. Feeling more and more like the complete outsider that I was, all I could do was smile. I tried to convey, with gesture and attitude, the warmest feeling of goodwill. Something along the lines of, *Hey guys, I'm just regular folk like we all are. No worries here mate. Just looking for a bite to eat is all.* The mood lightened. I tried asking for food again.

Despite having a couple of tables and some chairs, I was surprised to find out there was no prepared food to be had. Perhaps this was because it was after lunch time. Looking around further I spied a single shelf with a few dry goods. With relief I grabbed the only instantly edible thing on it—two cans of fish. At this juncture I noted one of the women slip out the door. I was too preoccupied with hunger to give it much thought, though I figured she had probably run off to fetch the mob. Hoping to get more sustenance, I made the motion as if eating rice. The proprietress caught on and brought me some cold rice from what appeared to be her own personal cooker located in a back room. Using my multitool, I opened the cans of fish and mixed the contents with the cold rice. What a feast. I added several glasses of tepid water and I was good to go. While I was eating, a man walked through the door. The moment I had been dreading had finally come. The authorities had arrived. My fate would now be decided.

It wasn't as bad as I supposed. Standing before me was an elderly gentleman. His wizened appearance suggested he was the village headman. He had the manner of someone who was used to being in charge. He sternly fixed his gaze upon me and then spoke in a language I couldn't possibly understand. I smiled a lot and let him know as best I could that I was harmless. I gave him a Canadian maple leaf pin that I occasionally handed out as a token of goodwill. I suspect it meant little to him as I am pretty sure he didn't even know Canada existed. I think my manners and actions assuaged his concern. I was young, my clothes were simple, my demeanour friendly and sincere. I guess he decided that there was to be no killing in his village that day.

After shaking his hand again, I stood up and beat a hasty retreat. I figured the less time he had to think about it the better. It looked like I would make a clean getaway. As I left town I passed an old woman bent over with age. The hatred in her eyes was too much to bear, and I averted my gaze. There was no doubt that these people had not forgotten or forgiven. Yet I was alive. Perhaps the old man recognized that I was not the cause of his grief. I soon passed a slightly larger enclave. I didn't even pause to blink. Children ran in terror as I passed. That was how I learned to distinguish whether or not a village in any remote area on earth had been corrupted by the presence of tourists. If the kids ran away in abject fear, they had probably never seen your likes before. Quite unlike my experience in touristic areas of Thailand or Burma, where they came begging for money or treats, or just to practise their English.

Making it past that town, I was relieved to be out on the open road again. Though I did wonder how much longer it would be before a contingent of mean, gun-toting Hmong rebels would come screeching up in a half-ton. For now though, the only things I spied out and about were construction trucks.

It seemed that tired old Route 13 was getting a complete makeover, the beginnings of the upgrade to a modern highway I mentioned earlier. This would be a slow process, as the work was being done almost entirely with the most rudimentary equipment. Vietnamese work crews were busy removing old material and resurfacing using little more than the sweat of their brow. I had the pleasure to become acquainted with work crews several times as I continued along the route. They were just as astonished to see me as the Hmong were—though very welcoming and friendly offering me tea, sweets and cigarettes (refused as I did not smoke) each time we met. I felt a special kinship with them. We were all a long way from home, and the constant threat of attack was over their heads as well as mine. Every camp did their best to get me farther down the line. Sometimes the construction truck provided for hitching purposes would only get me to the next gravel pile other times a little farther to the next camp. Then it would be back to walking. Once, though, I finagled a ride for a good one and a half hours or so. That would be the only long trip I managed. It was also the final time I rode with construction personnel. I had to pay the driver and believed that I had negotiated passage all the way to Luang Prabang. I was taken aback when the driver summarily dumped me at a non-descript roadside gravel pile, out in the middle of nowhere. My hopes of making it out of there before nightfall were dashed.

By now the soles of my flip-flop sandals were wearing thin and my blistered feet were aching. I walked down a hilly grade into a large valley and came upon a town. It appeared more prosperous than the previous hamlets I had passed through. Folks were most welcoming. Too welcoming it seemed. I felt an ominous, sinister vibe about the place. Despite the fact that the sun would soon set, it was clear I had to get the hell out of there and quick. A small group of people gathered around me. One guy grabbed me by the arm and implored me to stay. I politely declined and beat a hasty retreat out of town. I needed to conceal myself as quickly as possible. I figured a group would shortly show up and once again invite me to be their *guest* but this time it would be at the point of a rifle. It was with a sense of terrible dread that I could see no possible place to take cover. In front of me lay a wide valley, entirely covered by flat paddy fields. This was the most concerned I had been all day. I was quite certain that the sun I beheld, slowly disappearing before my eyes as it set, would be the last I'd ever see. That was, unless I could somehow figure out a way to pull off a disappearing act myself. Yes, a little timely stage show prestidigitation was certainly in order. Thankfully, that was precisely what occurred next.

It all happened so quickly that I could hardly believe my good fortune. Grace may arrive in many guises. The treatment administered to an African child dying of malaria, the timely shipment of food aid for the famine stricken, a refugee camp for those left homeless. In my case it came rolling down good old Route 13 in the form of a beat-up Japanese import. The cavalry had arrived!

A vehicle was fast approaching. In fact, it was the first half-ton truck of any sort I had spotted all day. Somehow I knew the driver was friendly. Now there was the matter of getting it to stop. I stepped halfway out onto the middle of the road and stood facing it. If manifesting one's personal reality were a possibility, then there was certainly no better occasion than that moment to prove it. I held my ground while putting intentional thinking to the test. In the fading light I clasped my hands together in a Buddhist pose and gave a little prayer. Then I bowed at the waist several times in the direction of the rapidly approaching vehicle and mentally implored it to stop. And by God it did!

The momentarily perplexed Laotian driver motioned for me to dump my things in the back. I greeted and then thanked him profusely. He relaxed visibly and in slightly formal, but fluent English, announced, "You are most welcome dear sir, wonderful to make your acquaintance. Simply wonderful. Sommai Rattanasamay (I recall his name was something like that) at your service." How moved I was at that moment. Overjoyed and quite overwhelmed with appreciation, I shook his hand and thanked him once again. He probably understood why my gratitude was so effusive.

After the introductions concluded and his truck was cruising down Route 13 as quickly as possible (best way to avoid the bandits, he assured me) there was time to talk. I was struck by how fluent his English was. I had never met a better speaker in the whole country. It turns out he had studied abroad during the short period of Laotian independence when such travel was still possible. After the French left and before the Americans had arrived. He had studied engineering at some British university. His combined British/Laotian accent was most charming.

He explained that he was the manager of a highway reconstruction project, north of Luang Prabang. He had been down in the capital on business and was now returning to his worksite. Sure he could drop me off in Luang Prabang on his way north, he assured me. At that point, curiosity got the better of me, and I asked him how he felt picking up a foreigner. Wasn't he surprised to find me in the hinterland at that time of the evening? "Not at all, and completely," came his paradoxical reply.

"How so?" I inquired.

Apparently when I approached his truck close enough for him to make me out in better detail, he was shocked to find a pair of blue eyes staring straight back at him. For a moment he wondered if his mind were playing tricks on him due to his many hours on the road. How was this possible he wondered? You see, he had taken me for a Laotian Buddhist monk. From a distance my completely shaved head and orange t-shirt (the exact same hue as Buddhist robes) had led him to believe that I was none other than a travelling ascetic. He was bowled over to discover, upon closer inspection, that I had morphed into an entirely different creature altogether. Momentarily he had wondered if I was a *pee* (Laotian term for ghost or spirit).

That explained the perplexed expression on his face when I first saw him. He said that if I had made any weird moves, or did not speak to him, he was going to hit the accelerator and get the hell out of there fast. We both chuckled at that. I momentarily reflected upon the good fortune of my choice of t-shirt. Though, in retrospect, I wonder if it was just dumb luck. Perhaps the change from tan to orange top was purposefully guided that morning. Call it intuition, divine providence or perhaps a bit of undigested beef, as Scrooge would have us believe. The miraculous or the mundane—it's all really a matter of perspective and belief isn't it?

The remaining trip passed in good cheer and conversation. I was surprised to learn how far away I really was from my goal. I thought that Luang Prabang was rather near. In fact I had entertained the possibility of finishing the remainder of the journey on foot. This seemed quite feasible as I had been led to believe it was not all that far away. The reason being that every village I stopped at, a local would invariably inform me that Luang Prabang was only a mere 10 kilometres farther up the road. Each time I heard this news I grew hopeful that my destination was just around the corner. After several inquiries, though, I noted a strange pattern. Every new village I came upon reported the exact same distance remaining to my destination. I was perplexed. Each time villagers reported, "Oh, just 10 kilometres more," I went the required distance, inquired at the subsequent village and found myself still no closer to my goal. What the heck was going on?

I later surmised that *Hill Tribe People* must symbolically use the concept of *greater than 10 kilometres* to connote something beyond easy walking distance. That's why my question always elicited a similar reply. I only registered the distance being 10, so thought it was only 10 kilometres farther, but they probably were saying something along the lines of, "Oh …. It's far away …. I reckon at least 10 kilometres for sure sonny boy. You'll never get there."

It turned out that never in my wildest dreams could I ever have arrived at Luang Prabang on foot. When Mr. Rattanasamay heard about my confusion, he laughed uproariously. In reality Luang Prabang was a good five to six hours away by Mr. Rattanasamay's truck. A slight miscalculation on my part. At that moment I must have appeared very worthy of the Lao nickname for foreigner, *Kii Nock*, which means *bird poop* (characteristically white and foul-smelling). I must confess that I was certainly feeling rather like a poopy head at that moment. Ah, ignorance truly is bliss. Nearing the end of this tale you may conclude that, *all's well that ends well*. Yet one remaining shock was yet to be revealed.

Upon reaching my final destination I settled into a Luang Prabang guesthouse, and the next day I had the good fortune to meet a taxi driver who spoke passable English. I chatted him up and in the course of our conversation he shared some confidential news. He told me that I would not hear the following anywhere in the local media, but he had it on good authority from his policeman brother-in-law that the previous day's night bus travelling north to Luang Prabang was ambushed along the way. As I recall, he said several people died. As the story unfolded, I began to connect the dots. Then my jaw dropped. That was the bus I was to have been on. The very same one I decided not to board up in the mountains. Ah, there but for the grace of quantum mechanics go I.

This brings us full circle back to the opening premise of the chapter. I opened by talking about the notion of impermanence and the idea of transcending fear in order to find freedom. As I have described, the fear that overcame me when setting out on Route 13 was all encompassing. Both mental and physical dread overwhelmed me. The gut-wrenching, elevated level of terror was unlike anything I had ever previously experienced. The fear of death in general is certainly the greatest one we have. Indeed it is the root of them all. My sense of it is that it is only at the moment when that primal fear has been totally transcended that one may consider life to have actually begun.

Standing out there among those Laotian rice paddies was the first time in my life that I really appreciated, or rather more like viscerally *grokked* to the very core of my being, the fact that I was not immortal. Like most young people, this thought never occurred to me before. In fact the opposite appeared to be the case. I thought I was somehow going to live forever. Or at least that was how I lived my life. Indeed don't most of us go around with that mindset?

Out there on Route 13 it became crystal clear to me that one day I would simply cease to exist. That reality could actually come to pass at any time, even in the next moment. My God, I was going to die! The realization was at first terrifying but ultimately a step in the right direction. The obvious was no longer deniable. I was impermanent. With that, *Reality* became a little bit sharper.

It is in knowledge like that one starts to move more and more in the direction of liberation. Accepting what is has made all the difference. As John Lennon said, "The unknown is what it is. And to be frightened of it is what sends everybody scurrying around chasing dreams, illusions, wars, peace, love, hate, all that. Unknown is what it is. Accept that it's unknown, and it's plain sailing."

All fear is bondage. After this experience I was convinced that I no longer feared death. I had confronted it head on, come to grips with my impermanence and found that fear was entirely optional. This brings to mind the Japanese samurai. It is suggested that the most refined of them had accepted the fact that they were already dead. This was in the understanding that they might better serve their master as a fearless warrior. Similarly, my experience, over time, has allowed me to better serve my master. That being *the ineffable nature of All*. While this experience was authentically liberating, I came to discover, during the later stages of the awakening process, that a far greater, quite unimaginable, level of fear awaited when I packed in the whole DJ story decades later. Transcending that fear led to final awakening.

Dare to Know

In a previous chapter, I mentioned the perfect storm that had been closing in on me for some time. Several conditions had combined to form a *spiritual super storm* that would ultimately force me to take action. This *perfect storm* metaphor has become somewhat of a cliché over time, but I feel it is an apt description in my case. Calling my situation a mere *tempest in a teapot* just doesn't work. A comparison to a natural calamity is a lot more visceral and closer to reality.

A *perfect storm* (origi-nating from the title of Sebastian Junger's book) is a descriptive expression of an event where a rare combination of circumstances will provoke a situation far out of the norm. In particular, the term is used to describe a hurricane that slams into a region's most vulnerable area, resulting in the worst possible devastation any such hurricane could ever produce. Calamity and death, or the threat thereof, was one of the driving forces behind the book's narrative. By novel's end, a full complement of fishing boat crew had perished. A similar kind of fate, though of a spiritual nature, eventually awaited me as well. We are talking here about the mother of all spiritual conflagrations. The ride was going to be a wild one. Though, like the ship's crew, I suspected not a whit of the incoming peril at the time. Let me now outline the final qualities that would whip the gathering storm into a chart-topping, full-blown, category five, ego-dissolving maelstrom.

As you may recall, some of the qualities of the approaching storm have already been mentioned. Certain foreshadowings like the spontaneous question that enigmatically presented itself several times in the form of, "Would you trade all your earthly treasures in order to gain enlightenment?" Then, as if in reply, experiencing a fire that actually destroyed all of those coveted possessions. Being plagued by ill health, particularly visual impairment which led to loss of employment and independence. Losing friends and family one after the other, in fairly short order. Studying ways to aid my chances of survival in an emergency situation. Getting into the best shape of my entire life was also thrown into the mix. Particularly important was the realization that there is more to reality than meets the eye. This arose due to exhaustive research into fields of a mystical, esoteric as well as sociopolitical nature. My increasing realization that beliefs are of dubious merit also surely increased the *barometric pressure* of the arriving gale force "winds" (biblical usage of the Hebrew word *ruach* denotes wind or Holy Spirit interchangeably). In fact, unless we personally experience something, Buddha would have us question the value of any belief whatsoever:

> Do not believe in any-thing simply because you have heard it. Do not believe in anything simply because it is spoken and rumoured by many. Do not believe in anything simply because it is found written in your religious books. Do not believe in anything merely on the authority of your teachers and elders. Do not believe in traditions because they have been handed down for many generations. But after observation and analysis, when you find that anything agrees with reason and is conducive to the good and benefit of one and all, then accept it and live up to it.

German philosopher, Immanuel Kant, during *The Age of Reason* (an 18th century movement) held a similar viewpoint, though for quite different reasons. His rallying cry of *Sapere aude*, translated as, "Have courage to use your own wise understanding and judgement," or simply "Dare to know" was seen as a necessary antidote to the dumbing down of humanity, which occurred through the simplistic mystical, religious and banal superstitious beliefs of the Middle Ages. While Buddhist doctrine concerned the realm of spiritual emancipation, Kant saw his as emancipation from anything religious, yet both movements perceived the absolute necessity of using one's own direct experience and reasoning to gain liberation. That is one of the reasons why I prefaced this book by asking you not to believe anything I say.

It is crucial that you determine what is not a fiction through your own direct experience. Knowing something gleaned by your own observations and wise analysis has a degree of certainty approaching 100 percent. That's getting much closer to *the truth*, isn't it? Believing in something without experiencing it directly is worthless. You can read all the books in the world, be advised by the greatest scholars or sagest gurus, yet still fundamentally be none the wiser. What you believe to be true may not actually be reflected in reality. I certainly found this to be the case. This idea is so important that it forms one of the cornerstones of the teachings of American spiritual guide, Byron Katie. She asks us to consider the simple question, "Is it true?" This is the first of four questions that she poses as part of her core teaching known as *The Work*.

When you wake up, you will find all of your beliefs, especially those you cherished most dearly, to be absolute rubbish. *Direct knowledge* that comes from transcending the thing altogether. That leads is where I found myself come easily. Especially not

conceptual mind is a different you to the *Truth* indeed. That headed though it did not at the start.

In fact, the decision to find the truth came as a bit of

actually begin my quest to a surprise. Quite suddenly I found myself with no caregiver at all. My wife and I had separated a few years back. The one person on whom I depended to get me places, like driving me once a month to the city for groceries or to medical check-ups, announced he was no longer interested in doing so. With no transportation whatsoever, even basic necessities could no longer be procured. Living any semblance of a life out in the rural countryside became impossible. For all intents and purposes, I was now alone in the world. I had come to a crossroad. At times it felt a bit like I had been pushed rather than voluntarily moved towards the place where I now found myself. Specifically, at the confluence of two diverging roads—shades of Frost's poem all over again.

I could once again attempt to pick myself up and try to continue in the direction things were presently going. Alternatively, I could elect to take the road less travelled. Looking carefully at my situation I had a sense that things were conspiring against me. But for what purpose I wondered? Why had my life been inexorably transforming me into a version of *DJ-lite?* It was simply a fact that, in the last few years, my life had decided to wholeheartedly express itself around the adjective *less*. As in, job-less, fat-less, belief-less, health-less, family-less, and home-less—hell even my hairline was shrinking! Like a character from a B-grade movie, I had become the *incredible disappearing man*.

I had no choice but to face the facts. My previous life was pretty much gone and what remained was getting less tenable by the day. Simply put—no food no life. With that the storm broke. Whatever was remaining of my life came crashing down. There was no option but to leave the countryside. And there was even more to it than that. I realized that the whole bloody DJ story had to go. A distinctly new way of relating to life would be sought out. The old paradigm was no longer tenable. Like an old romance, the time had finally come to admit it just wasn't working anymore and have done with it.

There really was no excuse not to. One way or another my load had been lightened to such an extent that an undertaking of this degree became quite possible. That was my epiphany. With my familiar means of transportation removed, I suffered the final bang to the head necessary to prod me into action. I realized circumstances couldn't have become more favourable for taking up the spiritual search. Socrates had talked of the unexamined life not being worth living. I could see that I was being offered the precious chance to explore this ideal as far as I possibly could. If only I dared to take it. That then is what I set out to do. Namely, find the *ultimate nature of reality.*

Truth or be damned became my rallying cry. I would pursue it with all my vigour. To pour all the energy I could muster into this search and be willing to keep at it until awakening occurred, or *death* caught up with me in the process. This, ironically enough, is exactly what happened on both counts. Nothing less would be accepted than a *do or die* ethos. I believed that if enlightenment were a possibility, surely I, above all other seekers, could find it. That sentiment may strike you as a tad arrogant, but I sincerely believed it. I knew that my personal strengths and quality of character, as well as my rich life experience, had all afforded me a great base from which to proceed. I was tenacious and patient by nature. If such a thing as enlightenment really existed, why should it not come to me as it had to others? But I needed more information. Did it really exist, or was it mere fable? Could ordinary people really achieve it? If so, how?

The prospect of beginning anew was both daunting and exciting. I decided to depart on January 1. Ring in the New Year with a spiritual *big bang*. Resolution—become enlightened. This was unprecedented. I had never made a resolution before. It seemed like a pretty good one to start with. If I succeeded, I would never have to make another one again, as *I* would no longer exist. I made that decision at the beginning of September. Four months remained. I would spend the time hunkered down on the farm. With no transportation, the food issue would be interesting. Always more than willing to try to make lemonade when handed those pesky lemons, I realized I could probably survive those four months in solitude with the food stores I currently had.

Except for going to a single medical check-up and conversing with a postman once, I didn't encounter a single soul during that entire time. In fact I didn't go anywhere or even talk to anyone on the phone. Total seclusion was the name of the game. It was a common spiritual strategy employed by many seekers, at one time or another, but was brand new territory for me.

I was living at the end of a dead-end road, with the nearest neighbour one mile away. Forest and field for as far as the eye could see. Autumn garden produce would provide sustenance for a while. As well there were emergency dry goods and 500 jars of salsa to draw upon. If I ate simply and in moderation (I was still dieting) I reckoned I could make it to January 1—fully four months away. Water was drawn by hand from a well. This was a great opportunity to test my survival skills as well as my resolve.

Life during that time was a peaceful, exceedingly simple affair. Not unlike that chronicled in Thoreau's *Walden; Or, Life in the Woods*, which was first published in 1854. His story was part personal declaration of independence, social experiment, spiritual voyage and manual for self-reliance. Like Henry David Thoreau's environment at Walden (though unlike myself, he received visitors and visited others, so was not a true hermit) a similar enclave had been constructed in my life. We both lived near a hamlet, yet far enough away to be totally secluded. My dwelling was of a similar size (both about 10X15 feet) to his and vintage as well. I was set up in the original farm homestead, dating from before the turn of last century. It had been long abandoned, as new housing was constructed elsewhere on the farm. Though it was very dilapidated and would be considered unsuitable for occupation by most, it was adequate for my needs. Composed of a single room and upstairs loft, the roof was prone to leaking during hard downpours.

In a sense, I guess I misled you about not having visitors, for on occasion two large snakes would slither downstairs from an unused loft. Particularly in the evening. This intrusion was originally rather unsettling, as they were a huge, black male/female pair, about six feet (two meters) long and as thick as a petite woman's wrist. An imposing sight to behold, especially if one was caught unawares while snoozing on the sofa. Though, in their defence, they usually heralded their arrival by slowly clunking their way down the stairs. I imagine they were simply looking for rats—their favourite prey. Living in such circumstances brought to mind Thoreau on simple living: "I went to the woods because I wished to live deliberately, to front only the essential facts of life, and see if I could not learn what it had to teach, and not, when I came to die, discover that I had not lived."

During this period, my attention was still directed towards weight loss and physical fitness. By this time, the remainder of the seventy pounds was getting increasingly more difficult to shed. The hours spent on the stationary bike afforded me much time to get an action plan together. Where does one start? I knew very little about spiritual seekers and what it was they actually did. I tended to be wary of the New Age brigade as they impressed me as non-rational, often gullible folk. When I cared to investigate areas of interest to them—such as channelling and séances or more contemporary avenues like the wellness blessing, theta healing and the information contained in *The Secret*—I had to shake my head in wonder. Some of it was nonsense to be sure. Be it New Age ramblings or messages from our corporate handlers, spread the bullshit thick enough and it seems you can get people to believe almost anything you want. I found it easy being a skeptic, but I made sure I never became cynical. There is a huge difference.

The potential avenues leading to enlightenment were as varied as Baskin-Robbins ice cream flavours. Mantra, yantra, tantra, chakra—on and on it went. One thing I had a sense of was that there were two broad approaches to spirituality. The progressive path and the direct route. The popular progressive path seemed far too convoluted and dreadfully slow for my sensibilities. It also often included elements that smacked of religiosity, which was of little interest to me.

My aim was to discover, as quickly as possible, if there were real, tangible merits to the spiritual pursuit. If it panned out, I saw no need to spend decades in the pursuit of realization. After all, how difficult could it be to discover *that* which I already *was*? A spiritual lifestyle held no appeal. It was only the final realization that I was after. The quicker the better as far as I was concerned. From the start I had an inkling that this thing could be accomplished if I had a mind to do so. But again ... where to start? I eventually decided I would direct my energies towards a twofold plan. I settled on utilizing entheogenic/psychedelic plants and the contemplative Tibetan Buddhist practice of realizing one's true nature through meditation and introspection. I suspected that they would complement each other well. This indeed turned out to be the case.

I was ignorant about both subjects. I had actually never experimented with drugs. In fact I had never even smoked a cigarette. I didn't experientially know the first thing about mind-altering substances. Sometimes I would stumble upon a positive report or mystical account of psychedelic use. The effects appeared interesting, but, admittedly, I largely bought into the government's propaganda that extolled the dangers associated with the use of evil psychedelic drugs. Carlos Castaneda's books mitigated that feeling somewhat. "How could they be so terrible when he had such positive spiritual results," I wondered? Then, Dr. Rick Strassman's book entitled, *DMT The Spirit Molecule*, was published, and it changed everything. Results showed that a powerful mind-altering substance posed no significant short- or long-term negative side effects to those taking it. However, the positive effects were extraordinarily profound. DMT appeared to literally transport you to a different dimension and provide you with insights, spiritual and otherwise, that could hardly be imagined. I decided this substance merited further study. Over the course of several years I had done a little cursory investigation. But presently my thoughts were mostly focused on the more pragmatic elements of my prospective journey. Particularly where I would I go and how I would get there.

I decided I would eventually land at a certain little Tibetan Buddhist retreat centre on Canada's coast. It was quite new, appeared to be struggling in its birth pangs and looked like a good place to get Buddhist teachings and learn about meditation. However, before settling there, I intended to experience what psychedelics had to offer. Having no contacts in the drug culture of any sort, and no past experience to draw upon, I needed to find some *tutors.* A youth hostel seemed a sensible place to find people knowledgeable in that area. I had no choice but to fly by the seat of my pants and see where I landed.

The decision to actually experiment with drugs came as somewhat of a shock. Something I could never have imagined doing a decade previously. As I have indicated, I was as straight as it got when it came to taking drugs of any kind. The plan was to temporarily set up shop for the winter in a youth hostel several hundred miles from the Buddhist retreat centre. Hopefully I could quickly learn what I needed to in order to actually begin experimenting with mind-altering substances as quickly as possible. That, and a fast Internet connection (in order to do further online psychedelic research) were my primary goals in seeking out a youth hostel.

The plan was coming together nicely. A few loose ends were left to sort out, like acquiring a new lightweight traveller's wardrobe. My new waist size had made the old one obsolete. Other lightweight gear appropriate for my few needs would be acquired along the way as well, until all my possessions fitted nicely into one small backpack. That's true freedom for you.

Finally the departure date arrived. It was an odd sensation phoning the cab company, since I hadn't spoken to anyone in months. Arriving at the train station, amid all the hustle and bustle of the holiday season, I marvelled at the mass of humanity. It sure was an eye and earful—momentarily verging on sensory overload. After four months of solitude it was quite an experience to simply hear the spoken word emanating from a living being. For a moment it all made me a little dizzy. But I soon got over the confusing hullabaloo. I couldn't let things distract me too much. I had a train to catch. It was with a certain sense of melancholy and apprehension, and also anticipation of the adventure about to unfold, that I waved goodbye to my life. I wondered if anything would ever be quite the same again.

Setting Forth

The ticket inspector clipped a small slip of paper over my seat which indicated my destination for this inaugural leg of the journey. I was glad someone knew where I was going. As I watched the ticket inspector disappear into the next carriage, I noted the unusual attire of the passenger seated across from me. Mennonite or Amish I surmised. What a coincidence. The last time I met a person of that background was during the very first solo journey I ever took as a kid.

A long time had passed since then, but the memory of travelling to the Pennsylvania Dutch Country to meet Old Order Amish, the *Plain People*, was still vivid. I had just graduated from high school. A friend and I had spent a year planning a grand adventure that would take us south into the Eastern Seaboard of the United States on our motorcycles. We planned to camp in the Catskill Mountain area in upper New York State and visit New York City, the casinos of Atlantic City and the Amish. We had little money but lots of enthusiasm and curiosity. In the end my friend failed to follow through on the plan, leaving me pretty distraught.

But I didn't let the opportunity pass. I set out alone. I just couldn't resist the urge to know what was *out there*. To see beyond the horizon. This interest, which actually bordered on compulsion, probably explained why the original *Star Trek* series was my all time favourite TV show. The opening refrain of, "Space … the Final Frontier …" always gave me goose bumps. In a previous chapter I mentioned the rallying cry of sapere aude, during the age of reason — *dare to know*. If you recall this was Kant's call for intellectual self-liberation. I like to think that the genesis for continuing my motorcycle trip originated with the original sentiment of the full quote from which this phrase originates.

Its first historical reference can be traced back to the Roman poet Horace's first book of *Epistles,* where he wrote, *dimidium facti qui coepit habet; sapere aude, incipe* (Book I, epistle ii, line 40*)*. Loosely translated it means *He who begins is half done. Dare to know. Make a beginning.* That is what drove me forward all those years ago. The simple desire *to know* proved irresistible. And so it was that once again I found myself seated next to an Amish gentleman as the desire continued unabated.

If we look at the definition of the word *know* we find it means *to perceive directly, to have direct cognition of.* To experientially know is to discover reality for yourself. According to Horace's words the very fact that I was now seated on a train meant that my quest was already half completed.

I marvelled at the beautiful scenery unfolding in front of my eyes as first hundreds, then thousands, of miles rolled by, but I knew it was ultimately of little import. It was not this experience that I was chasing. Rather my voyage of discovery was, as French novelist Marcel Proust expressed, *not in seeking new landscapes but in having new eyes.* That was precisely what I was after, and I reckoned psychedelics held a lot of promise and could quite possibly provide me with the new way of seeing Proust advocated. Before I proceed in greater detail, I would like to relate a story I picked up from the Internet a few years ago.

It was reported that a much respected 66-year-old Canadian psychologist pulled up to a border crossing with the intention of entering the USA to visit family. The guard turned up online evidence that the fellow had experimented with LSD for therapeutic research purposes some forty years ago in a university setting. With that he was banned from ever entering the United States of America again. No outlet for appeal. Case closed. This episode illustrated the very real consequences of living in the pathologically insane realm of Big Brother. Or *Bizarro World* as I thought of it. Bizarro was a planet of opposite sensibilities as compared to those on earth and originated from the pages of the Superman comic universe.

Here everything was transposed compared to normal reality—up was down, war was peace and the ugly and perverse were deemed the epitome of beauty. Unfortunately that's where we live today folks. Take your blinders off and have a peek. Bizarre doesn't begin to describe it. The American strategy of levelling whole villages during the Vietnam War, in order to *save them*, came to mind. The powers-that-be seemingly continued to employ such an insane strategy while conducting their *war on drugs*.

Ostensibly their professed mandate was to serve and protect the populace by eradicating the evil scourge that drugs posed. In their zeal to prevent as many people as possible from taking up such a potentially destructive lifestyle, one rife with destroyed families and ruined lives, the authorities deemed it in the best interest of all to incarcerate the unfortunate drug abusers for years. Consequently tearing apart their families and utterly destroying their lives. Of course this policy is not endemic to the good ole USA alone. This kind of madness is liberally spread throughout the world.

In order to avoid a fate similar to that which befell the psychologist, a personal disclaimer is in order. I want to again clearly state, as I did at the beginning of the book, that everything presented herein has no more truth to it than a fairy tale does. It's all fictional. Consequently, when I speak of personal drug experience, take this into account. All mention of drug use will always refer to SWIM (someone who isn't me). Any claim otherwise is purely a narrative device. Border crossing personnel and any other interested officials please take note—I have never used illegal drugs! I trust this disclaimer will ensure my safe passage around the globe.

Backpackers Guesthouse

As I walked up to the main desk, my senses were overwhelmed by a cacophony of sight, sound and odour. Amongst the smells were those of a freshly mopped floor and multicultural cuisine being prepared in the adjacent cafeteria. Several backpackers in their early twenties sat around chatting on funky couches in the far corner. A large bulletin board was covered with advertising promoting the underground arts scene or other venues that might appeal to the largely Generation Y/Echo boomers I saw milling about. I was encouraged. In the vernacular of the times, it held out high hopes for being an *epic* place to hang out. *Epic* of course related to the possibility of scoring drugs. I was pretty sure they were about. It was probably the blaring righteous sounds of Bob Marley that first tipped me off.

This guesthouse offered a discounted off-season rate on a few selected rooms. First come first served at the start of the month. No exceptions. I had arrived early to claim my spot. The cheapest possible accommodation would suffice as I was not here for the decor. And I had brought a roommate with me to further defray costs. He was a thin and pasty, though relatively handsome, young German man who aspired to make Canada his new home. As befits a pop star, which he so longed to be, he was thoroughly vapid and vain. We had absolutely nothing in common. His favourite topic was, of course, himself, but of this he had very little of interest to say. He seemed to have no appreciable skills outside of singing and that was mediocre at best.

We had met at another hostel. I asked him if he wanted to share a room for several months. The bargain basement rate of only $180 a month for his share appealed to him since he was presently living off the money his mommy would send him after he placed yet another desperate call home for more cash. I warned him it would be a small room for that price. He said anything would be fine as it would surely be an improvement over the single bunk he now occupied in a large dorm room. On that account he was not entirely correct.

I could see his growing sense of shock once the door to the room swung open. It was a windowless crypt that was literally just large enough to accommodate a single bunk bed. I had seen prison cells with more space. There was absolutely no place to stow anything so luggage was kept on the mattress top. Fortunately I am not so tall so there was still enough room for me to stretch out despite having all my stuff placed at my feet. It looked like it would be an interesting several months marooned with this guy.

I soon joined the local fitness centre to help preserve my physical well-being as much as possible, since I expected to spend many hours cooped up doing research. I set to work on the important matter of getting acquainted with someone who was trustworthy and knowledgeable about drug culture. At the same time, I had to devote myself to further academic research on the topic of psychedelics, since I had merely scratched the surface to date. What follows are some of my findings. In the first few months the topics were widely disparate. One day might be spent cataloguing the different categories of hallucinogens. The next day practical issues of their use might arise, or perhaps I might get sidetracked and start exploring the musings of a psychedelic or spiritual philosopher. As you are about to discover, some of it was pretty eye-opening stuff.

Perhaps many of you are inexperienced psychedelic users or complete neophytes much like I was. If that is the case you will probably find something of interest in the following pages. By way of an introduction to this fascinating and potentially edifying world of mind-altering substances, I would like to begin with their broad definition.

First let me explain that the drugs I am going to describe are not recreational in purpose. They do not get you high in order to have a few jollies or so that you may forget all your troubles for an hour or two. This class of substances does not produce the euphoric feeling most assume they might. Consequently they are rarely, if ever, abused. In fact you usually have to *screw your courage to the sticking place,* as Shakespeare put it, every time you jump back into the fray. Taking these compounds is a serious business indeed.

They are not narcotic in nature, though I have heard them incorrectly referred to as such. That class of substances refers to the opiate family, like morphine and heroin. Those get you high. The compounds under consideration here most assuredly don't. Throughout the last century quite a few terms were proposed to classify these compounds. This was due to the fact that there was so little agreement about what these substances were or how they operated. The etymology of the names of the most popular ones proved interesting from a philosophical viewpoint.

It is a fact that our perceptions of a drug often influence our experience of it. A placebo is a great case in point. Invariably, whatever label scientists or health care professionals chose to use to identify these substances, their own personal biases towards how they thought these compounds functioned were revealed. A shaman may refer to a DMT-containing ayahuasca brew as *plant medicine* or a *spiritual aid* while a doctor may call the very same beverage a short-acting *schizotoxin* that caused the patient to have a short-acting psychotic break with reality. One man's sacrament was another's doorway to pathological delusion.

One of the earlier and more commonly accepted terms was *hallucinogen*. It is still the most widely used clinical term, though it is perceived by some to have several shortcomings. Hallucinogen emphasizes the visual effects while totally ignoring the psychological or profound spiritual insights such a compound may afford. Furthermore, one may experience few, if any, hallucinations while actually under the drug's influence. That was often my experience. Objections also arise since many associate hallucinogens with delirium and insanity.

In my opinion, the term *psychedelic*, which is commonly held to mean *mind manifesting,* is a more accurate description of what these substances actually accomplish. Interestingly, when I looked at the etymology of the root word *psyche,* I found that the original Greek meant *soul, spirit or the invisible animating principle or entity which occupies and directs the physical body,* in addition to the commonly accepted *mind.* It seemed to me that when Dr. Humphry Osmond coined the term in 1957, he choose not to emphasize the spiritual connotations of the word. He was a respected man of science so, of course, he stressed the more prosaic reading of the term. Aldous Huxley, on the other hand, had suggested the more spiritual word *phanerothyme* (thymos meant *spiritedness* or *soulfulness*), but Dr. Humphrey objected. His stated reason was that the term was *too beautiful*. Actually, I imagine he felt Huxley's denotations smacked far too much of mystical mumbo jumbo nonsense—yet *psychedelic* carried with it the exact same connotations as Huxley's original *phanerothyme's* did. Humphrey just down-played the spiritual nuance and instead imparted a more acceptable *sober-minded* spin on it. Today academics and clinicians commonly accept psychedelic to mean *mind manifesting* just as Humphrey intended.

Unfortunately the term *psychedelic* carries with it all the negative baggage of the 1960s drug scene. When people of a certain generation hear the word psychedelic today they immediately flinch and associate it with LSD and crazed hippies. Initially I hesitated using the term myself until I experienced the effects firsthand. Now I use *psychedelic* without prejudice for it really does allow consciousness to be revealed in all its many guises.

The last classification commonly used to describe the drugs of interest to me is *entheogen*. *Entheogen* was proposed in the late 1970s as a more socially-acceptable, re-branded replacement for *psychedelic*. Entheogen seems the preferred term among hip, modern psychonauts and urban neoshamans. Examining its etymology we find, *en* (within, inner), *theo* (Divine, God) and *gen* (becoming, creating). An entheogen appeared to be something that filled someone with the Divine and revealed spiritual Truth. Entheogen seemed to really embody the spirit of my endeavour; though in practice I found the divine more reticent to appear than I had hoped. The pioneers who had preceded me were an encouragement.

Famous figures of the 1950s and 1960s, like Aldous Huxley, Carlos Castenada, John Lilly and Timothy Leary assuaged my fears with their own personal tales of spiritual growth through the use of mind-altering substances. If respectable, erudite pioneers such as these guys (there did seem to be a preponderance of male figures in this field for some reason) could jump into the great unknown, then what was there to stop me?

Castaneda's early work on peyote and shamanic practice was quite revolutionary for the time and great reading as a kid. Huxley's work in his seminal book, *The Doors of Perception*, described the mystical effects of mescaline (the active ingredient of peyote cactus). He was a very well-respected, sober-minded intellectual of the highest calibre. Though it was *DMT: The Spirit Molecule* that finally moved me to act.

Dr. Strassman's book was like nothing I had ever come across before. The other two components of the literary triad that inspired my curiosity enough to consider trying entheogens were Daniel Pinchbeck's *Breaking Open the Head: A Psychedelic Journey into the Heart of Contemporary Shamanism* and any material put out by Terence McKenna. Without stumbling across the works of these three provocative authors, I wonder if I ever would have taken the leap.

It all began by happenstance one day as I came across an Internet interview conducted to help publicize the launch of Dr. Strassman's new book. Hearing the term *Spirit molecule* alone was enough to intrigue me. Once I delved a little deeper into the subject, I was hooked. What I found astounded me. Dr. Strassman's clinical study seemed to demonstrate that a naturally occurring psychedelic, found in the human body, could launch your consciousness to-wards actual otherworldly physical realms where you could interact with real sentient beings. That seemed something worth investigating. I considered Dr. Strassman's work a touchstone as I discovered other researchers and authors in the field.

Terence McKenna stood quite apart from any other psychedelic researcher. He died only a few years prior to my discovering him. While not well known in mainstream literary circles, he was a giant in the field of psychedelic research and was probably the person most responsible for popularizing the use of DMT. This metaphysician, philosopher and botanist had a keen intellect and was also one heck of a raconteur to boot. A post-modern psychedelic bard extraordinaire. Strassman's work engaged me more in a sober-minded, rational, clinical way, while McKenna inspired through the emotions and the imagination. Giordano Bruno's words came to mind when trying to describe the McKenna mystique: "I cleave the heavens, and soar to the infinite. What others see from afar, I leave far behind me."

McKenna's tales of entering the drug-induced bardo state of hyperspace and engaging *bejeweled self-transforming machine elves* left me entertaining the possibility that the fairy realm really did exist after all. He assured his audience time and time again that all it would take was a long hard drag on a glass pipe to confirm this reality for themselves.

Authors such as these underscored that if psychedelics were taken in a responsible, well-informed manner, much could be learned about the nature of reality. Their material helped erode my fear and distrust of drugs. With enough research under my belt, I came to the conclusion that the powers-that-be (PTB) were misinforming the public about the dangers of these substances. It was obvious, even at this early stage, that the information about the evils of psychedelics, so stridently propagandized in the media, was nothing more than a load of hokum.

It became apparent that a long-running disinformation campaign was being employed. The PTB had decided long ago that we had no right to think outside the box. The act of exploring our own consciousness was verboten. Taking drugs jeopardized the status quo far too much to ever allow it to continue unchecked. They had placed themselves squarely in the position of *brother's keeper* and enforced a system that sought to maintain this position at all costs.

If you think I am prone to hyperbole, consider this snippet spoken by sociologist Richard Blum (at a Foothill College forum), transcribed from a 1966 CBC documentary entitled *How to go out of your mind— The LSD Crisis:*

> Many become less and less interested in the problems and affairs of the real world outside, and emphasize for themselves the real world inside. Then he blatantly reveals the government's real concern over drugs when he elaborates, what is the critical level for a given society before we begin to have troubles in keeping the ploughs and machines going?

This comes from a man awarded the Bronze Star for being the U.S. Army's first combat psychologist during the Korean War. He spoke of *machines* ceasing to operate. Perhaps he has some personal insight gathered during the years he spent employed in the military.

I am referring here to a military test in which soldiers were administered LSD out on the parade square. Not surprisingly the war machine came to a giddy grinding halt rather quickly. Happy and joyful soldiers do not an army make. These *machines* of war had ceased to function, just as Blum had warned us they would. Like the old film title suggests, *Suppose They Gave a War and Nobody Came?*

I fear it is a pool of largely biomechanical automatons, dumbed-down slaves of war and commerce alike, that the PTB desire most. Nothing must be seen to jeopardize this. It is interesting to note that Blum went on to work for the CIA around the time of the LSD forum. That agency now has a most sordid, unsavoury and perhaps even lethal reputation regarding its previous experimental use of LSD on unsuspecting test subjects.

Former Harvard professor, Richard Alpert (later to be known as spiritual writer and mystic Ram Das), comments in the CBC film about his reaction to attending the forum. He found the fraternity of anti-psychedelic presenters, such as Richard Blum, to be generally little more than a gang of knee-jerk noisy naysayers, totally committed to maintaining the status quo and frightened of anything that might change it. I think it is also correct to say that the apprehension about psychedelics also arose simply as a result of an egoic coping mechanism. Anything that threatened its hegemony was obviously an area of great concern since its very existence was put at risk. The ego's self-identification, which consists of thoughts, feelings and emotions, knows that its position is very shaky and rather untenable. In reality its existence is held in place by only the flimsiest of threads. Thus, allowing any kind of insight into its ephemeral nature was only courting disaster.

A parallel of sorts can be drawn with the Catholic Church's initial exposure to these substances in seventeenth century South America. Any spiritual ceremony utilizing sacred sacraments such as *flesh of the Gods* (sacred psilocybin mushrooms) or *vine of the soul* (DMT-containing brew called ayahuasca) or *divine cactus* (peyote) was certainly too great a threat to the Church's authority to remain unchallenged. Consequently such practices were ruthlessly suppressed or eradicated outright.

The Church's own largely ineffectual version of a holy sacrament paled in comparison to the real thing and must have appeared to be a sure sign of a bogus practice to the indigenous peoples. Those the Church wished to convert put it well when they said, "The white man goes into his church house and talks about Jesus; the Indian goes into his teepee and talks to Jesus."

Jesuit priests who tried ayahuasca for the first time were suitably impressed and horrified by the beverage, calling it a *diabolical potion*. And so it continues up to the present. That which is misunderstood, or perhaps understood only too well, is deemed evil and taboo by the authorities. What ignorance and arrogance expressed by those who would deny us our birthright to freely explore our own consciousness as we see fit. One day I had a good giggle when I realized that these people had the audacity to actually ban plants outright. How ridiculous. And to think that research has demonstrated much value in these substances. Is there no end to their lunacy?

Clinical tests and experiments carried out on psychedelics, beginning in the 1950s and continuing up to the present, have demonstrated promising results. Indeed several treatment centres, spread throughout the world, utilize the psychedelic ibogaine to treat various addiction problems. Early LSD studies indicated it might have proven an effective alcoholism treatment, but unfortunately research like this was cut short.

The spiritual use of the psychedelic peyote cactus by Native Americans dates back to before recorded history. A conservative estimate is at least 5,000 years ago. Modern studies of it began in the late 1880s and by 1897 its principal active ingredient, mescaline, had been isolated. Ernst Spath was the first person to synthesize mescaline, in his laboratory, in 1919. Amazingly, the last detailed analysis of the effects of mescaline was published in 1927 under the title "Der Meskalinrausch" (The Mescaline High). We're fast approaching one hundred years later and nothing further is scientifically known about it. Mescaline is still widely used by Native American healers. Obviously, the peyote ceremony is providing a service to the native community since it remains in high regard. It would appear that Western medicine is struggling to offer the same therapeutic benefits. Yet mescaline-containing plants and other psychedelics remain largely prohibited and ignored.

It wasn't until twenty-six years later, with the publication of Aldous Huxley's *The Doors of Perception* in 1953, that interest was renewed in the effects of mescaline. This influential book, which chronicled Huxley's profound and mystical mescaline experience, sparked a wave of interest among clinicians and others as well. The psychedelic revolution had begun.

Clinical trials began around this time designed to chemically induce psychosis, hence the archaic term *psychotomimetic*, in people who had no prior mental health issues. Later LSD was hoped to have a similar effect. The reasoning went that perhaps by inducing a temporary psychosis of sorts, the effects could be studied and applied to schizophrenia. This avenue of research was soon abandoned. They were completely barking up the wrong tree. Later tests showed quite the opposite effect. Psychedelics didn't cause mental problems but were rather well suited to treating them. People suffering from common depression and even those afflicted with more serious maladies like autism and schizophrenia responded favourably to doses of LSD. Other entheogens were similarly efficacious.

A 1945 discovery, that cacti other than peyote (*Lophophora williamsii*) contained mescaline, came unexpectedly to those who cared about such things. At that time nobody suspected that there were yet more psychedelics to be discovered. San Pedro cactus (*Trichocereus pachanoi*) contained a significant amount of mescaline and was used in ceremonial practice by natives of several South American countries like Peru, Bolivia and Ecuador.

In the early days of psychedelic research, mescline was studied widely for the treatment of alcoholism, neurosis and other mental disorders, until the discovery of psilocybin and LSD overshadowed it. With American banker R. Gordon Wasson's discovery of psilocybin mushrooms in Mexico, a whole new avenue of research was opened.

In 1955 he and his wife became the first Western participants in an indigenous mushroom ceremony carried out in a remote Mexican village. In 1957, an article on their experiences was published in *Life* magazine, creating a minor sensation. Up to that point Westerners knew little to nothing about entheogenic mushrooms—having thought them to have been entirely eradicated by the Spanish centuries before. In fact a handful of underground shamans somehow managed to persist throughout the years and to pass on their knowledge of the sacred mushrooms cult.

It was one such Mazatec shaman ceremony that afforded Wasson his glimpse of the netherworld. In 1956, Roger Heim named the first hallucinogenic mushrooms known to modern science as *Psilocybe*. In 1958 chemist Albert Hofmann (first to synthesize LSD) first identified psilocin and psilocybin as the active compounds in these mushrooms.

LSD guru Timothy Leary, intrigued by the Wassons' *Life* article, travelled to Mexico to experience psychedelic mushrooms personally.

Upon returning to Harvard in 1960, he and Richard Alpert started the Harvard Psilocybin Project aimed at studying the psychological and religious uses of psilocybin and other psychedelic drugs. Leary and Alpert were forced to leave Harvard in 1963. However, this did not stop them extolling the virtues of hallucinogens wherever they could find an interested audience.

The popularization of psychedelics by such luminaries as Wasson and Leary, and noted authors like Aldous Huxley, Ken Kesey, John Lilly and later Terence McKenna and Robert Anton Wilson for example, led to a huge mainstream interest in the use of psychedelics throughout the world.

Magic mushrooms helped spark the counterculture movement of the 1960s. By the early 1970s, many different psychoactive *Psilocybe* mushroom species had been identified from around the world. Presently they total more than 200. A manual published by the McKenna brothers in the mid-1970s offered, for the first time, a means to artificially cultivate *Psilocybe cubensis* in large quantity. The availability of wild and cultivated Psilocybin mushrooms, along with the profound effect they produced, made them a very popular entheo-gen indeed.

Psilocybin mushrooms do not create a physical or psychological dependency and are less toxic than aspirin. The possibility of overdosing is next to zero. This holds for DMT as well, which I will discuss later. A psychedelic mushroom trip typically lasts from three to seven hours depending on amount consumed and manner of preparation and intake. Your physiology and constitution may have some bearing as well.

After consumption, the onset, beginning around the 30 minute mark, may be noted by a tingling or numbing of the extremities accompanied by a subtle cognitive and perceptual shift. Given more time, sense perception may be altered. For example, sounds and voices may be heard with greater clarity or from a farther distance away. Visual acuity may be enhanced with colours appearing more vivid. Music may instil a profound sense of cadence, rhythm and *meaning* not normally perceived. One may experience synesthesia, which is a mixing of senses, such as when one sees an object and experiences a concomitant flavour sensation or perceives a certain colour upon hearing a sound. Odder phenomena, like halos, energy lines or surfaces appearing to ripple, shimmy or breathe, may also be perceived.

Of course, full-blown hallucinations often arise, with eyes either open or closed. Objects may seem to disappear, change shape and colour or melt into the environment. Time may appear to slow down, speed up or stop entirely. A large variety of physiological and emotional shifts may occur such as: increased heart rate, body temperature fluctuation, increased energy, feelings of well-being or euphoria, pupil dilation, stress reduction, feelings of greater freedom, emotions intensifying, novel ideas appearing and spiritual or mystical insight.

One's relationship to the cosmos often shifts radically and a feeling of communing with a higher power may temporarily overwhelm bemushroomed psychonauts. These experiences are very beneficial to the psyche and often have religious overtones. In fact, in the very early days of psychedelic research, an experiment was undertaken to ascertain whether or not genuine mystical insight could arise as a result of simply ingesting psilocybin.

The 1962 "Marsh Chapel Experiment," also referred to as the "Good Friday Experiment," occurred at Harvard Divinity School's Marsh Chapel on Good Friday. The aim was to discover how religiously predisposed individuals, in this case divinity students, would react to being administered an entheogen. Almost all of the subjects of the experiment reported experiencing profound religious experiences in ways that they could not have foreseen. They felt the experiences were entirely authentic and of great importance. Astoundingly, a long-term follow-up investigation carried out some twenty-five years later found the subjects still reporting positive results from the experiment.

The follow-up study reported that the respondents felt that they had been significantly affected in a beneficial and persistent manner and expressed gratitude for having participated in the experiment. Rick Doblin reports in *The Journal of Transpersonal Psychology*, 1991, Vol. 23, No.1 that the effects consisted of:

> Enhanced appreciation of life and of nature, deepened sense of joy, deepened commitment to the Christian ministry or to whatever other vocations the subjects chose, enhanced appreciation of unusual experiences and emotions, increased tolerance of other religious systems, deepened equanimity in the face of difficult

life crises, and greater solidarity and identification with foreign peoples, minorities, women and nature, among others.

Beginning in 2002, a more rigorously controlled version of this psilocybin and mysticism experiment was conducted at Johns Hopkins University by Roland R. Griffiths, Ph.D., yielding similar results. Subjects for the most part reported profound spiritual experiences with lasting positive benefits. No participants had had any previous experience with hallucinogens. One-third reported that the experience was the single most spiritually significant moment of their lives, and over two-thirds rated it among the top five most spiritually significant events experienced during their lifetime. Dr. Griffiths states that:

> This is a truly remarkable finding. Rarely in psychological research do we see such persistently positive reports from a single event in the laboratory. This gives credence to the claims that the mystical-type experiences some people have during hallucinogen sessions may help patients suffering from cancer-related anxiety or depression and may serve as a potential treatment for drug dependence.

New psilocybin research was begun in 2008 involving patients suffering from depression and end-of-life anxiety due to the complications of cancer. The results concluded that psilocybin was a very suitable treatment for reducing stress and anxiety. Subjects described ego disintegration as they began to identify with a more holistic state of consciousness in which their personal worries and insecurities vanished. They often reviewed past relationships with loved ones with a new sense of compassion and empathy. As one of the participants, retired clinical psychologist Dr. Clark Martin described in a *New York Times* interview dated April 11, 2010:

> It was a whole personality shift for me, I wasn't any longer attached to my performance and trying to control things. I could see that the really good things

in life will happen if you just show up and share your natural enthusiasms with people. You have a feeling of attunement with other people.

Even after more than a year had passed since being part of the cancer study Martin reported it continued to help reduce his depression and anxiety while greatly improving his relationships with his daughter and friends. He placed it among "the most meaningful events of his life." That's quite a testament.

This kind of reportage, though rarely featured in the mainstream media, greatly inspired me to continue my research on entheogens. After reviewing both historical and contemporary sources, I was quite sure knowledge and wisdom could be provided by these substances. I was very surprised at the paucity of negative reports. Where was all the hard-hitting science on the *evils* of these substances I wondered? How about chronicles relating the trail of misery and ruined lives these substances left in their wake? Was I missing something?

Mystical Experience

All of this talk about *spiritual insight* and *mystical experience* got me to thinking as I continued to peruse the Internet from the comfort of my hostel bunk. Just what the heck was a mystical state anyhow? Short of taking the drug myself, what could I conceptually learn about this most sought-after experience? I decided to see what I could find, but refrained from consulting contemporary New Age sources in doing so.

I thought it might be a good idea to see what the folks of yesteryear had to say about such things, since the few contemporary sources I had checked out left me pretty confused. After all, if there were but one truth running through all of spirituality, the *perennial philosophy* as it were, then what did it matter in which epoch I chose to begin my investigation? I hoped references from a century back might be more succinct and insightful than their modern-day counterparts. I often found getting back to the basics a good strategy for understanding the truth, so decided to check out what three authorities from the turn of last century had to say on matters of mystical significance. They proved to be good foils as their views differed quite a bit from one another.

I'd like to make one thing clear before proceeding—a great distinction must be drawn between the kind of experiences psychedelics can instil and full-blown awakening. Enlightenment is neither an experience nor a state of being. Rather it is *beingness* itself. Psychedelics provide an experience that arises and passes away just as all experiences do, while abiding enlightenment is simply resting in what actually is. For now let's stick to the possible physical, aesthetic, philosophical, psychological, emotional and cathartic responses these substances may evoke and see if any of them relate to the mystical experience in any way.

In trying to gain a better appreciation of what the mystical experience is, one thing became apparent quite quickly—there is no consensus on the matter. I could see that expressing the ineffable was about as easy as attempting to make a glass of water by trying to gather up steam.

There were a plethora of possible explanations and descriptions of what constituted the mystical state or mystical experience. Some of it smacked of religiosity and that was, as Huxley put it, "for people who have not yet had a spiritual experience themselves." Other writers seemed to describe a more authentic experience. As a means of contrasting these two poles of spirituality, I offer the following, which I found to be of some use in my own understanding.

The label philosophers, mystics, psychologists and scientists have used to describe the so-called mystical experience are numerous and include: *transpersonal experience, non-ordinary state of consciousness, union with the divine, religious experience, unitary state, unitive experience, sacred experience, non-local experience, Christ consciousness, cosmic consciousness* and one of the newer ones presently being proffered, *quantum consciousness*. The experience is typically a highly subjective one, though sometimes seemingly devoid of any personhood whatsoever, where some kind of contact with a transcendent reality or encounter/union with the divine is experienced.

To flesh out these concepts a little more, I would now like to turn to the first of three writers I wish to mention. Namely noted American psychologist and philosopher, William James. In James' *The Varieties of Religious Experience* (1902), which is one of the best known works published on the mystical experience in the last one hundred years, he describes four marks of the mystical state. These are:

Ineffability
The mystery beyond all mysteries, described not by what it is but rather by what it isn't. If there is an object of contemplation, it defies description. Its content can never be adequately articulated to others in any meaningful way. Direct experience is seen as the only route to understanding. Feelings are often described in order to relay to others some semblance of what is going on but the experience is often

so inexplicable that little in the way of meaning is imparted. Mystical literature is filled with paradox and metaphor.

Noetic quality

Besides feelings, mystical states seem to also impart knowledge. They are states of insight unfathomed by the normal egoic consciousness. Offered are insight, awareness, revelation and illumination full of significance and meaning, brought forward with a startling sense of authority. Often an overwhelming perception of unity with the *All* or a sense of transcendence is felt. A sense of a timeless, spaceless void is often perceived. Great truths are realized as the *me identity* evaporates into the nothingness.

Transiency

James gathered that mystical states were fleeting and could not be sustained for very long. Usually no more than half an hour or at most an hour or two. Once faded away, their quality could be imperfectly recalled.

again, there was a sense and a continuation experience. It should be were thought able to sustain samadhi and other so-called

Though, if experienced of recognition, familiarity or progression of the noted that certain adepts prolonged periods of *higher states of consciousness,* for

much longer periods of time. Though again I stress that these are just examples of state-bound phenomena and not enlightenment itself.

Passivity

Swept up and overwhelmed by the reality of the moment, the mystic's *will to act* is subverted or controlled by some greater power or influence beyond them. This was often accompanied by a loss of body awareness (similar to an out-of-body experience). Related phenomena might also be apparent such as: a mediumistic trance, automatisms, healing powers, visions and voices. James said these were regarded as states of pseudo-enlightenment, not the mark of a fully enlightened being.

Though James' work was a popular pioneering study, not everyone agreed entirely with his approach and understanding of mysticism. Particularly outspoken was influential British spiritual writer Evelyn Underhill.

Her seminal work, entitled *Mysticism*, was published one year after James' death. She dismissed James' work for being too clinical and scientific for her liking. Compared to her work, James' *The Varieties of Religious Experience* read too much like a textbook, she said.

I would say his insights were not without merit. I certainly experienced all the categorized qualities he spoke of. The difference in Underhill's approach to understanding mysticism compared to James' can be put down to conflicting sensibilities. The devotional or heart-centred, emotionally driven practice seemed to resonate more with Underhill than did James' more contemplative insight and wisdom-based approach. I found equal measures of these components were essential to the awakening process. Underhill seemed inclined to stress the heart over the head in the majority of her writings.

Thus her style was evocative, romantic and practical in nature. It was not overly historical or scientific in presentation as she so critically recognized James' work to be. In response to James' four tenets she offers up her own:

- Mysticism is practical, not theoretical.
- Mysticism is an entirely spiritual activity.
- The business and method of mysticism is love.
- Mysticism entails a definite psychological experience.

Her work, in turn, has been criticized for being far too subjective, quite imponderable at times and lacking analytical and logical reasoning. For example, consider her definition of mysticism: "Mysticism is the art of union with Reality. The mystic is a person who has attained that union in greater or less degree; or who aims at and believes in such attainment."

A lot of words that said very little, if anything, of substance.

The insights she offered regarding the fledgling science of psychology now appear dated. At times she came off as being a tad sanctimonious, too. Her criticism of James' scientific approach is a case in point.

Apparently her wisdom was in part derived from her own direct experience. Perhaps debatable, but the implication was that James' understanding was not, thus inferior in some regard. James was forced to admit that his own spiritual make-up precluded him from having direct mystical insight for the most part. By his own admission, most of his understanding of mysticism was purely objective. Despite James' admission, I wondered if Underhill's criticism of him was well founded for James was known in some quarters to be the *Godfather of American Psychedelia*.

The movement began with an anonymous article published in 1874 in *The Atlantic Monthly* that was in fact written by James. "The Anaesthetic Revelation" and "The Gist of Philosophy" suggested that the essence of mysticism and spiritual philosophy could well be found in nitrous-oxide inhalation, more commonly known as laughing-gas inebriation. James experienced ecstatic visionary insights that clearly impacted his philosophical outlook, and these extraordinary revelations were noted to be an abiding positive influence for the remainder of his life. James was known to have used other psychedelics available at the time as well, including peyote.

Significantly James felt it imperative to submit his first article anonymously. This inclination persists today as my desire to use a pseudonym can attest. Over 100 years have passed and still this avenue of research has a certain unsavoury reputation about it. No wonder James felt obliged to downplay his personal spiritual insights, for, after all, they were *artificially* induced and therefore deemed to be less than authentic by Underhill and others of her ilk.

James' writings don't seem to support the supposition that these drug-induced states were not really legitimate. In *The Varieties of Religious Experiences* he includes such passages as:

> One conclusion was forced upon my mind at that time, and my impression of its truth has ever since remained unshaken. It is that our normal waking consciousness, rational consciousness as we call it, is but one special type of consciousness, whilst all about it, parted from it by the filmiest of screens, there lie potential forms of consciousness entirely different.

An article in *The Atlantic Monthly* (May 1996) written by Dmitri Tymoczko validates the authenticity of James' experience with the following passage:

> Drugs helped James to understand what religious belief was like from the inside. When he took nitrous oxide,

he was for all intents and purposes a religious mystic. ("Thought deeper than speech!" he wrote while on the drug. "Oh my God, oh God, oh God!").

This kind of insight seems to be getting closer to the heart of the matter, but was spiritual truth actually being relayed to James through the drugs he took? Was he really learning anything of true value?

Apparently the majority of his skeptical peers at the time felt his experiments misguided, if not downright reckless. Religious sorts were threatened by the comparisons this *nitrous-oxide philosopher* was making with what they considered to be the real thing. This debate rages on unabated up to the present.

Insight from a gas canister, what rubbish! This sentiment is not at all surprising given that it arose from a Western mindset bent on vanquishing psychedelics to the dustbin of history for their so-called profane and anti-religious nature. This, in part, explained James' initial reluctance to pub-licly acknowledge his experiences. Evelyn Under-hill's negative perception of the man's work probably stems in part from a similar bias. James should have counted himself lucky though, for a few centuries earlier his musings might very well have aroused the ire of the Church and earned him a session with the Inquisitor.

I think that something I call the *proximity test* can be a helpful concept in ascertaining the validity or relative merit of potential spiritual guidance. It is a gauge that measures how close to the source of direct mystical inspiration the teacher's or writer's experience actually lies. Primary sources of knowledge, by my definition, would be the most valid and are considered to be embodied only by fully realized enlightened so-called *masters*. Direct interaction with these individuals is, of course, superior to reading their texts. If you are not certain of someone's status, ask them directly. Don't assume anything. Chances are great they aren't abiding in Reality. If they indicate that they are fully realized ask them how so? If someone replies, "Those who say don't know. Those who know don't say" you'd be advised to walk away or get clarification. That reply is often a ploy used by the ignorant to keep their true status hidden. I know of at least one great teacher who *knew* and said so to as many people who would listen— Siddhārtha Gautama Buddha, The Awakened One.

Secondary sources would include those individuals with some actual mystical experience or insight, though not a complete and abiding realization. These folks often draw inspiration from and cite primary sources, as they endeavour to deepen their own understanding. That is where I would place James and Underhill. Tertiary sources would be those who quote the primary and secondary sources since they lack any direct experience themselves.

Direct personal mystical experience is essential to anyone who seeks knowledge of the Absolute, but a crucial distinction must be realized. Namely, understanding the difference between putting your faith in belief systems and actual authentic direct experience itself. Only one carries with it the possibility of discerning the Truth for yourself. The other assures the delusional state is maintained.

Truth is a bit like the binary system. Binary holds information in an on or off relationship. Plus or minus, yes or no. Similarly truth is either completely true or 100 percent false. There are no half-truths to be found in reality. Beliefs do not work the same way. They are

relative in nature. Truth is
to escape a lot of people. I
which people proclaimed
valid as mine was.

I pointed out to them that
truths at all. Sure I held beliefs

not relative. This fact seems
have had conversations in
that their *truth was just as*

I didn't actually have any
but truths were self-evident so

there was no need for me to prop them up. It was true that the earth was a sphere. I never felt I had to defend that statement. It is true that I am wearing shoes and it would seem ridiculous from your point of view if I attempted to convince you of this fact. You could clearly see that footwear was affixed to the bottom of my feet. It was not *my truth;* it was simply an accurate statement of fact. It is true that the world is round — full stop. Truths have no relative degree of validity. Truths and beliefs are obviously not the same thing, yet countless people fail to make this distinction.

Realizing what is actually true and not merely a reflection of your belief system can ultimately lead you to liberation from illusion. Beliefs keep you firmly embroiled in delusion and sadly that is where most of humanity lies. When you are stuck identifying with an illusory state of being, everything you perceive is premised upon the fact that it is not *authentic* in any real way. Reality from this perspective is just varying degrees of deception. Everything is relative and speculation abounds. Magical thinking prevails around every corner—if we believe something, ergo it is true. Nonsense!

Reality for most is experienced as a kind of witch's brew. Into the cauldron they stir beliefs, along with a large dose of speculation, usually followed with a dollop of conjecture and a pinch of hopes, wishes and dreams. Voila—a sure recipe for confusion.

If a genuine elixir of knowledge were ever formulated that allowed the imbiber a chance to actually awaken to the Truth, to become instantly enlightened, the result would be skepticism, distrust, disbelief and, mostly, sheer panic for the egoic centre. That is because consensual reality is composed solely of beliefs. The egoic *me sense* doesn't actually know how to relate to reality as it actually is. I experienced my ego reacting in precisely this manner.

This brings to mind the story of Galileo Galilei. Most of us know the story of how he held a heliocentric view of the cosmos. The earth was not the centre of the universe as the Church held but rather the sun was the centre of our whole solar system. By holding this contrarian view he paid dearly for it with a life of imprisonment. He assured the Church hierarchy that his views were sound, and all they had to do was look through his telescope to come to the same conclusion.

The reason the Church hierarchy refused to do this was that they knew that the Devil was quite capable of making anything appear in the telescope, so it was best not to take a look. Why let a little common sense and reason stand in the way of great story? Don't bother me with the facts Galileo, *my mind is already made up.* After all who, other than the Church, would be better placed to know the ultimate nature of reality? Damned be any who claimed otherwise, direct experience or not. Galileo was obviously a madman or a heretic. The flat earth, disease caused by bad air, the impossibility of heavier-than-air machines taking flight, the theory of evolution and the Big Bang are several more examples of man's ability to thoroughly deceive himself.

All we have are our beliefs. Direct mystical experience will show you the false nature of holding up beliefs as your only arbiter of reality. Abiding in the Truth as an awakened soul is just that. All beliefs are ultimately of no value if one is seriously enmeshed in the Truth game. *Beliefs are bullshit* through and through. I hope you understand this. If you get nothing more out of this book than that single concept, you will be doing well. This is so important. All I ask is for you to do is recognize the truth of my statement, beliefs are bullshit—and if you do then you have just fallen victim to bullshit once again—it's all bullshit, that includes everything I have put down in words here. Only your own direct experience will reveal to you what's what. That is why I keep saying, "Don't believe anything I say." Go and experience it for yourself. I guarantee you will never figure out what enlightenment is by reading this, or any book. You've got to live it to learn it—to Be it.

I wish I had been aware of that fact years ago. As I indicated previously, I read a library's worth of esoteric books but never got any wiser. It was like I spent thirty-five years furiously spinning away on my bike never realizing the rear wheel was being held aloft by a bike stand formulated entirely out of beliefs. *Standing down* has made all the difference. When you no longer prop up your false sense of self by constantly referencing beliefs, thoughts and desires, you will be amazed. Of course, the psychedelic path was rife with belief systems. Let's see how we might avoid these pitfalls shall we?

Consider Terence McKenna, perhaps the most influential *altered* *statesman* of psychedelics alive after Leary left the scene. I thoroughly believed his mushroom/ DMT experiences could serve as a good model for understanding what I would likely experience myself. His talks were always entertaining and provoked a flurry of thought. Whenever I listened to one of his presentations, I became entranced by his ability to entertain and articulate the most amazing things imaginable. I became a believer in his *True Hallucinations* (title of one of his books) and thoroughly enjoyed myself in the process. There was but one problem. When I actually took the drug, my experience was widely different from his. In fact, I could hardly believe we were engaging in the same practice.

During a video interview taped near the end of his life, he described himself as a *story teller* whose role was to inform people that the psychedelic trip was a safe one, no more dangerous or scary than a particularly engaging roller coaster ride. He believed people drew *permission* to enter into the psychedelic experience through his assurances that all would end well. On this count he was, of course, correct. I give kudos to Terence for assuaging my own fears. Certainly his reassuring words made my decision to test the psychedelic waters that much easier. It was his inability to illuminate spiritual truth that concerned me.

There was no doubt Terence was a brilliant man. Conceptually he could hold his own with the best of them. As an authentic *truth-teller* he didn't even rate. Terence had little, if anything, of value to say about matters of a transpersonal nature.

In my experience, I rarely, if ever, went to any realms where bizarre machine elves and self-dribbling bejeweled basketballs engaged me in strange rituals, as Terence commonly described. Or at least, if I did, I have no recollection of such. In fact, what I refer to as *weird shit* was almost entirely absent from my experience. The few hallucinations I do recall were never mistaken for anything more than distractions that did not interest me much at all. For Terence they were the whole purpose of the endeavour. I viewed them as beside the point, superficial and banal. Apparently he never discovered much in the way of what I found psychedelics to do so well on occasion—reveal truths detached from the ego.

Terence was a great thinker so I believe he must have been frustrated when the drug experience created for him, as he said, "a place where language finds it very hard to pull over and look around." In essence an un-Englishable experience. Of course that description of his is what naturally happens when the ego steps aside. In my estimation, for the most part Terence had purposely avoided this state of being. For him it was all about what thought, idea or information he could conceptually tease out of hyperspace. It seemed that this mindset held him back from a fuller, deeper and richer encounter with the unknown. In his desire to parse conceptual significance, to go *fishing for ideas* as he put it, he most assuredly sacrificed a lot. With entheogens it's either one state or the other. Concepts gleaned come at the expense of spiritual insight. Being the ineffable mystery meant there remained nothing left to understand or articulate to anyone—least of all to yourself.

But what the heck, if someone wanted to go fishing, more power to them. I spent decades doing so myself. There were certainly worse pastimes. The confusion about Terence's true motivations and insights were to a large degree created in my own mind, not Terence's. I thought that when he regaled us with his weird and wondrous revelations brought back from DMT hyperspace, he was referring to meaningful spiritual insight—he was telling us the Truth. Experience showed me otherwise. What occurred to him, or at least the bit he shared with us, was mostly egoicly derived projection and, as such, wasn't really pertinent to the kinds of Truth I was in search of. I view McKenna as a kind of *psychedelic bodhisattva*, spreading the *good news* to whoever would listen while forestalling his own enlightenment right up to the very end. Which in his case arrived at an early age in the guise of brain cancer.

I suspect he was actually quite hip to what was *really* going on (that being that nothing was really going on) but preferred instead not to dwell on it too much. Telltale signs were evident like when he related a ketamine (anaesthesia favoured by some for its illuminating dissociative properties) experience he once had. On that occasion he said reality was seemingly an impersonal realm where all that was experienced was pure awareness with nothing whatsoever to be aware of. However, being ever the empiricist, he could not help but then add, "This is not a very sense-making perception." Of course it is not, that is the whole point!

I only wish Terence had chosen to share more of his *non-sense* perceptions with us. But again Terence was clear that these matters did not interest him much, or at least were not worthy of sharing with his audiences. In my opinion, his take on enlightenment missed the mark entirely. It essentially hearkened back to the *Age of Reason* and supported Kant's call for a more measured, reasoned, empirical and rational view of reality. Terence held most contemporary mystics, gurus and sages alike in low regard and once said of meditators, "They were always looking for the gas while psychedelic users were perpetually searching for the brakes." He couldn't have been more wrong on that count. First of all meditation had nothing to do with the cheap thrills a carny barker might extol. Besides which, it could be an exceptionally intense experience in its own regard. I found it exceedingly so on occasion but not in the way Terence might have imagined. Returning to the historical perspective once again, let's see how it may aid us in our further understanding of the mystical experience.

In this case let us now look at the work of Richard Maurice Bucke, a contemporary of James and Underhill, who was an important Canadian progressive psychiatrist in the late nineteenth century. His most famous work was published in 1901 as *Cosmic Consciousness: A*

Study in the Evolution of the Human Mind, and he is credited with coining the term *cosmic consciousness*. It was to this concept that many hippies turned their attention during the Sixties. I was particularly taken with a direct mystical experience that occurred to him one day in 1872 while he was in London, England. Bucke's *peak experience*, a fleeting mystical realization that he regarded as but a few moments of *cosmic consciousness* occurred as follows:

> Like a flash there is presented to his consciousness a clear conception (a vision) in outline of the meaning and drift of the universe …. He sees and knows that the cosmos … is in fact … in very truth a living presence. He sees that instead of men being, as it were, patches of life scattered through an infinite sea of non-living substance, they are in reality specks of relative death in an infinite ocean of life. He sees that the life which is in man is as immortal as God is; that the universe is so built and ordered that without any peradventure all things work together for the good of each and all; that the foundation principle of the world is what we call love, and that the happiness of every individual is in the long run absolutely certain.

Bucke's description of cosmic consciousness was certainly compelling and struck me as being an authentic experience of the Divine. This direct mystical experience made all the difference regarding the validity of his insights. He believed those who experienced cosmic consciousness displayed certain common characteristics such as:
- Subjective experience of light (inner light)
- Sudden appearance
- Intuitive understanding
- Moral elevation
- Loss of sense of sin
- Intellectual illumination
- Sense of immortality
- Loss of fear of death
- Definite moment or period of transformation

His understanding was less conceptual or speculative than that of James or Underhill. The nine defining qualities he set down were clear and specific. The man *knew* of what he spoke since he lived it. Particularly pertinent was his last point which suggested that cosmic consciousness involved transformation.

True mystical realization is transformative and Bucke's recognition of this fact separated him from his peers. If the case was very much business as usual after a spiritual experience, then it was no more than a mystical dalliance, or worse yet nothing but delusional ego-based fantasy. Bucke was talking about a realization that permanently changed the way a person fundamentally perceived and related to reality ever thereafter. Before looking any further into the concept of transformation as a means to acquire liberation, let's take a little detour to see what kinds of psychedelic substances SWIM actually utilized during his quest for spiritual insight.

Liberation Technology

In the third or fourth minute after the injection, vegetative symptoms appeared such as a tingling sensation, trembling, slight nausea, mydriasis, elevation of the blood pressure and an increase of the pulse rate. At the same time eidetic phenomena, optical illusions, pseudo- hallucinations and later real hallucinations appeared. The hallucinations consisted of moving, brilliantly coloured oriental motifs, and later I saw wonderful scenes altering very rapidly. The faces of the people seemed to be masks. My emotional state was elevated sometimes up to euphoria. At the highest point, I had compulsive athetoid movements in my left hand. My consciousness was completely filled by hallucinations, and my attention was firmly bound to them; therefore I could not give an account of the events happening around me. After 3/4–1 hour the symptoms disappeared, and I was able to describe what had happened.

In the annals of psychedelic research, those words you have just read chronicle a groundbreaking experience. They record the very first occasion of human exposure to a fully psychedelic dose of synthesized N,N-Dimethyltryptamine, DMT for short. It is structurally analogous to the neurotransmitter serotonin. The experiment occurred in April 1956 and was a self-administered injection by Hungarian chemist and psychiatrist Stephen Szara, whose report appeared above.

Another form of DMT is found in magic mushrooms. Psilocybin, which is chemically known as 4-PO-DMT, is metabolized in the body into psilocin, or 4-HO-DMT (4-hydroxyl dimethyltryptamine). Ultimately it is the psilocin that is responsible for the mushroom's psychoactive effects. Both drugs are members of the tryptamine class of psychedelics, which was my favourite. Pure *N,N*-DMT (Dr. Strassman's test drug), unlike the 4-PO-DMT of mushrooms, is not orally active. If you were to eat N,N-DMT by itself it would have no effect whatsoever. The chemistry of 4-PO-DMT differs just enough to allow it to be assimilated by the digestive tract directly. This bit of chemistry explains why mushrooms or ayahuasca can be eaten while pure DMT powder must be smoked or injected.

DMT fascinated me. The tales of altered states, mystical insights and myriad sentient beings awaiting discovery were a strong testament to its ability to alter consciousness as well as a powerful inducement for me to throw caution to the wind and actually try it. As mentioned previously, I first stumbled upon DMT through references to Dr. Strassman's clinical trials, which began in 1990 and lasted for five years. This kind of research was the first to be undertaken since those pioneering studies completed in the 1950s and early 1960s. Unlike its more famous counterpart LSD, not much was known about DMT at the time.

The onset of response to injected DMT was very rapid, beginning in only a few heartbeats, and the duration of the response relatively short. Doctor Strassman described the experience as peaking within two to three minutes of the injection, and then the subject gradually headed back to relative sobriety some fifteen or so minutes later. Though the subjects would still be pretty high at that point and eager to share their experience, Strassman encouraged them to keep their eyes closed for another ten or fifteen minutes because some pretty interesting residual effects could still arise. Dr. Strassman said that patients would usually open their eyes again at around the half-hour point, feeling almost normal. While Strassman's study involved IV injections, it was also possible to smoke DMT. The effect was nearly the same as injected DMT and lasted a similar duration, depending of course on dose and physiology of subject involved.

I never smoked or injected *regular* DMT but did inhale its more potent cousin 5-methoxy-dimethyltryptamine (5-MeO-DMT). That compound completely destroyed any semblance of my humanity. It was the single most amazing transcendental experience, via an entheogen, I ever had. A near-death experience would be putting it mildly. Saying that I outright *ceased to exist* would be closer to the mark. What does one then become when this happens: A*ye there's the rub.*

Even the experience with the weaker, normal DMT can be earth-shattering. Reports have compared it to parachuting at night into the midst of a tribe of frenzied New Guinea natives at the height of an elaborate war-dance or being fired out of the barrel of an atomic cannon. It was clear no one could ever know what to expect except that it would be one hell of a ride.

DMT experiences are relatively free of danger. No one has ever overdosed on DMT in all its various forms that I am aware of. Smoking cannot lead to serious medical distress since the onset is so quick that only a limited amount of vapour can be inhaled before the effects become overwhelming. Usually the problem is not getting enough in, rather than too much. That being said, certain provisos should be mentioned such as cautioning people with severe cardiovascular problems or other health-related issues centred around anxiety (i.e., stress-induced asthma, vertigo, etc.) to consider refraining from the experience. Those with a psychiatric history or the emotionally unstable should also be cautious. People taking certain antidepressants, such as SSRIs and other medications with an MAO inhibitor-like function should also avoid the DMT experience.

Finally, use common sense to ensure that your immediate environment is safe and secure. Don't take DMT next to an open window or near hot objects, etc. and, if outside, avoid an elevated location or open water unless a sitter is present. This is just a brief indication of what to look out for. For more details consult certain Internet web sites like erowid.com for more details related to health and safety issues (such as food to avoid, etc.). All in all, it is a ridiculously safe compound to use. Nicotine is more toxic than DMT.

It's very reassuring to know that however much you might screw up the dosage, the results will be harmless. If you consume too much, you might have a terrifying experience or perhaps even be rendered unconscious, but death is out of the question. Having said that, please try to ascertain the correct dose as carefully as possible. No need to scare yourself if you can avoid it.

Start with a low to moderate initial dose and see how you react to it. Then increase the level until you find the *sweet spot*, yet not enough to render you completely insensible. What I am talking about here is a stiff dose perhaps approaching what Terence McKenna referred to as a fully psychedelic heroic dose.

Be aware this is not a *how-to guide*, nor am I even advocating psychedelics in general. All I am saying is that I found a *heroic dose* to be beneficial for purposes of gaining insight. Of course the amount varies from person to person. Terence reckoned that five grams of psilocybin mushroom was the mark to aim for. I needed at least thirteen grams to degrade my ego sufficiently. I think the difference in amount is significant and may explain why my experiences differed so much from McKenna's. I wanted transcendence not *eye candy*.

Anything you can do to improve *set and setting* will go a long way to ensuring a rewarding trip. I am referring to the present mindset of the practitioner and the actual physical location where the drug will be consumed. Never take psychedelics if you are depressed, upset or psychologically disturbed in any way. The immediate surroundings where drugs are taken should be relaxed, peaceful and comfortable. Taking the drug alone, in subdued lighting or even entirely in the dark, adds another dimension to what is often just a social experience. I would advise against taking psychedelics in a noisy, frenetic, party type environment. Do everything you can to bring about a positive, upbeat mindset prior to taking the drug.

Fostering a positive mindset is partially a matter of intention. Upon awaking in the morning and several times throughout the day that the psychedelics were to be taken, I reflected upon the wonderful experience about to unfold. I always vacuumed and tidied up the spot where the experience would happen. When it was a communal experience, we all might listen to uplifting music or tell jokes. I can't stress enough how important set and setting are. Your intentions and the correct dose will ensure the most favourable outcome possible. You never know what may come your way so stacking the deck in your favour is the best way to avoid a bad trip.

During the 1960s, taking DMT was reputedly referred to as the *Businessman's Lunch* or *the Businessman's Trip* due to its brevity. In trying to describe the effects of DMT you often needed to resort to metaphor and poetic language in an attempt to get your ideas across. This was particularly true when describing the more profound spiritual effects. The vivid hallucinations of fractals, sentient beings and weird landscapes were much easier to articulate. The following is a broad characterization of the four phases one may chance to encounter while on a trip:

Level 1: Threshold experience.
Characterized by an interior flow of energy or movement of consciousness. Shock and surprise may result due to the rapidity of onset and overwhelming effects. An intense feeling may arise, though you may not be quite sure what is causing such an odd impression. It may be positive or slightly uncomfortable. Colour shifting of the general environment may ensue. For example, a golden-yellowish or greenish hue may develop. The distinct impression that something *big* is about to unfold is often present at the peak of this phase. If not enough DMT was administered, baseline will soon reappear.

Level 2: Intense sensual experiences or perpetual distorions arise.
If more DMT is consumed, you may observe a coloured, patterned, two-dimensional field with closed eyes. Many speak of seeing a richly coloured, ornately patterned *chrysanthemum* pattern or seeing lovely tapestries or wallpaper type vignettes morphing into ever-changing patterns of complexity. With enough substance, open-eye visuals are also possible. The visual field, as well as sound, may have a pulsating fluctuating quality to it. This effect is very distinctive and will be familiarly recalled with multiple experiences. Multi-coloured bursts of light or fractals may also appear.

At this point a typical fight-or-flight stress reaction often occurs. Heart rate and blood pressure dramatically rise. Pupil size may increase by up to double. Pituitary gland hormone levels shoot up. An overpowering rushing sensation, along with vibrations, may be experienced. A powerful, high-frequency energy may be perceived as coursing through your entire being. Often a loud buzzing or humming/roaring sound is heard that increases in volume/pitch just prior to the onset of full-blown psychedelic breakthrough. Terence McKenna likened this sound to that of cellophane tearing or crumpling, but in my experience, 5-MeO-DMT produced a sensation more akin to that of an out-of-control rocket-powered freight train barrelling down the tracks with many of the ties under it missing, while a ram's horn, perhaps louder than the one that knocked down the walls of Jericho, frantically sounded the alarm in hopes of attracting attention.

With stronger visual effects comes an increasing sense of dissociation of mind from body. The first time you experience this fragmentation of being, it is very startling indeed. Some find the weirdness of it quite uncomfortable, scary even. It is at this point that some believe themselves to be dying. To experience radical ego loss you must experiment with high doses of 5-MeO-DMT, and I wouldn't necessarily recommend that experience to anybody. I have heard (and found through ayahuasca experimentation) that a really high, truly heroic dose of regular DMT can facilitate near complete release as well, though I wouldn't go so far as to call that ego death.

The feeling of dissolution into the ground of being can be entirely blissful and liberating or panic-inducing as hell. Fortunately for those who are seriously taken aback, this second phase passes quickly. Less than thirty seconds is typical. Hopefully at this juncture enough DMT has been taken in to ensure the much sought after breakthrough experience.

Level 3: Entering hyper reality. The breakthrough experience.

This phase is often associated with the perception of intense light. Like those described in reports of the near-death experience. You may travel through a tunnel or some other portal to the next level. A gauzy veil may part or a membrane may be pierced. This part of the journey is very brief and may be disorienting for many until the new reality reveals itself fully. On the other hand, the transition from Level 2 to Level 4 may be as instantaneous as suddenly switching on a light.

Level 4: Accessing the transpersonal state or spiritual realm

Immediately you find yourself transported to a new realm that many describe as astonishingly real and convincing. Here the magic, fun and games may begin, and, most importantly, profound insights arise. The spiritual component of DMT is much more elusive than the far more common eye-candy is. Strassman's study only mentioned a mere handful of such cases out of the approximately 400 hundred trips his volunteers underwent. I checked on sources outside of Strassman's study and similarly found few references of spiritual significance arising while under the influence of lab-synthesized DMT. As a personal note, though I did successfully break through, there is not much I can say about this component of the journey because there is not much anyone can say about this experience. I leave it up to you to formulate your own impressions by trying the drug yourself.

I wondered why there were so few case reports of people having the so-called *religious experience* while on DMT. A very high dose was required to even stand a chance for an insightful experience to arise. Often people didn't take enough. Furthermore, it was extremely difficult to totally surrender yourself to the unknown. Finally, if you did happen to take enough, you were often in such a discombobulated frame of consciousness that conceptualizing anything was next to impossible. And, even if you could understand what was occurring, you would in all likelihood forget what happened once you sobered up.

This was an all or nothing affair. You either utterly relinquished control and whole heartedly embraced the Divine or else you remained within the confines of egoic illusion and projection. Admittedly, SWIM doesn't recall any unequivocally full-blown, totally-transcendent religious experience unfolding while under the influence of high doses of ayahuasca/psilocybin mushrooms (though at times it sure seemed pretty close, details are lacking) but did find total release with 5-MeO-DMT. I do not, however, discount the fact that DMT can be spiritually beneficial to a degree. It sufficiently eroded my ego to allow increased clarity and presence of mind.

The tryptamine hallucination was truly remarkable. Everything was hyper-real. Things appeared so pristine, freshly rendered, starkly crisp and clear that many considered this drug-induced reality to be actually real. *How was all this possible*, the tripper's mind screamed out in bewilderment? It has to be real ... doesn't it?

That is one of the amazing things about DMT—you usually still had the capacity to think quite rationally. If the dose was not too large, leading to total befuddlement or unconsciousness, you still basically had most of your wits about you. Sometimes, though, you may have wished that this wasn't the case at all. That you could just tune out the whole crazy thing.

As you gain experiences, you may find you begin to develop the ability to shade, slant or outright control the experience unfolding before you to ever-greater degrees. I found I could pay attention to or pretty much ignore the hallucinations at will. They seemed pretty trivial and insignificant. As William James put it, "We see only what we do not see through." This was a good skill to acquire since some of the visuals were quite intense and disturbing.

Most inexperienced neophytes took the reality that was unfolding before them to be entirely real. The experience they reported was of being in an *objective* reality. A space or landscape opened up before them complete with real objects, though inexplicable and bizarre at times, or even sentient beings or entities. These entities may have remained silent or their appearance may have been fleeting and transient in nature, but often they were willing to interact with the tripper. It must have been occasions like these that caused the term *mind blowing* to arise. It was all so weird and wonderful. McKenna said that initiating this kind of psychedelic journey was quite likely the bravest thing you would ever do. Earning your *laurel leaves* was how he put it.

Portions of Level 3 or 4 may be extremely frenetic, with everything happening incomprehensibly fast. On the other hand, things may be relatively coherent and explicable. Astonishing thoughts and revelations may arise. Dr. Strassman reported that most people found high doses of DMT to be *exciting, euphoric and extraordinarily pleasurable*. Sometimes this ecstasy related to the visions themselves. So just what kind of specific things do people perceive while under the influence of DMT? Answering that adequately could well fill a whole book in itself.

Constantly morphing abstract imagery, to realistic recognizable landscapes, to a four-dimensional (or beyond dimensionality) space, can be expected. Strassman's patients related such specific things as: a fantastic bird, a tree of life and knowledge, a ballroom with crystal chandeliers, a merry-go-round, crazy circus sideshow, DNA, apartment complexes, palaces, computers' circuit boards and inner workings of machines.

There seemed to be no limit to what the imagination was capable of bringing forth. And it wasn't confined to visuals only.

On occasion, you might hear audio hallucinations involving the ambient sounds of the room itself, but more commonly the perceptions of sound, weird noises or voices are internally generated by the hallucinations themselves. If a sentient being chooses to communicate directly with you, it often does so through telepathy. The words may be expressed in ordinary English or alternatively may sound like incomprehensible gibberish which McKenna likened to the glossolalia (speaking in tongues) one might hear a Holy Roller uttering. Reports of these beings proved highly disturbing to Strassman. It is to this provocative and contentious area I would now like to turn.

Entities?

Dr. Strassman's book was well received but it is important to remember that it employed a fair bit of speculation. Unfortunately, many have confused Dr. Strassman's thought-provoking conjectures for fact. Let's be clear, Dr. Strassman did not claim any of the following to be scientifically proven, and, since publication of his book a decade ago, the conjectures remain unverified. He said:

1. The pineal gland is the source of endogenous (self-synthesized) DMT in the body;

2. A fetus is exposed to a large release of pineal DMT at 49 days as its *soul/spirit* enters its body. (I had to question whether a fetus even had a functioning pineal at that point, never mind nervous system. Of course the mother could release the DMT but that remained to be seen as well.);

3. The pineal releases a massive dose of DMT at death thus freeing the spirit/soul from the confines of the corporeal body;

4. A release of nocturnal DMT could be responsible for alien abduction lore. The pineal gland is most active in the early morning hours. This is the same time that alien abductions are often said to occur;

5. As the sub-title of his book, *A Doctor's Revolutionary Research into the Biology of Near-Death and Mystical Experiences*, suggests, DMT is an efficacious agent for inducing an OBE (out-of-body experience) or authentic mystical state (it seemed the actual results of his study suggested that the opposite was

really the case);

6. DMT allows one to engage with sentient beings that inhabit free-standing, ontologically real realms. All it took was a large enough dose to allow one to break through to a world as real as our own.

7. The mechanics of this breakthrough experience are mediated through a detuning of normal consciousness (channel normal) and, through the effects of DMT, a retuning to another realm (channel dark matter). Much as you would change a channel on a TV set. These parallel realities are always present, we only have to acquire a new station to experience them in full vibrant Technicolor and digital surround sound. These realms were suggested to be autonomous, free standing and independently existing. As real as real gets; and

8. These multiverses are hidden in dark matter (proposed invisible matter comprising 95 percent of the total matter of the universe).

I grant you that all of this conjecture was very thought-provoking, and some of it certainly was within the realm of possibility. Unfortunately, none of it has yet been supported by any empirical evidence. I mention this because the field has been tainted by a certain level of mythologizing carried out by authors who should know better. I wanted to discover what was really going on when the body's system was flooded with DMT. It was clear Strassman struggled with this question himself.

Strassman stated that the beings his volunteers encountered could either appear human-like or quite alien. Non-human entities might be recognizable creatures such as spiders, mantises, reptiles or weirder projections like the reported saguaro cactus. Invariably his subjects believed that these were *real* beings inhabiting some actual otherworldly realm. They felt that their interactions with these creatures were just as valid and authentic as any normal encounter here on terrestrial earth might have been. When painfully invasive medical procedures, or, worse yet, rape, occurred to a test subject, these experiences were all accepted in stride by Strassman as being in some way reflections of a real encounter. I have a huge problem with this and feel it is time for a little reality check.

Entities?

I don't question the fact that the trauma perceived *felt real* enough. My own hallucinogenic experiences often seemed very real indeed. But it was all just smoke and mirrors, projections thrown up by my ego or subconscious mind due to my radically altered brain chemistry. My point is simply that I never confused DMT apparitions for anything more than just that.

Strassman, while considering the veracity of what his patients were telling him, decided that he would accept their testimony at face value—that their DMT experiences were *more real than real*. In a sense he elected to go along to get along. He decided to, in his own words, *conduct a thought experiment* and suspend his disbelief. If his subjects believed that what they had experienced was a genuine realm inhabited by real creatures or, as Strassman put it, *autonomous, free-standing and independently existing realities*, then he would treat them as such.

Strassman considered standard religious philosophy, be it Buddhist, Jewish or Christian, and saw that it offered little in the way of explanation. He also explored psychological explanatory models such as those offered by Freudian or Jungian analysis, but those failed to address the complexity of the experience as well. He felt biological explanations such as straight-forward hallucinations or waking dreams also failed to agree with the volunteers' reports. For them it was a real experience, and they were very reluctant to consider any other possible explanation. Why did Strassman's subjects so adamantly declare that what they experienced was something *genuine* when I believed nothing of the sort?

I grant you the DMT-manifested hallucination was very realistic and compelling. I just didn't make the leap and conclude that what I perceived was a real *nuts-and-bolts* reality. What seemed to be occurring was far more interesting than that. Somehow this was all being created somewhere within myself. Though I could never figure out precisely where that *self* actually resided. Fantastic new levels of consciousness popped up, and it had nothing to do with any outside influence whatsoever. In a *Pogoesque* moment, I realized that *I had met the enemy and he was me.* For the most part the experience was hallucinatory and dream-like. But not the typical dream state most people are aware of. No, what I experienced was much more akin to lucid dreaming. Let's now see what this avenue may offer us in hopes of better understanding the DMT experience.

Trance Formation

Regarding this notion of the DMT experience arising from the dream state, Dr. Strassman had the following to say, "The rapid eye movements that sometimes took place in our subjects may have indicated the presence of a 'waking' dream state." After the publication of his book, Dr. Strassman elaborated on this concept with the following excerpt from an online chat:

> The DMT dreaming connection is very relevant. Pineal function is highest at 3 a.m., and so is dreaming activity. I propose, in the book, that DMT is a sort of spirit gland, with the highest level of precursors and enzymes of any organ in the body. Jace Callaway, in Finland, has proposed a role for pinoline, a beta-carboline, in boosting the effects of naturally released DMT during REM sleep. Along those lines, we did notice that many of our volunteers showed rapid eye movements during the peak of the DMT trance. So, it's an extraordinarily relevant relationship.

Strassman touched upon Dr. Jace Callaway's (University of Kuopio in Finland) long-held supposition that DMT may play a role in the creation of dream imagery. "We experience psychedelic states on a regular basis while dreaming," Dr. Callaway assured us (*New Scientist* vol 182 issue 2453).

Radio host Laura Lee interviewed Strassman in 2002 when he

added additional supporting comments for the *DMT experience as dream* hypothesis:

"There are parts of the brain responsible for visual phenomena, and obviously DMT is affecting those fairly profoundly." When asked by Lee about the possibility that the DMT experience is merely a product of dreaming, he elaborates with the following, "Well, I think that is a very strong possibility that the production of dreams is mediated through elevated levels of DMT. Some visions are just residual psychological detritus just left kind of floating around.

Does the following case report taken from Strassman's book sound more like a dream to you than it does a first-hand encounter with an alien universe?

> I was on a merry-go-round! There were all these dolls in 1890s outfits, life-sized, men and women. The women were in corsets. They had big breasts and big butts and teeny skinny waists. They were all whirling around me on tiptoes. The men had top hats, riding on two-seater bicycles. One merry-go-round after another after another. The women had red circles painted on their cheeks, and there was calliope music in the background. And there were some clowns, flitting in and out, not really the main characters, but busier, somehow more aware of me than the mannequins.

Not unexpectedly Strassman noted that this sounded like a dream to him as well. I think one would be hard pressed to conclude otherwise. Strassman also added, "Dreams are a basic tool for any personal growth and understanding, and DMT may generate highly symbolic dreamlike images."

So there it is. Dr. Strassman conceded the possibility that the so-called *spirit molecule* may very simply be a compound which elicits dream-like responses in people. I would go further and postulate that the DMT state most closely resembles that of *lucid dreaming*. The reason that the subjects were so adamant about the reality of their experience is that this is exactly how any lucid dreamers worth their salt perceive conscious dream imagery. When lucid dreamers are fully lucid, what they experience for the most part can not be distinguished from normal waking reality. In fact, when I elected to fully investigate lucid dreaming after my awakening, I was bowled over by how cleverly this mind state manifested a totally immersive, seemingly real world. At first I could hardly believe that what I perceived was not at least in some way quite genuine. Lucid dreams really are, as Strassman's subjects put it, *more real than real*.

This kind of dream state is remarkably detailed, vivid and logically coherent. Imagery is crisp, sharp and vibrant. Bright colours, the likes of which you have probably never seen, dazzled me with their richness. Sounds seemingly originated from a real place and behaved in ways terrestrial acoustics demanded. For example, once, in a lucid dream, I heard a radio playing in a room, and, as I left that space, the sound naturally muffled and reduced in volume as I made my way to an adjacent corridor. Remember, this kind of phenomena occurred all by itself and didn't seem to be dependent on whether I was aware of it or not. If I did happen to pay attention I could hear anything that might also be heard in our world. For example, I recall unseen birds singing noisily, insects chirping away, the sound of waves crashing or the whistling wind beating against my face. The fact that the voices of all dream characters I heard were distinctly different and never sounded artificial in any way always amazed me. This was not like hearing a high quality Dolby surround sound recording— this was hearing someone speaking as they normally would. If you have seen the film *Inception*, you may get a sense of what I am talking about but that is just a film. The reality I perceived was as convincing as what greeted me when I awoke in the morning. In fact, lucid dreamers, myself included, often experience *false awakenings* where they believe that they have actually woken up, shaved and drunk their first cup of coffee before realizing that they, in fact, are still dreaming. They may then *wake up* again only to realize several minutes later that they are, in fact, still dreaming. Occasionally this may go on long enough to get very annoying.

While lucid dreaming, all of my senses are keenly active. For example, once I felt the texture of individual strands of a woman's shaggy mane of hair and even smelled traces of her shampoo. Looking to the ground another time, I spied some gravel. I picked a handful up and rolled it around in my fingers. It even tasted real! Adept lucid dreamers use terms like *hyper reality* or *reality on steroids* to describe the verisimilitude of the space. I don't think it was mere coincidence that these were the same expressions DMT users bandied about. I dare say that anyone coming back from their first very conscious lucid dream will find it to be the most amazing thing they have ever experienced. If you were not shocked and amazed by it you simply were not lucid enough. In case you are interested, this experience is open to anyone who cares to learn a few simple techniques.

Lucid dreaming first arose spontaneously for me during my meditation period, but I ignored it so it eventually went away. When I got back into it, after my awakening, I was faced with a conundrum. The lucid dream state seemed entirely real, yet I knew it wasn't. This was difficult for me to come to grips with. Were my dreams at least partially real I wondered? That is, at least partially drawing upon elements of our normal world. The dream landscape I beheld was often unknown territory so I knew I wasn't exclusively referring to past memories to create the experience. So where was this novel landscape originating from? Was I subconsciously accessing some pool of information and then somehow manifesting it in the form of a dream? I was curious to know if there were any elements at all of this experience that somehow reflected our reality. I decided an experiment was in order. I would try to figure out if I was actually in a real place during a dream.

By this time lucid dreams could arise spontaneously for me but I could also create them on demand. The technique I employed was known as WILD—wake-induced lucid dreaming. This meant I woke up in the early morning hours and then remained totally conscious as I slipped back into the dream state. Apparently it was similar to a technique employed by monks to induce Tibetan *dream yoga*. I gradually slipped into a dream.

Great lucidity resulted this time as I was highly motivated to get to the bottom of my conundrum. With a sense of urgency and strong purpose, I resolved to discover the name of the town I had just popped into. Immediately I could sense that the place was a relatively small urban centre, quite unknown to me, yet in some ways eerily familiar. I could not account for this strange feeling. I instantly *knew* a few general characteristics of the place without even thinking about it. As my eyes focused, I beheld a body of blue water in the distance. I sensed I was in the United States, somewhere in the South. Not west, perhaps one of the Carolinas or Alabama …. There was no evidence to indicate the exact location, but I felt certain I was in the Southern USA.

I quickly ascertained that I was in the middle of the crest of a road that gently sloped down towards the water many blocks in the distance. I could see sidewalks on both sides of me as I was apparently in the middle of some kind of downtown commercial area that reminded me of small-town USA. It all seemed entirely real. I could even hear the sounds of traffic mixed with the conversation of passing pedestrians.

"Ah the ocean," I thought as I reflected upon the blue water in the distance. This idea momentarily seemed to be supported by the rack of bright yellow commercial fisherman's rain gear I spied on display in front of a nearby shop. I had seen a similar view once in reality while visiting a Canadian commercial fishing port. But confirmation of an ocean location was not forthcoming as the rain coats and coveralls morphed into some kind of casual outdoor wear. Nope that water was definitely not salty I concluded. Apparently I was near a fairly substantial body of water yet I was in a downtown core. It now had some historical significance. Keeping focused, I got off the road and walked toward a store front, hoping to see some kind of geographical reference. I wanted so much to shout out, "This is so fucking amazing," but instead retained my composure for fear of awaking.

I had to squint through a reflecting window pane as I struggled to read the signage affixed to it from the inside. It was of no help, just typical commercial advertisements. My capacity to reason was fully functional, so at that point I knew I had a problem. Towns don't generally advertise their name except at the town limits. Grabbing a local paper might have helped, but that did not occur to me at the time.

Two middle-aged ladies presented themselves. Why not ask them? But with that thought I realized I would look silly since nobody in their right mind would approach anyone with such an outlandish question. Of course, I knew I was in a dream, so could have asked them anything I liked, yet for some strange reason I felt inclined to observe social norms. Some dreamers liked to break all the rules and acted totally out

130

of character or even committed crimes. I've never felt that being able to access this realm lucidly was a licence to act foolishly. Given that, I wondered how I could tactfully ask my question and not provoke suspicion.

"Excuse me ladies, can you tell me where I am?" came my first question. But as it came out I knew exactly how they would respond. With a quizzical look on their faces they asked, "You mean like where you are now, right?" Much as I would have preferred not to, I nodded in affirmation and they proceeded to give me directions and get me all straightened out. Rats, still no town name. I pondered again how to get the identification I was after without arousing suspicion. Time was running out.

Next a *distraction* occurred. A *distraction* was a term I applied to describe a common ploy my mind used to try to involve me in some little activity, sidebar or intrigue such that lucidity was eroded to the degree that conscious dreaming ended. In this case my subconscious went all out by manifesting a full-blown parade, complete with marching band and majorettes only one block in the distance. I was having none of it so turned away and preceded with my mission. After crossing the street and walking a little ways down the sidewalk I spied a likely prospect.

He was wearing khaki shorts and sandals, was shirtless and had a long grey pony tail running down his back. Now this was the kind of guy I could relate to. At that point I decided to throw caution to the wind and bluntly asked him what the town's name was. He looked like an old hippie who had probably wondered the same thing several times himself. Seemingly unperturbed by the absurdity of my question he answered but all I caught was some muffled garbled nonsense that sounded like "... orja ...." Puzzled, I said, "Sorry, did you say Florida?" My question instantly made no sense to me as I had requested a town name, not a state. Surely he hadn't mentioned a state I reasoned.

He replied with a sweep of his arm and a shake of his head, "No that is down there (in reference to Florida). This here is Rome." At that precise moment a dog barked nearby. By this I mean a real dog, and so I awoke. I was not too disappointed because I had managed to finagle an identifying name out of the experience after all. As I contemplated the results of my effort, it seemed that I must have failed. For, after all, I only knew of one Rome and could not imagine another existing in the

States. Still I decided to check the Internet and confirm my suspicions. The results surprised me.

I found two towns called Rome in America, one in New York and one in Georgia—the epitome of the South. More in-depth research showed that the town was located at the junction of three rivers and the downtown section seemed almost entirely surrounded by water. If I were indeed in downtown Rome, a body of water, much like the one I observed, could in all likelihood not be missed. I found a short video of the actual downtown core and was impressed by the similarities of the real architecture compared to my dreamt version.

The reference to Florida really astonished me. It turned out Rome is located in the extreme northern section of the state. Across the state border to the south is Florida! Just like the pony-tailed pedestrian intimated with the sweep of his arm. All in all pretty compelling stuff, but what did I make of it? Was I really in Rome?

Of course not, I was in a dream. Admittedly an entirely convincing dream that may have somehow incorporated paranormal elements into its fabrication, much like military remote viewing does, but a dream nonetheless. Did this episode actually reflect the real world in some way? That question begs another; how do we go about defining what is *real* in the first place? The more I accessed the lucid dream state (as well as that of DMT) the greater my confusion grew.

I found out that the brain has an interesting proclivity. Regardless of its state of consciousness, whatever can be *conceived* or *perceived* is generally *believed*. Simply put, the brain tends to accept any perception that floats its way as being a reflection of something real. The brain's ability to suspend belief and thereby perceive whatever arises in its field of awareness, including those cognitions of a hallucinatory nature, in a rational and dispassionate manner is severely, if not entirely, curtailed most of the time. For some reason we are hardwired to accept all experience as genuine—imagined or otherwise. I would suggest that is because ultimately no experience is real. At least not in the way you commonly suppose, so distinguishing fact from fiction is impossible. It seems everything is make-believe.

I came across a recent case in point, entitled "Pain relief—it is just an illusion," from *The Telegraph* dated April 14, 2011. Test subjects were asked to watch a very realistic computer simulation of someone massaging their arthritic hands. Despite no one actually ever touching them, the mere act of watching a simulated massage markedly reduced the discomfort of osteoarthritis. A similar phenomenon has been noted to occur in those amputees suffering phantom limb pain. If they gaze into a mirror at their remaining healthy arm, which convinces the mind that they are now whole again, drastically reduced pain and discomfort levels result. *The Telegraph* article concluded with the statement, "Arthritis Research UK said a simple optical illusion that can halve pain without the need for drugs has 'a lot of potential.'" Potential, yes, but surely it also demonstrated the nebulous nature of consensual reality. Once again, whatever can be conceived or perceived is generally believed. And like this example, often goes on to affect your personal reality in a very genuine way.

You probably aren't aware that there is another state of consciousness preceding full-blown dreams known as hypnagogia, the transitional state between waking and sleeping. Here you encounter simple rudimentary sounds and imagery such as multicoloured flashing lights, specks or lines and sometimes more complicated things like geometric shapes and patterns. With the passage of a little time they become more elaborate and often coalesce into recognizable static or morphing photograph-like snapshots/tableaus that fleetingly arise and pass away again. This brief portion of the sleep cycle is highly reminiscent of the latter part of stage one or the early part of stage two of a DMT trip.

I was intimately familiar with this state of consciousness since I sometimes passed through it prior to lucid dreaming and discovered it was, at times, just as weird as the initial DMT flash. In both cases I found sounds could accompany the imagery. Sometimes just simple sound bites but often quite elaborate passages as well. Once, a masterfully produced techno-song struck up in my head immediately before a lucid dream broke out. Its complicated electronic score and driving beats were indistinguishable from any commercial rendering I had previously heard, but this one was unfamiliar. I listened to it more intently and was shocked to find it suddenly change from mono to full stereo. Simply amazing. Equally fascinating was the reference I found to a lucid dreamer who experienced a hypnagogic radio commercial advertising a product he had never heard of before. Later, in real life, he searched for the item but didn't come across it. Two years later he stumbled upon it. Perhaps that song I heard has been recorded by now.

In my case I noticed that as hypnagogia progressed, elaborate silent images would often arise displaying fully realistic short scenes. It was shortly after this that outright dreaming often commenced.

Almost all of us unconsciously experience such phenomena each and every night. We are just oblivious to them for the most part. A veritable nocturnal three-ring circus strikes up practically every time you lay your head down on the pillow, but the price of admission is obliviousness. On the other hand, complex hypnagogic imagery was sometimes skipped entirely as I rapidly transitioned from simple abstract imagery to full dreamscape. This manner of progression could occur in the DMT dream as well. It's curious how both situations employed an intermediate step, as if it took some moments for the dream machine to fully power up.

One astute Internet forum member wrote the following on the subject:

> Sometimes hypnagogic visions can be intense, almost
> like   a   DMT   flash   (medieval   Incubi
> and   Succubi   have   been   blamed   on
> hypnagogic imagery).   Then   the   dream
> world seems to form   from a grey-black
> mist, if you've gotten   this far you should
> be having a lucid dream.

I have read many similar anecdotal accounts, by other lucid dreamers, that corresponded with my own experience as well. The following forum quotes seem to suggest a striking similarity between conscious dreaming and the DMT experience:

"In fact, at the moment I realized I was dreaming, I experienced the same 'rush' that smoking DMT gives."

"I've done DMT twice before and I must say the 'rushy' feeling in the dream was very similar to what I feel in the first few seconds of a DMT trip."

"… lucid dreams are almost reminiscent of the way tryptamines affect me with closed eyes/in a hypnagogic state … and the buzz peculiar to tryptamines."

The following report sounds very much like it was taken directly from the pages of Dr. Strassman's book but actually occurred merely as a result of lucid dreaming:

> I can feel myself leaving my body. I then am catapulted into a psychedelic dreamscape, with thousands of mirrored hexagonal cubes mirroring my face in a honeycomb of light. I can feel myself flying around this land and it is so intense and scary I usually wake up. This then cycles for about thirty minutes of me waking up and then being thrown back into this intense psychedelic land. It reminded me a lot of what I have heard DMT trips are like.

Bloggers have chimed in on the subject as well with articles like "Hypnagogia: Who Needs LSD When You Can Just Sleep," (from the Serendip website). In part it read:

> Hypnagogia induces strange experiences that are similar to those triggered by hallucinogens such as LSD and DMT. The person's imagination takes over: He or she can hear random voices, see imaginary objects ranging from people to mysterious worlds; his or her body can experience strange sensations such as floating or becoming bigger, and the brain can spit out random and origin-less thoughts. The experience can be anywhere from fascinating to utterly terrifying.

Or another,

> I think pretty much all three (LSD, psilocybin mushrooms, DMT) can be described as a waking dream experience. DMT has a sort of cosmic dreamy feel; you don't know what's going on but it's so instant and mind-blowing that it doesn't matter, and you're blown away anyway. Psilocybin, in low to medium doses, is like having a dream where you realize you're dreaming,

but it's not lucid because you can't control what you see.

Finally this account from noted ayahuasca researcher Dr. Erik Hoffmann: "Ayahuasca increased the 'twilight state' between sleep and awake, the so-called hypnagogic state. It is interesting that the ability to dream lucid is being highly stimulated for a period after the intake of Ayahuasca."

The previous blogger's point about lack of control is very telling in my opinion.

The ability to manipulate the experience can help us to distinguish the two states to some degree. I discovered that lucid dreaming provided a much more controllable experience than that of DMT. For the majority of people, the DMT experience presented itself to them, and they were just a passive observer going along for the ride. On the other hand, in lucid dreaming it is possible to create scenarios and narratives from scratch or alter a story already in progress. Manifesting dream objects, characters or carrying out actions (like flying) is no more difficult than just thinking about it. Adept lucid dreamers are more or less *Masters of the Realm*. When I considered the two experiences, I realized that the main differences could be summed up as varying degrees of the three Cs— *control, coherence and clarity*.

The lucid dreaming experience simply had more pronounced levels of those three characteristics. Lucid dream researcher, Dominick Attisani, has commented on the lack of control during ayahuasca ceremonies versus what he experienced while lucid dreaming. He said ayahuasca was *similar to*, but not *the same as*, lucid dreaming and made it clear that taking DMT "is not a paranormal experience in the way most people talked about it." By this I gather he meant DMT does not manifest a real *nuts-and-bolts reality* outside of our own.

Pioneering dream researcher, Dr. Stephen Laberge, as well as other researchers and writers such as Professor Benny Sannon, Martin Ball and Dr. James Kent, also held that the DMT state was not ontologically real. I would like to now specifically examine Dr. Kent's position a little more closely in order to appreciate why it is so diametrically opposed to that of Dr. Strassman's. The material cited is drawn from an article entitled "The Case Against DMT Elves," which in turn draws heavily upon ideas presented in his book, *Psychedelic Information Theory:*

Shamanism in the Age of Reason.

Dr. Kent's well-considered research and wealth of personal experience (some twenty years of psychedelic use) places him in an excellent position to demythologize the DMT experience as presented in some circles. He succinctly stated:

> I do not believe DMT is a gateway to an alternate dimension, nor does it induce contact with autonomous elves and alien entities. Yes, DMT produces a vivid other-worldly landscape when ingested, often including elves, aliens, insects, snakes, jaguars, etc .... But when you try to shine a light of reason on them, they dissolve like shadows.

I concur. As I mentioned before, my experience showed them to be mere mental apparitions that rarely persisted if rationally scrutinized, or, alternatively, were ignored entirely. We really do only see that which is not *seen through*.

This position was similarly echoed by Nicholas Sand, who, over the course of more than forty years, had in excess of 1,000 DMT trips. Sand is the chemist responsible for synthesizing *orange sunshine,* a particularly renowned form of pure LSD that was popular in the late 1960s and early 1970s. He also was the first to realize that DMT can be smoked in its freebase form. In a 2001 article entitled "Moving into the Sacred World of DMT" he wrote a response to excerpts of Strassman's soon-to-be-published book. He felt it important to address several points of contention. He stated:

> DMT is not a re-run of the *X-Files*. There are no aliens squiggling through psychospace to do experiments on us. That idea is just plain silly. It is fine to wonder how these perceptions occur, but it's another matter to jump to conclusions.

Returning to Dr. Kent's informative article, let me now quote a passage that directly points out the insubstantial nature of DMT entities:

> I initially found it very surprising to be confronted by

elves in my DMT experiences ... and did indeed perceive them as externalized, morphing, disincarnate beings .... However, the more I experimented with DMT, I found I could think them into existence, and then think them right out of existence simply by willing it so. Sometimes I could not produce elves, and my mind would wander through all sorts of magnificent and amazing creations .... A wide variety of archetypes and just plain-old whacked-out stoner shit creeps into the mix.

I never saw much in the way of elves or aliens myself, though I can recall several faint recollections of encounters with clown/harlequin-type characters. I was intrigued why so many people reported interactions with the *wee folk*.

Perhaps they were archetypal figures and you simply saw that kind of thing while under the influences of DMT. I wondered, though, if there wasn't a bit more to it than that. Then I discovered *Charles Bonnet syndrome*, which demonstrated to me just how powerful the human imagination can really be.

Hallucinations may be willingly induced through means other than drug-taking or arise spontaneously due to illness. Examples include prolonged rhythmic dancing/drumming, chanting, hyperventilation, sleep deprivation, sensory deprivation and, like in the case of those afflicted with Charles Bonnet syndrome, a medical problem. This long obscure and poorly understood malady is known for its ability to create astonishing visual hallucinations reminiscent of DMT creations.

The syndrome was first described in 1760 when Swiss writer Charles Bonnet chronicled it. It took over 200 years for the modern health care establishment to acknowledge its relevance. Mentally healthy people, whose only significant problem was gradual vision loss, started to experience daytime hallucinations as their situation worsened. It has been demonstrated many times, through careful scientific experiment or even by those folks just relaxing in their own flotation tanks, that sensory deprivation can ultimately cause people to hallucinate. This fact was probably at the heart of Charles Bonnet syndrome.

The brain likely compensated for the sufferer's failing vision by creating its own imagery out of thin air. More particularly it has been postulated that in a desperate attempt to continue to make sense out of a world that is slowly disappearing, the brain resorts to filling in the gaps. The realism reported is astonishing. Apparently it was often very difficult to distinguish self-generated *virtual reality* from the real McCoy. The hallucinations could last from a few seconds to several hours. Keep in mind that these folks were mentally healthy individuals. I reasoned that if they couldn't resolve reality clearly due to the powerful hallucinations they were experiencing, why would DMT users be any more able to do so?

Hallucinatory content generated by this syndrome can be familiar to the sufferer or decidedly not and includes both animate and inanimate objects. Mundane things like furniture, vehicles or plants and animals can manifest, but the mind seems unusually preoccupied with facial imagery or the creation of entire people/beings. This probably results from the primal survival urge to distinguish friend from foe. Not surprisingly, alarming entities can appear that would be right at home in DMT land.

Like the *fleeting improvised men* of Shreber's own creation, the unfortunate Bonnet sufferers similarly manifested characters unknown to them, and these were often distorted or grotesque in some way. Sometimes they appeared realistic in detail but were smaller than normal. Insubstantial ghost-like images or even some resembling cartoon or caricature figures could also erupt into consciousness at any time. Precisely like those in the DMT reverie. Even more amazing—*DMT-like* clowns, jesters, harlequins and even the renowned elves were reported on occasion!

These Lilliputian characters have been variously described as ranging from diminutive policemen to stovepipe-hat-wearing chimney sweeps to stereotypical Irish leprechauns. Other hallucinations shared by both camps included abstract light effects, geometric patterns and other *trippy* visuals. Insects or insect-like beings were common to both as well. Even lizards and snakes, a recurring motif in the ayahuasca ceremony, popped up from time to time. A 64-year-old woman described her encounter with serpents as follows: "snakes crawling out of people's heads and onto my body." (*International Journal of Neuroscience* 1982, Vol. 17, No. 1: Pages 13-15).

While those afflicted with Charles Bonnet syndrome were often distressed by the disturbing reality of their visions, I gather none felt that they were actually being whisked off to another realm. Mostly they just wondered if they were going crazy or not. Not a bad supposition since various kinds of mental health issues may cause vivid hallucinations to arise.

The hallucinations caused by organic delirium, the *delirium tremens* of the alcoholic, are thought, in some quarters, to most closely resemble the kind of realistic perception experienced in natural REM dreaming (same state as lucid dreaming).

These hallucinations proved so vivid and disturbing that they were colloquially referred to as *the fear* or *the horrors*. These predominantly visual and auditory hallucinations featured the *usual suspects*—insects, animals, reptiles and people (often grotesque just like in the case of Charles Bonnet suffers) or other beings like monsters, angels and, of course, the elf. The following is a case report of someone suffering from alcohol-withdrawal-related delirium tremens:

> He started seeing little people all over the house. They were about a foot high, with funny colourful dresses, weird faces, big eyes and mouths. Some of them were also wearing spectacles. They would follow him all around the house and he could hear their footsteps. (*German Journal of Psychiatry* ISSN 1433-1055 "Understanding a Strange Phenomenon: Lilliputian Hallucinations")

Those suffering from epilepsy and even severe migraines also reported weirdly vivid hallucinations, including those of the Lilliputian kind. In fact, the more I looked into it the more I started to see elves everywhere … at least in the literature.

I was beginning to understand that the brain is quite capable of creating astounding, totally realistic and engrossing imagery all by itself. No need to resort to exotic otherworldly explanations to help shed light on the mind's ability to deceive itself. It is far more relevant to realize that each one of us is capable of manifesting whole worlds, universes even, utilizing nothing more than the power of our imagination. Let us empower ourselves with the realization that we create our own reality. Like Christ said, "The Kingdom of Heaven is within you." It became quite obvious to me that Dr. Strassman's thought experiment was a little off the mark. I could not support the model he used to explain the significance of what seemed to me to be little more than banal and trivial hallucinations. The Divine was not to be found in some far-off parallel universe but much closer to home.

My thesis is supported by the fact that Dr. Strassman's so-called autonomous universes were never the same twice. Nick Sand reported, "I have taken DMT thousands of times. I never had two trips that were the same." Some DMT trippers reported a continuation of the narrative as they re-entered DMT space. The setting and story seemed familiar and occasionally picked up from where it had left off. Strassman felt that this point was significant and supported his model. I would like to point out that normal dreams, as well as those of the lucid variety, work in exactly the same manner. I have had one or two recurring story lines running throughout my dream life for decades.

I also found it curious that these so-called *entities* were always described as being distinctly different from tripper to tripper and, as Sand noted, even *from trip to trip*. The way that these entities reacted to you when you stumbled upon them was highly suspect as well. Not at all the kind of reaction you would expect from a real being if you were to suddenly pop up in front of them out of thin air. What would be your reaction if the reverse were true and a weird creature suddenly manifested in front of you? I asked myself why it was that they never seemed to know anything more than I did. They were just as dumb as me. Of course they were, since they were me. They were no more than figments of my own imagination. But then if you consider what Dr. Laberge has to tell us, we are dreaming all the time anyhow.

Whether we find ourselves in bed or at work, reality is entirely a mental projection. The difference between the waking and dreaming state is just a case of sensory input. Dreaming while asleep is perception unconstrained by input from the five senses. The corollary is that perception while awake is dreaming constrained by sensory input. Awake or asleep, dreaming is occurring. I repeat—**you are now dreaming!**

What we take to be reality is actually the brain's best guess at analyzing the sensory input it is, or is not, being provided with. As we have seen in the case of those afflicted with Charles Bonnet syndrome, the brain can get mighty creative in its guesswork. At first glance the idea that we are dreaming all the time may seem like a preposterous notion, but it is not as ridiculous as you may think.

Reality is fundamentally mediated by the senses, though other factors such as experience and conditioning come into play as well. We have never actually experienced the physical world directly. There has always been something separating it from us. Our perceptions of reality are a purely mediated experience. In a very real way a *middle man*, taking the form of our senses, has always been in the way.

Take vision for example. You have never directly perceived anything and never will. Photons bounce off of an object and then impinge on your retina. The sense of these photons is then converted into an electrical impulse which eventually causes a virtual image to almost magically appear in your field of awareness. Although it certainly seems like it, you are not, in fact, actually peering out of a *window* onto the world at large. Isn't your *mind's* eye just creating a virtual representation of reality?

Your *wetware* takes all of the perceptual data presented to it by the senses, filters most of it out and, with what remains, tries its best to model a coherent picture. This *re-presented* creation is what you ultimately perceive as reality. It's all smoke and mirrors. You have never actually touched, tasted, heard, smelt or seen anything at all. Reality is just a bunch of electro-chemical interactions impinging upon your awareness. We truly do live in *dreamtime*, and, as the Australian aborigines tell us, we are all simply *singing* (conceptualizing) ourselves into existence. Whatever, if anything, is *really* out there (the volume of an atom exceeds 99 percent empty space, and, at the subatomic level, matter doesn't really *exist* at all), will never be directly known. It seems counter-intuitive and defies commonsense but our experience of reality is fundamentally created entirely in our minds. Consciousness manifested matter. Matter did not manifest consciousness as was normally supposed. Pleasant dreams all. Now let me share one of my dreams with you.

I began dreaming vividly one night but did not become lucid in the process. In this dream I dreamt I was dreaming. And in that dream within a dream, I realized I was merely dreaming. So I started to become lucid. And then it appeared as if I actually awoke. I believed I had, and yet I wondered … was I now hallucinating that I was dreaming or rather dreaming that I was hallucinating? The distinction was lost on me. And still is I might add. Fourth-century Chinese sage Chuang-Tzu apparently once had a similar conundrum:

> Once upon a time, I, Chuang-Tzu, dreamed I was a butterfly, fluttering hither and thither, to all intents and purposes a butterfly. I was conscious only of following my fancies as a butterfly, and was unconscious of my individuality as a butterfly. Suddenly I was awakened, and there I lay myself again. Now I do not know whether I was a man dreaming I was a butterfly, or whether I am a butterfly now dreaming I am a man.

Ayahuasca

My research showed that ayahuasca, also called *yagé, nepe, kabi, natema, hoasca* and *daime*, was starting to make some slow inroads into the consciousness of mainstream culture. It had been featured during an episode of a popular American TV show several years back, and a British reality TV show also devoted a slot to the topic. Several documentaries and a couple of movies also used it as a narrative device. More authors were referring to it in their work during the last decade and there was recently even a two-part radio show dedicated to it. It played on Canada's national radio network.

Ayahuasca's growing popularity has even created a tourist industry of sorts in places like Peru and Brazil, where serious-minded spiritual types flock, as well as those seeking just another cheap thrill. South American society had relied on its healing powers since preliterate times. Shamans (*ayahuasceros/curanderos*) still utilize it today for purposes such as giving them the ability to speak to all manner of flora and fauna, for contacting the dead, for telepathic communication, for divination and for treating a patient's physical, emotional and spiritual ailments.

Evidently it is of such value that beginning in the early part of the last century it was incorporated into the practices of several syncretic religious organizations. These religions, perhaps most notably those found in Brazil, combined indigenous ayahuasca practice with African spiritualism and Christian liturgy. The organizations officially sanctioned included the Santo Daime, founded in the 1930s, the União do Vegetal, founded in 1961, and the Barquinha, a group that parted ways from the Santo Daime in 1945. In both the traditional practice as well as its modern-day counterpart, ritual is an important element. During the later part of the twentieth century, chapters of the Santo Daime and the União do Vegetal spread outside of Brazil's borders, travelling as far afield as Australia, Canada, France, Germany, Japan, the Netherlands, Spain and the United States. In some of these countries it is now legal under religious freedom legislation to consume ayahuasca as part of a church's sacrament.

The drink is composed of two constituent ingredients that must be combined for the effects to take hold. Ayahuasca is the common name of a particular jungle vine as well as the brew it is a constituent of. This woody plant, Latin name *Banisteriopsis caapi*, is referred to as the *vine of the soul or spirit*. It's pounded up and boiled in combination with its DMT-containing companion plant. The leaves of this second constituent are often commonly referred to as *chacruna* (Latin names *Psychotria viridis* and *P. carthaginensis)* and are found in the jungles of Peru, Ecuador, Colombia and parts of Brazil. The beverage must contain at the very least these two main ingredients for it to be orally active. It may also include various admixtures like tobacco, coca, datura or san pedro cactus. These add additional distinctive psychoactive properties to the brew.

As I mentioned before, you can eat as much DMT as you like and feel no effects whatsoever. This is because the body contains an enzyme called monoamineoxidase that deactivates N,N dimethyl tryptamine as soon as it enters the stomach. In order to enjoy the effects you need to inhibit this enzymatic activity. This component is an MAOI (monoamine oxidase inhibitor). Plant-derived DMT, in combination with enough MAOI from the vine, will allow a full-blown, long-lasting trip to ensue. This is known as the ayahuasca experience. Typically a high dose would last from two to six hours. Some antidepressants in the SSRI family (like Zoloft) are MAOIs so you must take care to never consume ayahuasca if you are taking this kind of medication.

Once the ingredients are boiled long enough to release the active elements, it is simply a matter of getting enough of it down your gullet for the drug to take effect. The taste is quite unpalatable, though I have experienced worse. Vomiting, or *purging* as it was known in some circles, usually ensues after half an hour or so, but this is not always the case. The physical discomfort that results from drinking ayahuasca is one of the reasons it will never become a mainstream recreational drug.

Unlike Western medicines, which usually taste sweet going down but often cause long term negative health repercussions, ayahuasca is a bitter pill to be sure, but its long-term positive effects are truly impressive. Terence McKenna said of the experience that ayahuasca was the only drug he knew of that not only had no debilitating morning-after side-effects, but actually made participants feel substantially better on the morning after. Indeed long-term Uniao do Vegetal ayahuasca drinkers, studied by Western scientists a couple of decades ago, had nothing but very positive mental and physical health benefits as a consequence of their long-term use of the medicine.

Regarding the biochemical, pharmacological and physiological tests carried out by the researchers, no perceived negative complications were ever observed. The test subjects passed various psychological examinations with flying colours. In fact they scored higher than their non-drinking control group peers did. Contrary to the control group, ayahuasca users were found to be more trustworthy, loyal, optimistic, spontaneous, energetic and emotionally mature. Additionally, their short-term memory and ability to concentrate were superior. Overall not a single negative side effect was noted. I don't know of many Western medicines that are so overwhelmingly positive over such a broad range of areas.

Other studies have also been conducted which corroborate the fact that ayahuasca is harmless and in all likelihood an excellent medicine. Dr. Erik Hoffmann, part of the team that gathered to carry out EEG studies on ayahuasca drinkers, has suggested that the altered state of consciousness induced by ayahuasca had similarities to that of meditation. This was of interest to me as the purpose of meditation for me was simply to improve clarity, presence and awareness.

On that note, some brain researchers believe they may know precisely which part of the brain the sense of awareness actually resides in. I am talking about the part of the brain which perceives *How do I feel right now?* The ME centre if you will. If the researchers are correct, the sense of human awareness may actually originate in the *anterior insular cortex*. And perhaps not coincidentally, a recent study entitled, "Increased Frontal and Paralimbic Activation Following Ayahuasca, the Pan Amazonian Inebriant" (2006), mentions the significance of that region as well.

The study, which utilized modern high-tech brain imaging equipment, discovered that the effects of ayahuasca were quite pronounced in the anterior insular cortical region. Certainly, if an awareness centre really did exist, stimulating it beyond its norms might cause *the doors of perception* to be flung open as Huxley suggested. Could this explain why that particular region was so active during ayahuasca use?

As the centre of awareness, the anterior insular cortex may very well be the place where the *sense of I* is mediated. Perhaps by psychedelically tweaking this area, a fuller, richer experience of reality results. In a sense the awareness of self and its place in the world is temporarily heightened. Huxley used the analogy of a valve, like in a water main, being opened, which allowed consciousness to be freed up to perceive a much broader spectrum of reality.

If psychedelics affected the anterior insular cortex in a temporary manner, might something like long-term meditation actually cause a permanent physiological response to occur there, I wondered? I could well imagine such a direct cause and effect relationship arising given the dramatic way prolonged meditation affected my own sense of awareness. I just so happened to locate a research project that suggested this very relationship might actually exist.

The results of a magnetic resonance imagining (MRI) study published in 2005 show that long-term meditators displayed increased cortical thickness in the anterior insular. The fact that a simple meditation practice could actually stimulate the brain to react in such an amazing manner was incredible. Something very significant seemed to be going on in the anterior insular cortex. Could it be that this part of the brain was responsible for manifesting *us*, that is our very ego, into existence? Research seemed to suggest it was quite possible. Therefore modifying the anterior insular cortex through drugs or meditation could actually change the nature of reality itself. Precisely what the mystics and shamans have been telling us all along.

Curious and Curiouser

It was with a sense of relief, but also a tinge of trepidation, that I first tumbled down the psychedelic hole. Let me catch you up on how I got there. It turned out to be more difficult than I first imagined. Sourcing recreational drugs was no problem. Mind expanding substances—forget about it. In my neighbourhood, all it took was a casual saunter down the street to score some heroin, but getting your hands on something as benign as MDMA (ecstasy) was a whole different story. I found it incredible that psychedelics had somehow gotten listed as a Schedule 1 drug in the USA. These compounds, which had demonstrated so much positive potential, were lumped together (along with cannabis, equally ridiculous) with the terribly destructive opiate class which included things like heroin; while opium, morphine and even cocaine were placed in the less harshly prosecuted Schedule 2 category. To be deemed a Schedule 1 drug a substance had to fulfil the following three conditions per the United States Controlled Substances Act:

1. The drug or other substance has a high potential for abuse.
2. The drug or other substance has no currently accepted medical use in treatment in the United States.
3. There is a lack of accepted safety for use of the drug or other substance under medical supervision.

Of course, substances like ayahuasca or psilocybin mushrooms failed to fulfill any of those criteria. Not a single one. So ask yourself, then, what is the real reason for scheduling them? Recently a UK study considered how their drug classification system might be flawed, since there was a concern that the current practice did not accurately reflect the actual harm the rated substances posed. Exactly the same weakness the US system suffers from.

The new updated classification system suggests that tobacco and alcohol are in the mid-to-high range in terms of potential harm, while cannabis, LSD, MDMA and DMT-containing compounds are all deemed much less problematic than those two legal drugs. Ecstasy is considered to pose essentially the same level of risk as anabolic steroids, while common household solvents are seen to be potentially more dangerous than LSD. Let's be clear here, common nail polish remover poses more potential harm to health than LSD! Pretty eye-opening stuff, eh?

But getting back to the matter at hand—how was I going to secure my drug of choice given its relative scarcity? I was getting increasingly frustrated with my lack of success at the hostel. My metrosexual roommate was, as far as drugs were concerned, as straight as an arrow. No help forthcoming from him. Seemingly his only passion was singing mediocre karaoke most evenings at night clubs. Not so bad as far as vices went, but he would insist upon serenading me from his top bunk bed at every opportunity. He slept in late most mornings, which fortunately afforded me some quiet research time. I always dreaded the thought of him awaking, as it invariably lead to excruciatingly painful renditions of some current pop song bouncing off the walls of the room. In fact, now that I carefully reflect back to those moments, I recall that there was no echo at all, since our 7X5 foot cubicle was too small to actually sustain such an effect.

Nope, it was just pure unadulterated misery. As I lay stretched out on my bunk, much as I might have appeared if placed on a medieval rack, I thought how wonderful that fate would have been. Short and sweet. Then the Karaoke King bought himself an electric guitar which he was even less proficient at. My God was there no end to the evil tools of torture this mad inquisitor had at his disposal? I would have pled to being the worst kind of heretic, to fornicating with old Beelzebub himself, if only asked. Oh the horror, the horror ....

My plan had always been to find someone in the hostel who was an experienced and knowledgeable psychedelic drug user. Someone who might take an interest in my quest. After a few weeks passed I finally chanced upon a likely candidate.

A Fleeting Improvised Man

As I made my way up the hall one morning, I heard the familiar sloshing sound of the floor being cleaned. Turning a corner, I found my way blocked by a large raggedy mophead made from numerous strands of twisted cotton fibre. Working my gaze up the handle, I was immediately taken by another stringy mop of sorts—a magnificent corn-rowed head of black shiny hair. "Sorry," he said with a beaming grin as I halted in front of him. "Never mind, just walk on through. It's just gonna look like shit again soon anyhow."

I thanked him and from there a casual friendship struck up. Tunji was a tall black man in his thirties who had decided to make a break from his old life and start afresh out on the coast, just like me. He was intelligent and articulate. The ladies found him quite irresistible. He also smoked a lot of dope. Over the course of several days during his morning cleaning job, which earned him room and board at the hostel, we had the opportunity to learn a bit about each other. It turned out he was a writer of sorts as well as a dub poet and a good conversationalist. Since he was a newcomer, he could not help me out immediately but promised to keep his eyes and ears open. He was guarded and a little suspicious of my intentions at first until I assuaged his fears that I was not a cop. While I bided my time, I decided to rank the entheogens I would use in order of preference from first to last. Last being considered the most potent drug and thus the best candidate to produce the insight I was seeking. I didn't think it was necessary to try them all, but I felt the first should be *Salvia divinorum* and the last definitely DMT, since it seemed to be the entheological Holy Grail. The proposed list ran in my mind as follows: first *Salvia divinorum*, then MDMA, to be followed up by magic mushrooms, possibly peyote, and finally DMT. Ayahuasca was not in the running as that would have required a trip to South America. As I learned more, I considered doing ketamine and LSD as well, if the opportunity arose. Conceptually it seemed a pretty sound plan. Simply start with the weaker substances and, as experience was gained, work up to the more profound medicines. But the plan suffered from at least one major flaw which will become apparent shortly.

One day Tunji finally came through and announced that he had found some *Salvia divinorum*. This was not such a big deal as it was not a scheduled drug in Canada. Freely available for purchase if you knew where to look. However, Tunji informed me that there was to be an added bonus. A guy staying at the hostel had it in quantity and wanted to get rid of it all so he said the first dose would be free. If I liked it I could take the rest off of his hands for a good price. I didn't know much about salvia but I figured that since it was legal, its effects must be moderate at best. It was the new hallucinogenic kid on the block. A great way to gently pry open those perceptual doors just a crack and take a peek in. With the first toke it became only too clear that my supposition was not entirely correct and also explained why this guy had so much of this stuff on his hands.

The green leafy substance I was presented with originated from a bushy Mexican plant commonly known as Diviner's Sage. Unbeknownst to me the psychoactive chemical in *Salvia divinorum* was by mass the most potent naturally occurring hallucinogen in the world. LSD was more potent but was semi-synthesized. Somehow salvia's notoriety had escaped me. I guess Tunji was out to have a good laugh, so didn't inform me about its true strength. He mentioned his own harrowing encounter with it, where he came face to face with his dead father, only after my own experience had ended.

Tunji filled a pipe bowl about half full with leaves. That may not seem like much but this was 20X fortified salvia. Literally twenty times stronger than just natural leaves. I asked the guy who gave me the free sample not to be stingy. Turns out he wasn't. He assured me it was a hefty dose that was certain to work its magic. On that count he was entirely correct. In retrospect I wish I had just kept my big yap shut. I simply had no idea what was about to unfold during the very first drug experience of my life.

What seemed like a never-ending stream of hot smoke entered my lungs. Just as I managed to exhale this single huge toke, reality, as I knew it, completely disappeared in an instant. No lead-up at all. One second sober, the next completely out of it. As salvia-land popped into view, I heard a sound like a row of windows being slammed shut in quick succession—bang, bang, bang, with a mechanical regularity. Accompanying the sound was a startling sight. The realization of what I beheld shocked me thoroughly. *My God will you look at that ... it is a whopping big ...* but I could not finish the thought. I had become totally unconscious in the space of a second or two.

Blacking out could have simply been a dose response, but I rather think it was more likely a coping mechanism for dealing with the horror that confronted me. What I beheld was so disconcerting that I suffered a complete mental shutdown. It would have probably remained that way but for the urgings of Tunji. He called me back and was inviting me to look out the window. What a crazy notion I thought! To do so would have meant I was mobile. The plain fact was I was paralyzed, my head canted at a bizarre angle. Pronounced *energy lines* that felt like strong electricity were coursing up and down my chest. Conceptualizing anything was extremely difficult, if not impossible. I tried to explain to him what I was experiencing but could barely get a word out. What I beheld was a partial cartoon reality superimposed upon things in the room. My chest showed vibrant patterns of energy running up and down it, which matched the sensation perfectly. I was wearing Charlie Brown's famous V-patterned sweater. Some of the wide Vs represented the actual energy meridians, while the other coloured portions helped form the rest of the patterned patchwork. The more I tried to explain the situation to Tunji the more hysterical I became.

There were other elements of cartoon simulation spread about the room as well, but they were difficult to discern since I could not rotate my head. A very bizarre situation that only intensified as the seconds ticked by. A maniacal laugh was all I could muster. I think the worst part was the sheer helplessness and lack of control I felt. I had never been so incapacitated before. An irrational terror arose as I felt more and more like a trapped animal. How I so wanted out of there.

I finally gave up any further communication with Tunji and lapsed back into unconsciousness. Perhaps a minute later, I partially regained consciousness (the whole affair lasted but four to five minutes total). Once back I still felt this tremendous energy, and it was now coursing through my thighs and lower legs. It was an entirely unpleasant sensation—like someone had jabbed the leads of a 12-volt car battery into me. My whole lower body appeared to be a crude cartoon rendering. I seemed to be wearing big blue clown booties, and they were topped with vivid crimson socks. My pants were equally outlandish. How much longer was this purgatory going to continue, I wondered?

There was nothing for me to do but wait until I was released from the grips of this terrible compound. Within a minute, I could finally move my fingers, but the hallucinations still persisted as did the weird energy coursing through my body. With a little more time, the visions finally subsided, and I could rise from my chair. I just wanted to get the hell out of Tunji's room as quickly as possible, though I was obliged to first answer a question. I simply told Tunji I doubted I would ever try that nasty shit ever again. Indeed I never did.

Later I came to learn that salvia is a dissociative and apparently not everyone's cup of tea. For many it is simply a roller coaster ride to hell and back and most never repeat the experience. The whole episode had really sinister, creepy overtones to it, but these were difficult to articulate. Having my ego eroded to such a degree, so quickly, was intolerable.

I reflected back to the experience and recalled how I was freaked out so much by what transpired as the hallucination first kicked in. It was no more than a momentary flash. What I could recall was a loud bang, bang, bang sound accompanied by the visual impression of huge snapping cartoon dentures seemingly placed only a foot from my face. Later I learned that the dental work belonged to a giant jeering cartoon face which seemed intent on my demise. This was not recalled immediately but later brought back to memory thanks to an ayahuasca trip.

In that instance, ayahuasca told me in no uncertain terms to stay away from salvia. It retrieved dramatic buried memories of the original salvia encounter, to reinforce the point. It showed me that, after I noted the chomping teeth, my perspective pulled back in a desperate attempt to figure out just what the heck was going on. Revealed was a huge rotund cartoon face appearing very much like a malevolent ivory-coloured giant snapping beachball. It had no torso whatsoever. Since salvia is a dissociative, I had no way to place what I was seeing in context. My personal history had been erased, so the knowledge that I had just taken a drug was not present. At that point I didn't even know that I was a human being. But there was no confusion about my reaction to the situation—pure unadulterated terror. Lurching backwards away from the monstrosity, I whirled around but that only increased my fright.

It appeared I had somehow gained admission to the psychiatric ward that housed all of the dysfunctional, psychotic toys of the world. Like a scene straight out of the movie *Toy Story: The Troubled Years*, I found that the lunatics had clearly taken over the asylum. It was a madhouse of animated cacophony and bedlam. Various stuffed figures, as well

153

as all manner of mechanical wind-up or vintage battery-powered toys drunkenly careened around while some attempted to bash each other to bits. Hysterical laughter as well as sobs of misery mixed with the bell, chime and drum sounds the careening wind-up toys made. It was all so ghastly it's no wonder I chose not to acknowledge it and passed out instead.

One of my childhood fears involved the thought of dolls animating to life. Mr. Peanut Head and Howdy Doody, for instance, used to really creep me out. Here they were before my very eyes, and there was no escaping them. These insane hallucinatory phantoms, seeming relics from an abused child's toy box, seemed to be deliberately trying to unhinge me. Thankfully the terrible tableau ceased at that point. The ayahuasca recollection had driven the point home. No more salvia for me. I struggled to make sense out of the experience. Could it be relevant in some way, I wondered?

Psychologist Carl Jung's concept of the *shadow* came to mind. Considered by Jung to be part of the unconscious mind, the shadow, or *shadow aspect*, consisted of repressed instincts, weaknesses and shortcomings we all held. Things we found distasteful or rejected about ourselves were warehoused here. The shadow may link us to the more primitive, irrational, animal instincts which are mostly superseded during early childhood by the conscious mind.

Jung strongly felt that all humans embodied the shadow somewhere in their psyche and the less it was expressed in the individual's conscious life, the darker and more disturbing it would prove to be in its obscured state. If I had indeed managed to make it to *shadow land*, I did not relish the thought of ever returning.

The salvia experience was my one and only bad trip. It took me a few days to regroup and let the trauma work its way out of my system. Wow, that experience turned out to be all that I feared and then some. What about the future? If this was a *soft* hallucinogen, what would the *hard* stuff be like I wondered. Could I actually bring myself to continue down this road of exploration?

Mulling over the experience, a few thoughts came to mind. My salvia experience demonstrated to me that my ranked list of potential psychedelics was probably ill-conceived and of little value. There seemed no way for me to accurately ascertain what these compounds were capable of doing beforehand. From now on I would take whatever came my way without distinction. The thing that I most wanted to avoid, the so-called bad trip, had already occurred. It was traumatic, but I had survived. I couldn't conceive of a worse experience so I reckoned I could proceed and know that psychedelics would not be the ruin of me. My commitment was intractable. I could not help but see this thing through to the end come what may. I was seemingly alone in this venture. I never did find a willing ferryman to extend me aid in crossing to the underworld. Though Tunji offered a little encouragement from time to time, the final outcome rested squarely on my own shoulders.

Gone Fishing

I was pleased when Tunji located a supply of psilocybin mushrooms for me. I purchased five grams. The exact amount Terence said was required for full release. Since this was my first experience with mushrooms, Tunji advised me to err on the side of caution and take only two grams (normal recreational dose) to start. I ensconced myself in the dimly lit cell (the Karaoke King had left early for his nightly song fest) and began the experiment. Once again my hopes ran high. I proceeded to remove from the plastic baggy some suitably sized dried caps and stems, which approximated two grams, and then proceeded to masticate them thoroughly in one mouthful. I adore fungi of all sorts so my taste buds enjoyed the pleasant mushroomy flavour. I chewed on the pieces for about ten minutes before swallowing. The idea was to allow the mucous membrane of my mouth the opportunity to pick up some of the psychedelic component quickly and actively transport it to my blood stream immediately without having to pass it through my gut first. Others choose to simply make a tea out of the pieces, though I would recommend you eat the sodden remnants as well. One way or another, mushrooms will begin to take effect in about twenty minutes.

Eventually I began to feel a slight tingling in my extremities. This feeling became ever so slightly more pronounced as time went on. Perceptually nothing much of interest happened. After an hour had elapsed, I knew that this was not going to be the day that I discovered what all the fuss was about. The next day I reported the results to Tunji and asked him if he could get more, as the remaining three grams would be of no use on their own. I waited and waited but there would be no more forthcoming. Many weeks had elapsed, and I was growing impatient with my lack of success. Taking matters in hand, I decided a weeklong trip to the Big City was in order.

A change of venue, particularly to a larger fishing hole, could only increase my chances of catching the kind of fish I was after. Utilizing my current strategy, I looked for a hostel that might be home to the kind of people that could be of service to me. An Internet search brought the perfect location to my attention.

Numerous negative reviews presented a dirty, low-rent kind of place, in theory restricted to those under the age of thirty five, though, hearing I would stay a full week, the owner was happy enough to take my money. What kind of people would hang out in a cheap, bug-infested hovel, I wondered? Probably just the kind that had the specialized knowledge I required.

The Ameridian Hostel, or flophouse if you prefer, was located in the worst part of town. People had warned me to stay away from such a seedy area. Apparently drug pushers plied their trade throughout it. Perfect. All the easier to find the kind of people I was after. "No," my friends told me, "you don't understand! You could very well end up looking at the business end of an AIDS-infected hypodermic needle, wielded by a desperate user trying to shake you down." Even better! No need to seek informants out. They apparently would come to me. Of course, the *charms* of the Ameridian were attractive as well.

While there I met ultra-low-budget backpackers just passing through, but it was the long-term residents that interested me. Third World students, the newly emigrated, Canadian day labourers supporting various habits and teenage runaways all called this place home. The level of decrepitude and squalor of the place was astonishing even to a well travelled backpacker such as me. I fondly refer to this place as the *Hostel from Hell*. Certainly the worst I had ever encountered in my life. The fact that it existed in one of the most developed countries in the world was all the more amazing. A dirt-cheap pricing policy seemed its only virtue. A bed in the dorm cost a mere sixty bucks a week or thirty five dollars if you slept on the roof. I found the bedbugs intriguing. I had backpacked all over South-East Asia and they had never once crossed my path. I see them reported in the news these

A Fleeting Improvised Man

days as a growing American scourge, but a few years back they were virtually unknown. I tried to avoid these by getting a top bunk.

The dreadful matron was a force to be reckoned with. She was outright scary … and crazy! An old shrew of a woman, clearly psychotic (though the owner calmly assured me she was only suffering bipolar mania), with a slash of the brightest crimson lipstick smeared across wrinkled lips, which perpetually clenched a dangling cigarette between them, and dark sunglasses planted firmly on her head to shade her bloodshot eyes from any rays of hope. She was exceptionally rude and ill mannered. Central casting could not have done better when the call came in to find a suitably wretched overseer for what was in all likelihood the worst hostel in the world. Things were really looking up as far as I was concerned.

My room was so dreadful I had to prevent myself from retching upon first entering it. Barns at home smelled better. The stench was horrible—a mixture of rank body odour combined with ancient urine-stained carpeting—topped off with appallingly dirty pockmarked walls. In an attempt to hide all the foulness, my roommates would spray room deodorizer around from time to time, but this just intensified my nausea. I had occasionally smelled a similar, though less offensive version, wafting up from the chronically homeless. The three bunks jammed into the room were seemingly WWII relics topped with nasty soiled mattresses. One corner contained graffiti covered security lockers, and open duct work and rusty pipes hung down from the ceiling that was illuminated by a single bare bulb. My spirits continued to run high as the place seemed to hold great potential. Unfortunately, I encountered the exact same stumbling block which had hampered my progress back at the Backpackers Hostel.

There were lots of drugs about but nobody was interested in hallucinogens. One of my roommates suggested I go on the *anti-drugwar tour* since it was a prerequisite for getting into *The Herb Shop* which might sell what I was after.

The tour guide spread his pro-drug, anti-establishment rhetoric pretty thick while he showed us the downtown sights. We were advised to remember three tour *facts* since they were the ticket required to gain us entry through the electronic security doors of The Herb Shop.

When the double security barriers of The Herb Shop swung

158

open, I was presented with a novel sight. Four, or perhaps five, men were seated behind a row of plain wooden tabletops offering some pretty funky herb-based wares. What was all this weird exotic shit I wondered? Someone asked me what I wanted, but I didn't have a clue what I was looking at. "Well," came my faltering reply, "I was wondering if anybody had any mushrooms."

He said, "No," and explained how this space was really devoted to the pleasures of herb, but he was kind enough to check around and found out that, if I came back the next day, a certain seller might be present who could help me out. That was encouraging news.

For good measure, the guy helping me asked again if I might like something. My inclination was to decline a second time but I reflected back to something the tour leader had said an hour earlier. His statement that those "who have never tried herb had no right to hold any opinion about it" came back to me. I could not argue with the veracity of his words. I decided I would buy three cookies in the hopes of educating myself a bit. Later that day SWIM ate one.

At most the effect was similar to drinking several beers. Not as dramatic as I expected but I didn't care because that was not what this trip was about. I was anticipating the results of my follow-up to The Herb Shop the next morning. Things looked very promising, though a problem arose that threatened to upset the plan.

Turns out I couldn't find the damn shop again. The previous day's tour had so discombobulated me that all I could recall was the street name. I walked up and down the long thoroughfare with no luck. Then I spied The Drug Museum which I recalled was somehow associated with The Herb Shop. Just pop in for some quick directions and then be on my way I thought.

The museum chronicled the commercialization of drugs throughout the ages from their original nonprocessed natural form, through the patent medicine phase, right up to the present control of pharmaceuticals via multinational corporations. A charming, articulate curator, looking ever so much like Niles Crane (of sitcom *Frasier* fame) but sporting a long greying pony tail, described various points of interest among the display cases. Eventually I got the directions and was about to leave when he asked me if I might not enjoy a nice cup of legal herbal coca tea. Why not?

A Fleeting Improvised Man

We passed into a curtained-off lounge area of sorts. Several couches and oversized stuffed chairs were set out for people to relax in. He went over to the small kitchenette and started preparing the tea. There were two people chatting next to a coffee table, one of whom came over and introduced himself. He was a New Zealander, of probable Maori ancestry, who had an impressively extensive knowledge of drug use and lore. Apparently he had tried almost every substance known to man and could rattle off the exact chemical structure and class of each compound, like a housewife could cite her favourite soup recipe. Just like my gracious host, he impressed me with his charm and good manners.

On the coffee table sat an impressive shiny stainless steel cone-shaped contraption measuring perhaps a foot tall. I asked him what it was. A German sounding brand name was provided for what was apparently a state-of-the-art vaporizer. It carried a whopping $700 price tag. Not the typical stoner paraphernalia one usually associated with this drug. "How does it work?" I inquired. His reply was most unexpected.

He asked me if I wanted to try it out for myself. That stopped me cold in my tracks. I had come here looking for an address, certainly not to get stoned. That was the furthest thing from my mind. All my life I had made a very conscious decision to stay away from what he was now offering me. My present goal did not include recreational drug use, and I certainly had a very negative view of the kind of drug culture associated with this substance. But the people here did not fit my stereotypical view at all. They appeared to be highly educated and wholesome. What to do? I hesitated and waffled but in the end decided to inhale, if only for the sake of my education I assured myself.

Sucking the smoke through a valve fitted to a plastic bag was very easy and elicited not the slightest cough on my part. Moments later it hit me. Wow! Yet another sacred cow was on its way off to the abattoir. It was obvious I had been deceived once again.

This was no evil substance. What outrageous negative propaganda had been spread about its nature. Quite the opposite seemed true. It struck me as a far healthier choice than alcohol. It's beyond me why it was prohibited, but it may have had a lot to do with its propensity to make us passive and pensive. Keeping us as perpetually dumbed-down, hard-working schmucks seemed always to be the order of the day. The propaganda about it being a gateway drug was laughable. It certainly never inspired me to use any harder drugs. In fact that single encounter remains my only recreational experience with that particular drug to date.

I spent the rest of the afternoon there getting very inebriated. The few people who came and sat down to enjoy the volcano were all lovely souls. I talked to the Kiwi as best I could about psychedelics but eventually could no longer articulate much of anything at all. I just sat back and enjoyed the moment. At 5 p.m. I learned that the place would close for several hours and then reopen as a social club. *Niles* asked me if I wanted to return, and I thought about it for all of one second. "Sure, I would love to," I said. I did not want to miss the opportunity to talk to the Kiwi some more as he was such a wealth of information. Furthermore, I wanted to experience this drug to its fullest.

To that end I went back to the hostel and consumed the last two cookies. The effects started to kick in around the time I made it back to the museum. After indulging myself moderately for about an hour, I asked the Kiwi if I could buy some of the herb myself to share around with the kind folks. He said sure. All I had to do was wait my turn, and then I would be invited upstairs where a seller waited. After about fifteen minutes I was directed to a door and told to ascend the darkly lit staircase. Normally I might have been a little wary but the effects of the smoke took care of all my worries. Getting to the top of the dark passage, I momentarily looked around in confusion until I spotted a rickety ladder that led to the attic. I ascended again, and this time found a man illuminated by a single bare bulb that dangled on the end of a long black cord which threw shadows all around the place as it oscillated back and forth. His balding pate and facial features made him appear very much like John Malkovich, particularly in the poor light and my creative mind state. "What an appropriate *mis en scene* for my very first drug deal," I mused.

I was soaking it all in, momentarily mesmerized by his uncanny appearance and the mysterious ambience of the crawl space, when he broke my reverie with a brusque business-like, "What do you want?" Sputtering, I confessed I didn't know as I had no idea what I was looking at.

Looking down at his professionally packaged product and then back at me he gruffly barked, "What the hell you are talking about?"

161

I only managed to make matters worse by divulging my ignorance concerning such products, explaining that today was the first time I had ever laid eyes on such stuff. Oh dear … with that he momentarily flipped out, first accusing me of being a cop and then asking me how the hell I ever got permission to come up there in the first place. I said Jason (the Kiwi's real name) told me to go on up. "Jason! How the fuck do you know Jason's name?" he bellowed. There was going to be hell to pay, that was sure, as nobody was supposed to know the Kiwi's given name—nobody! I explained that when I met him he introduced himself as such. Well that infuriated him even more. He pounded the table and started to rant on once again about me having no business up there, security concerns and how they had to get to *know you* for some time before revealing this side of their operation.

I just sort of whimpered and pleaded my innocence. "You should take all this up with Jason, oops … shit I mean the Kiwi," I suggested. I was just a naïve bystander. At that he calmed down a bit, suggested something that might be of interest and allowed the sale to proceed.

With my bright shiny foil-covered treasure in hand, I descended the stairs as quickly as possible, feeling relieved I had managed to make it out in one piece. It turned out that this little brown cube I had just laid down twenty bucks for was about to initiate the first insightful psychedelic experience of my life, and I had not the slightest clue it was even possible. After all who had ever heard that this drug could be strongly hallucinogenic? Though I stumbled upon the technique by chance, I later learned that eating and smoking it at high levels was the secret to my success.

I had told the Kiwi that I wanted to try a lot in one go to see what might happen. "Oh, you want to *bogart* it all then," came his response. Bogarting meant taking more than your fair share.

"Precisely," I said and explained that I wanted to experience overpowering effects if possible. He seemed happy to oblige me.

I took several long hard drags from the vapour filled plastic bag. I can't say that the effects were unexpected, since it was all new to me to begin with, but I can say I was delightfully surprised. Combined with the cookies, a pretty extraordinary shift of consciousness resulted. In several ways it differed remarkably from that which DMT produces. But I had yet to bark up that particular tree, so I had nothing to compare it to at the time. It was an entirely pleasant experience, no fear or apprehension whatsoever. Truly a great introduction to the world of psychedelics and one that most people aren't even aware is possible.

The first thing I noticed was the increasing vividness of colour and the way objects seemed to now be rendered in what I can best describe as high *definition*. I was fascinated. I had never had occasion to view reality in such a realistic manner before. Everything vied for my attention as it was all equally fascinating. *Oh look at the charming chair with vibrant red leather upholstery over there* or *how marvellous that wood grain coffee table top looks,* sort of thing. How utterly amazing reality appeared at that moment!

Then my perspective started to alter. I had the distinct impression that I was at home and was entertaining guests in my living room. These people were not strangers but rather old familiar chums, and we were simply enjoying ourselves like we had done many times before. The large, very brightly lit room I was actually seated in now appeared to be a much smaller intimate and cozy venue, with a welcoming golden hue cast over everything. It was uncanny how familiar this place and these people had become. My rational mind could clearly discern that this was not really my living room at all, and these people were perfect strangers. Yet my heart told me otherwise.

This new perspective arose if I simply relaxed and allowed it to manifest itself. I was tempted to immerse myself in this new reality and allow myself to be fully swept away, but I resisted. From time to time I shook my head and was completely back in normal reality. The switching back and forth was controllable.

This feeling eventually faded only to be replaced by a new perception. Everything started to take on a 2-D computer-rendered feel. It was like I was looking at a computer screen and viewing a convincingly modelled 3-D presentation of reality. If you have ever looked through virtual reality goggles, you will know what I mean. I think my depth perception was being altered since the figure/ground relationship became skewed and difficult to discern. It was odd how the environment in totality appeared less convincing, yet, at the same time, individual objects in it seemed hyper real. The impression evoked was similar to looking at a single cell of an animated movie. The sense of place became more static, time and space less distinct. The immediate surroundings were now like a freeze frame that I could manipulate at will.

A Fleeting Improvised Man

I was looking at several unoccupied couches and chairs, and, with no effort at all, I could move my perceptual gaze at least forty-five degrees around an imaginary arc from where I was actually seated. I could view anything I liked from new angles without moving my position. The basic qualities of those things under my scrutiny did not change, merely the angle from which I perceived them. This effect was reminiscent of how the angle of view rotated around a static character in the *Matrix* movie. I could manipulate the experience with no effort at all. One moment seeing everything as it ordinarily appeared from my seated position and the next moment as a 3-D rendering, and I had somehow skewed my view as if seated elsewhere.

Playing around with this new ability was highly entertaining and metaphysically rewarding as well. The mystics had gotten it right; reality was far less solid and intractable than imagined. I was amazed at how easy it was to come back to the normal way of perceiving things and then relax and be off to the races once more. I felt quite lucid and rational during this phase of the experience. Then it dawned on me, I had finally found the vindication I had long sought. Reality had divulged its true nature to me—it was as fake as a Canadian $2 bill. Just as I had suspected all along. With that realization a voice soon interjected. Speaking in my head it said:

"Hi DJ. This is the *real DJ* speaking. Yes, that is correct—the real you—and I, or should I say you, are actually elsewhere right now and the real you is speaking presently. You do indeed exist but not as you presently believe yourself to be. Actually what is occurring presently is I—the REAL I—am writing the thing you perceive yourself to be into existence as we speak."

I was flabbergasted. Not only was reality fake but this presence claimed that I was as well. Apparently some form of *me* really did exist in some other place or manner of being. What did the voice mean when it said it was *writing me into existence*? Was that implied in a literal sense I wondered? As a reply came a mentally projected picture in my head of pen in hand writing on paper. It was confirmed. Apparently I was just a bunch of words, a narrative in some other guy's story!

I was a little bit awe-struck in having the opportunity to communicate with my real essence yet wondered how it was possible that I was being constructed or *conceptualized* into being as one would have a story written about themselves. The author was apparently real enough, but I was not. If I were to believe it, then the Arabs had gotten it right when they used the preface, *So it was written ...* at the beginning of something they wished to impart to another.

Several Biblical quotes like "You saw me before I was born. Every day of my life was recorded in your book. Every moment was laid out before a single day had passed." from Psalm 139:16 or from John 1:1, "In the beginning was the Word, and the Word was with God, and the Word was God." as well as, "And the Word became flesh and dwelt among us." from John 1:14.

I took away several revelations from that experience but ignored the most important one. I loved the fact that I finally had confirmation that reality is not all it is cracked up to be. But the deep ramifications of being told that I am no more substantial than a word were lost on me. I continued to ignore this fact and chose instead to keep the charade going. Let's face it, how many amongst us really want to embrace the notion that we are *nothing*, that we are *empty*, as empty as any hollow word ever was.

The time had come to leave the social club. I sobered up enough to not be concerned about my fifteen-minute walk home to the hostel. Deciding to skip the worst part of town, I chose to make my way through the deserted streets of Chinatown. It was an exceptionally quiet neighbourhood since the tourists had abandoned it many hours earlier. It seemed like a nice place to go for a stroll.

After several blocks, I saw pedestrian movement up ahead. A congregation of people moved off the sidewalk to occupy the centre of the road. Perhaps seven or eight young men milled about, dressed entirely in black, including what I took to be leather jackets. They all seemed to be of average height and quite slim with dark features. Their attention, as well as mine, was drawn toward several more people moving up the sidewalk in the direction they had just come from. This new grouping numbered three and all were dressed as the others. As they got closer one of them began yelling at the larger congregation.

He was extremely aggressive in manner and hollered very loudly while shaking his arms in the direction of the larger group. They definitely took note. His two sidekicks stood ready to back him up if need be. I was a little worried as this maniac was on the other side of the road, directly in my way if I were to cross.

I took this to be a gang related matter with an *alpha dog* male, perhaps even leader, venting his rage in an attempt to cajole his cohorts into compliance. The situation looked like it would soon escalate, so I started to cross the walk and aimed to scoot behind the leader while his attention was focused elsewhere. I made it about half-way across the road, and then things took a turn for the worse.

The leader was now slowly advancing on the larger group, continuing his rant as he did so. The level of ferocity in his voice was alarming, though I could not make out precisely what he was saying. The larger group reacted defensively by scattering to create a defensive semi-circle and then started to reach into their coats. "Oh here we go … guns," I thought. I was pretty close to the line of fire, so I needed to get cover fast. I walked straight backwards without turning around and found the safety of a nearby building. The situation was incredibly tense. Surely someone was about to suffer violence, but incredibly everybody held their ground without doing anything rash.

The leader managed to diffuse the situation enough that nothing was drawn from places of concealment. Somehow he persuaded the gang to listen to him. He continued to bark out words as a semblance of order was restored. The main grouping maintained their defensive posture for several more minutes by which time he had appeared to have won them over. They broke their ranks as the leader approached slightly closer to them—stepping several paces off of the sidewalk as he did so. He continued to cajole them, though less aggressively now. I thought my opportunity to escape had arrived. I would slip behind his back and make my way up the sidewalk post-haste. I crossed the street, approached his rear and as I got directly behind him, no more than four feet away, he briefly turned and glowered at me.

He was wearing black well-tailored slacks, fresh white shirt and black jacket. He was taller than the others, somewhere in his mid-thirties I guessed. His dark black hair was fashionably coiffed and his complexion was the olive hue of someone having a Mediterranean or Middle Eastern background. As he turned, our eyes momentarily locked and a spark of recognition was born. A dread and fright overwhelmed me to the core of my being. The fight or flight instinct kicked in as adrenaline flooded my system.

Not including my recent salvia episode, this was the most

frightening experience I had had in decades. He glared at me for only an instant, but I could tell that this was not a man to be trifled with. He looked at me in such a dismissive manner that I felt like a mere bug that he could squash at any moment—inconsequential, less than nothing to him. His disdain for me was extraordinarily palpable. I had never before had occasion to feel so insignificant in the presence of another. This guy was a consummate leader. The ultimate *man of power*. A commander who could attract legions of followers to do his bidding. The kind of figure that caused men to lay down their very lives at a moment's notice, if he but gave the word. Follow him to the ends of the earth and beyond if so ordered. His overpowering charisma was such that, for a moment, I imagined I could be one of those people. If I were ever to be a follower, this was the one man who would lead me. I could well imagine becoming a centurion to his Caesar. I've met prime ministers, princes, millionaires and other assorted potentates but they were all poseurs compared to this figure.

Repulsed, I turned away while I still had a chance. I was terrified by his strength and what that represented, and also by my own weakness. For a brief moment, I could see the allure such raw unadulterated power afforded one. To control men's lives and conquer worlds—that was the ultimate aphrodisiac for a commander. Yet an instant later I recognized this for the pure hollow illusion it really was. This man actually wielded no power whatsoever. What his sycophantic followers appeared to grant him, free rein to wield the *will to power* in any way he saw fit, was no more tangible than a collective thought. It was all mind stuff to begin with. To believe otherwise was delusion. I turned and walked away. The ephemeral phantom still barking out his insane orders as his existence soon faded from my awareness.

After that intense encounter, I thought a stroll in the park might do me some good before tucking in for the night. From the vantage point of my park bench, I saw a light shining down from a pole in the corner of the park, some 100 feet in the distance. Beyond that more lights illuminated a store from several hundred feet farther down the way. Though the lights were clearly separated by a great distance, they could be seen to be on the same plane by my currently inventive imagination. Figure/ground relationships could be easily altered, as had been the case several hours before. Once again my mind employed this effect for its own amusement. Using the row of lights as a starting point, my imagination proceeded to assemble an exceptionally realistic-looking Japanese curbside food stall right before my eyes. This kind of portable cart was a regular feature around subway entrances late at night in Tokyo.

First the basic plywood shell appeared with lights affixed at the top as they normally would have been. Next a brightly coloured awning manifested overhead. I focused my attention exclusively on the lights. The stall evaporated in an instant, and all I saw was mundane reality. Simply a park and streetscape with lights receding into the distance. Relaxing my focus again, the lights proceeded to once again all merge into the same plane, and voila, there was the stall again demarcated by the lights on top. However, now the awning was freshly adorned with Japanese writing and colourful geometric patterns, unlike before. Next came cookware and gas burners. Again focusing in the distance, I could clearly see how my mind was utilizing the distant lights as inspiration for the stall. It was completely apparent what was going on, but the hallucination was entirely realistic if allowed to manifest.

Next time I looked, vegetables were strewn about on a newly created chopping board and steaming pots of food bubbled merrily away over gas flame. The last element, surely about to appear, would be a boisterous Japanese cook beckoning me over to sample his fare, but that was a bit too weird to contemplate so I broke off the reverie there.

I am convinced that hallucination had the same startling realism that Charles Bonnet sufferers experience, but in my case I could control it. If I hadn't known better, there would have been no way for me to distinguish what I was seeing from the real thing. That cart looked entirely authentic in every detail, indistinguishable from what I had actually stood in front of in Japan. That realization tumbled around in my mind long enough to cause an epiphany the next morning.

It occurred to me that the whole Chinatown drama was simply a hallucination which went along totally unsuspected at the time. I took the whole episode to be completely real. Several clues forced me to rationally concede that I had been duped. Though to this day, the memory of it still seems to recall an incident that was as real as real could be.

The gang's outlandish dress was a huge giveaway. Such garb, all identical and definitely 1950s retro tough guy attire (think Fonzi from *Happy Days* fame for instance) was terribly inappropriate for the current era. Nobody would ever go around dressed like that, certainly not gang members. Imagine the looks they would invite. The more I thought about it, the more it all seemed quite amusing, and I marvelled at how readily I accepted such an obvious charade as the real thing.

Their ethnicity was also rather odd. While mulling over their heritage, I realized that the language they spoke was unknown to me. A dead giveaway was how the main body of thugs formed their defensive semi-circle. It looked much too choreographed, like something straight out of *West side Story*. My extreme reaction to the leader was very strange as well. So many sensations and impressions were conveyed, yet he said not a single word to me.

However visceral and deeply felt the experience was, I simply wasn't buying it. As far as its level of realism went, this hallucinatory experience stood above all others to date. The other hallucinations, or even lucid dreams I have had, have always had little telltale signs that allowed me to question their verisimilitude very easily. In this case, it was only the contextual content of the dream, not its actual visual representation, that gave away its false nature. Rational reflection did reveal the truth of the matter in the end. Was *the great man of power* I met some kind of archetypal encounter, I wondered.

Perhaps it was a powerful, masculine yang-like expression which served as a foil to the previous hour's delightfully gentle and sensual yin-like reverie back at the social club. A kind of positive versus negative balancing out, good versus evil duality, if you will. The concept of Satan came to mind as I reflected upon this being.

Not the common Biblical interpretation or Hollywood depiction of a supernatural fire-belching horned demon, but something far worse. A psychopathic (incapable of displaying empathy or regards for others) monstrosity so full of hubris, jealousy and spite that it delighted in leading others to their downfall at every opportunity. Since the beginning of time this so-called *fallen one* had perpetually failed to recognize anything outside of itself. The son of God now lost in delusion. Unknowing and uncaring and uncaring to know. The eternal quest for illusory power its only goal. The original Hebrew term for

A Fleeting Improvised Man

Satan was a noun from a verb and meant primarily *to obstruct or oppose*. This being represented that which eternally opposed the Divine. Put more clearly, it endeavoured to prevent reality from appearing as it really was. This was what the Great Deceiver really represented and I, like you, had long ago fallen under its spell. But it could easily be seen through if you dared look. Its transparent insubstantial nature was obvious once I shone the spotlight of awareness on it. It is possible for all of you to walk away just as I did. Simply turn from ignorance and the Truth will start to reveal itself. Enlightenment is simply no longer opposing what actually is. That archetypal hallucination, so convincingly manifested out there on those lonely streets of Chinatown, represented the real terror that perpetually haunted humanity. Ignorance.

Ultimately, I failed to get the magic mushrooms I so longed for but did have one final interesting experience before returning to the Backpackers Hostel. I really had to thank my lucky stars it worked out so well. You see when I returned to The Herb Store the next morning to finally get my hands on some of that ever so elusive sacred fungi, the shop was being busted by the cops! This place, as well as the drug museum, was shut down permanently that day after being in operation for over three years. I guess the attic-dwelling *Mr. Malkovich's* security concerns were well founded after all.

As I made my way up the sidewalk towards the shop, oblivious to what was unfolding before me, the guy who looked like Niles Crane pulled me aside and drew my attention to several cop cars parked some fifty feet in the distance. The look of concern on his face was evident, particularly as he was unsure of his brother's fate. I was overjoyed not to have been found in the shop myself. It very well could have turned out that way but for a lucky turn of affairs earlier that morning.

You see I fully intended to visit the shop earlier in the day. Instead things had worked out a bit differently. Originally I had set out in the direction of The Herb Shop but instead got distracted with a side visit to the local Chinese gardens first. That little jaunt took just long enough to save my ass. After that I decided to get hell out of Dodge. The Karaoke King was pleased to see me on my return and immediately started serenading me. Grudgingly I had to admit his charms were growing on me as I laughed aloud and flopped onto my bed.

Vine of the Soul

After my long struggle, I finally chanced upon an inexhaustible source of DMT that had been staring me in the face all along. I never imagined I was only a charge card away from success. The raw ingredients for ayahuasca were legally available for purchase over the Internet. All SWIM had to do was brew it up. I was so happy and relieved to finally have the opportunity to get down to the serious work of using plant medicines. The ingredients were ordered and would take a week or so to arrive. This waiting period gave me an opportunity to do more research on the brew. My abandoned list of hallucinogens had ranked DMT at the top. It would soon be time to finally ascend that pinnacle, but to date I had done little research on it since I never expected to get the opportunity to sample the orally active form.

I needed to investigate more trip reports, find the best brewing techniques and gather any other pertinent information that might be potentially useful. This long-lasting entheogen was the best I could ever have hoped for. I dared not leave any room for error to avoid a repeat of my salvia experience. Figuring out how to process the raw ingredients was the first order of the day.

The plant materials would arrive in pencil-length, tough, fibrous strips of wood, resembling kindling. After reading various trains of thought on the subject, I formulated the best recipe I could. My scientific background aided in understanding the simple organic chemistry required to extract as much of the active ingredients from the plant material as possible. First the woody fragments were reduced

171

in size, and then it was simply a matter of boiling the pieces in several batches of acidified water. Later on the pH of the final solution could be brought back to a more neutral level with the aid of baking soda. If the bitter tannins were a concern, these could be dealt with by dissolving some gelatin or egg white into the final mix. This last step proved unnecessary, and I soon abandoned it.

I brewed the authentic Amazonian botanicals in three separate washes of water and strained accordingly. This took the course of an afternoon. While stirring the brew, I would send out a prayer or positive intention over it from time to time. Some people are known to whistle or sing incantations of good will and healing as well.

This was an important part of fostering a positive mindset, for as you may recall, set and setting were crucial to having a good experience. I also cleaned and tidied beforehand the space where the ayahuasca would be consumed. Finally, I thought a trip to the park several hours before the ceremony began would be an excellent way to further raise my spirits. To increase the positive vibe, find those things that distinctly resonate for you. In my case I liked to listen to uplifting music or get on YouTube for a little comedy in preparation. If it was a social gathering, I encouraged those attending to tell jokes or briefly recount amusing anecdotes about their lives, just before the brew was consumed.

For this first occasion, a university student staying at the hostel expressed an interest in joining me. He was a regular pot smoker but had little psychedelic experience, so we were both neophytes in this regard. A modified fast was followed that day—light lunch, no supper. Prohibited foods associated with ayahuasca drinking were avoided. We gathered in my room around 8 p.m. My friend brought some world beat music. All appropriate research and preparation had been completed. The stage was set. Now it was time to drink. Though we tried our best to relax, the tension was palpable.

This was to be a two-staged affair. The MAO inhibiting ayahuasca vine and the DMT containing *Mimosa hostilis* bark were in two separate containers. The strategy was to first deactivate the MAO enzyme in the body and fifteen minutes later follow that by drinking the DMT found in the bark. With music playing in the background, I said a final prayer that has become a standard ritual for me.

It was inspired by something Terence used to say just before inhaling DMT smoke. I invoked the spirit of ayahuasca and basically pleaded for her gentle guidance and mercy. I humbly promised to always take the highest useful dose possible—to never cut it back out of fear—and in doing so was willing to submit to whatever came my way. My sincerest desire was to learn whatever she thought appropriate to teach me. I only asked that she be easy on me if the situation allowed. Particularly the first time out, I wanted to avoid as much unnecessary trauma as possible. I was but an ignorant fool throwing myself at her feet. Somewhere in the back of my mind salvia loomed large. I prayed that that kind of experience would be avoided this time. The initial dose was calculated to be moderate.

There was nothing left to do but get on with it. Mugs were clinked together in one final show of goodwill, and then the foul tasting contents were forced down. The taste was made even worse by the fact that I had used too much citric acid in the recipe, which resulted in a mouth-puckering experience akin to biting on a lemon wedge. After this slight error, I utilized neutralizing baking soda to help make future batches more palatable and also switched to using vinegar to acidify the solution rather than citric acid. Fifteen minutes later the second quarter-cup was forced down. We had buckets ready for the retching that was predicted to follow.

Minutes passed as we held our breath in anticipation. Had I understood the formulating process correctly I wondered? Was the dose too small? Would it simply fizzle out like the previous failed mushroom experiment? We both asked each other if anything unusual was happening. Nothing worth mentioning. At around the twenty-minute mark I noticed an extremely subtle perceptual shift. Was it real or imagined? A minute or two later there was no doubt about it. SWIM had crossed the Rubicon ... or rather was it the River Styx? I would soon find out.

The white walls had begun to take on an increasingly greenish tint. Moments later everything was painted in this garish hue. I asked my friend if the brew was working, and he confirmed that it sure the hell was! We both laughed at that. I felt a sense of relief. I had spent so much time and effort in this pursuit. What a relief to finally see it come to fruition. Yet this was but the start of a new chapter. I momentarily felt relief, but it was quickly replaced with trepidation. There would be no turning back now. A rather odd unsettling sensation began to grow and envelope me. The feeling was not at all like my previous psychedelic experiences. My consciousness was being shifted and my perspective and grasp on reality altered in a totally novel way.

My life had been spent seeing reality in one consistent narrowly defined manner, and now other possibilities began to present themselves. "Isn't this fantastic?" I exclaimed. Nods of affirmation came in response from my friend. Soon, "Oh my God," and "Holy crap," were the best articulations we could muster. There was no doubt that Lady Ayahuasca had begun to reveal her charms. She was so tender and sweet. I had found my ally.

My ego had a hard time with the experience in the beginning. In that first forty minutes of increasingly intensifying effects, much was experienced, but it was difficult to say exactly what. My ego protested at no longer being totally in control and the centre of attention. A little alarming at first, ego dissolution was just something that had to be gotten used to. Eventually it became second nature to me.

The predominant feeling at that point was a sense of joy and open-heartedness. This was certainly not a whacked-out dopey type of inebriation which caused a brief respite from all of one's troubles. Rather, it was a case of meeting reality head on. The background music sounded terrific. Thoughts were no longer linear but increasingly freely associated. The first few ayahuasca encounters were very much about probing my subconscious mind. I knew something was going on in that department, but for the most part it remained unknown to me precisely what was occurring. It didn't matter. The point was ayahuasca knew, and the effects were terrific!

A curious sensation arose which I can only describe as my mind being rewired or reformatted in some way. Perhaps this response was being evoked due to the drug's stimulation of the anterior insular cortex spoken about previously. This strange feeling occurred during the first four or five sessions. Then all this wonderfulness came to a crashing halt as waves of nausea overwhelmed me. Despite trying my best, I could not keep the brew down any longer. After recovering I immediately drank more. I could only keep this subsequent dose down for five minutes or so. This certainly was strong medicine alright. With the extra dosing, the magnificent feelings returned along with a major vision.

Wow, what an amazing hallucination appeared during the post

purge-portion of my *tryp*. With eyes closed, I beheld what looked to be a full-figured Indian deity. Or at least a statue of one—I wasn't sure. It appeared convincingly real but I was having a hard time determining if it was sentient or merely some incorporeal chunk of stone. I knew nothing about Indian mythology, so could not place it in their pantheon of Gods. If indeed it even originated from there. It just sat silently meditating on a raised platform in seeming equanimity. Its eyes mesmerized me. The eyelids drooped in a sleepy sort of way but looked like they were about to open at any second. For the duration it simply sat quietly. If its purpose was to relay some kind of message, it came free of words. Its mysterious expression struck me in the way the Mona Lisa had when I saw her portrait at the Louvre. I was captivated by the deity's ambiguous nature. I couldn't even determine its gender. A uniformly unnatural azure blue colour covered its entire body.

Hundreds of dazzling gems adorned it, contrasting sublimely with its shocking skin tone. These sparkling stones outlined the meditation platform as well. Most amazingly the gems blinked on and off as Christmas lights would. These gems were self-illuminated. I have always been intrigued by gems, even accumulating enough for a small collection of sorts at one time. The finest terrestrial jewels I had ever beheld could in no way compare to these magnificent specimens flashing before me with an inner warmth and beauty quite unparalleled. Why did jewels captivate me so?

Humans have always been attracted to shiny polished pebbles. Huxley has pointed out that man's fascination, indeed compulsion, to adorn himself with such baubles stemmed from the psychedelic experience itself. In his follow up book to *Doors of Perception*, entitled *Heaven and Hell*, he posits that "To acquire such a stone is to acquire something whose preciousness is guaranteed by the fact that it exists in the Other World."

A gem's intrinsic nature reminds us of the glowing marvels seen with the inner eye of the visionary. With my first ayahuasca vision, I was granted the opportunity to marvel at these very wonders myself. Those treasures are referred to as *stones of fire* by Ezekiel and *masses of transparent fruit* by physician Weir Mitchell. Terence sometimes called his DMT elves bejeweled *self-dribbling basketballs*, which were noted on occasion to manifest the most amazing Faberge Eggs, "things made of pearl, and metal, and glass, and gel." My impression of beholding such a jewel was akin to catching the glint in God's eye. Indescribably sublime.

I recall little more detail of that first trip. I can tell you it was all I hoped for and more. I knew I had found a wonderful teacher, dare I even go so far as to say lover, in ayahuasca. I was sure she would never betray me. This was the medicine I had long searched for. The alchemical elixir of old. The metaphysical Philosopher's Stone—capable of transmuting not base metals, as was commonly supposed, but *base instincts*. When a catalyst of *sincerity* approaching 100 percent purity was employed, exceedingly difficult to acquire I might add, the ensuing reaction sometimes saw the dross of ignorance driven off to a very great extent. If the process could be contained long enough without it blowing up in your face, occasionally unadulterated Spirit remained. Ayahuasca's portent was clear to me from the onset. McKenna's self-coined *archaic revival* was really afoot. If only I had the balls, integrity and fortitude to see it through.

I learned quickly what separated the truth seekers from the dabblers and poseurs. Those that surrendered to ultimate reality did well. It was this aspect of ayahuasca that proved most beneficial to my spiritual quest. Ayahuasca helped to erode those last remnants of wiggle room that still afforded me the ability to turn away from reality. The authentic spiritual realizations ayahuasca helped facilitate had nothing to do with astonishing hallucinogenic eye candy.

To that end ayahuasca helped guide me in the correct direction, not so much by revealing the *big picture* but rather by simply showing me how much I was deceiving myself and dwelling in delusion right here in ordinary reality. It functioned as a sort of cosmic lie-detector. It all boiled down to seeing the truth in whatever form it presented itself and never ever turning away. Step by step, session by session, the brew eroded my precious *empire of shit* sufficiently to see it for what it really was. A banana republic ruled over by a deluded and impotent tin-pot dictator. Thankfully, ayahuasca pointed out my nobler aspects from time to time as well, which helped reduce the shock to my system.

Cogitating the illuminating nature of DMT further, I wondered if I could actually place the jewel-encrusted hallucinogenic deity I met on my first ayahuasca trip somewhere in actual mythology. Could I find it represented in the Indian pantheon of gods or perhaps elsewhere like in the Tibetan Buddhist texts for example? Where to begin?

The word *Shiva* sprang immediately to mind, which was strange as I was not at all familiar with this being. In fact I knew nothing about Hinduism at all. The only reference to Śhiva I ever recalled hearing was when the father of the atomic bomb, Robert Oppenheimer, commented, "Now I am become Death, the destroyer of worlds," upon seeing the results of the first A-bomb explosion. He was referring to the line in the Bhagavad Gita "Behold! For I am become Śhiva, Shatterer of the World." As a lark, I web searched Śhiva and up popped an almost identical image to what I had seen in my hallucination. The giveaway was its colour. Śhiva is always portrayed as blue. Many pictures showed a seated figure in meditation, just as I had seen. Perhaps I had come across such an image somewhere in my travels, but I could not recall doing so. As I dug a little deeper, the significance of Śhiva became apparent to me.

Hindus have a key concept called the *trimurti*. Here cosmic reality is seen to be the eternal interplay between creation, maintenance and destruction as personified by Brahmā (the creator), Vishnu (the maintainer or preserver), and Śhiva (the destroyer or transformer). These three deities comprise the Hindu triad or Great Trinity.

Śhiva was the great cosmic dancer, the grand liberator of the universe. He was the most well-known and revered icon of Hinduism. To understand that he had shown up on my hallucinatory doorstep was a bit of a shock, for the significance was immediate. You have to understand this was my very first and last significant ayahuasca vision. After this experience I never paid much heed to them. This one was different. It was by far the most realistic DMT vision I ever beheld. Out of all the possible apparitions to appear, I could think of none more spiritually significant to the task at hand. This figure, above all others, represented the pinnacle of my goal. If you haven't realized it yet, the enlightenment game is all about destruction. You find the biggest wrecking ball you can and have at it. From a mythical viewpoint, no being is more dedicated to the fine art of annihilation than Śhiva.

While still on the topic of destruction, I recall a detail from the first ayahuasca episode in which my buddy commented that he had *died*. He could not elaborate much further than to tell me that he ended up in some kind of realm with nothing there at all. Generally speaking these occasions occurred infrequently, and varied as to degree of *emptiness* experienced. From a spiritual perspective, these episodes were always rewarding. Some people referred to this experience as *ego death*, but that is a bit of a misnomer, since nothing really perished at all. Rather the ability to conceptualize was reduced to some degree, and with that the *me identity* was eroded, sometimes dramatically enough to be perceived as a death of sorts.

During these occasions, space and time ceased to have any relevance. These experiences could be uncomfortable or blissful depending to a large degree on how able and willing you were to let go. I must confess I struggled long and hard with this issue. I would take a massive dose of ayahuasca in order to create favourable conditions for ego loss to arise and then scramble around so that I might avoid the consequences. If possible, just relax into it. Much easier said than done. As you repeat the experience it gets easier. Or you may simply be one of those that slip into it the first time around and find nothing but bliss. I resisted a little less on each occasion until one day Śhiva finally brought the whole house of cards crashing down. That was during my meditative phase when drugs were no longer employed, but I feel ayahuasca helped to pave the way in.

Though I am getting a little ahead of myself in this narrative, I would like to mention an incident that occurred during the early stages of the contemplative/meditative phase of my awakening. It was during this period that SWIM decided to once again try some psilocybin mushrooms. Typically the effects were very similar to those of ayahuasca. Psychedelics were used very infrequently during this time, but I had an inclination to discover what a heroic dose would be like. I also wondered if my many weeks spent meditating would modify the experience in some way.

I consumed a huge 13 gram dose while listening to uplifting techno/trance music. When I regained consciousness, I was experiencing the most pleasurable, orgasmic bliss of my entire life. It was like waking up inside the *orgasmatron* device featured in Woody Allen's 1973 film *Sleeper*. Unabated waves of ecstasy of a very high intensity, almost electric or kundalini in nature, coursed up and down my body. My heart was just about ready to explode. The kind of music I awoke to always evoked pleasure, but this feeling was tremendously euphoric.

The mushroom had somehow amplified the joyful feeling the music usually instilled. Using my self-coined *orgasmascale* for reference, I would rate the experience as a four or five—one being the normal level of pleasure experienced during sexual release. The ecstasy just went on and on, never wavering in intensity. A minute or so of this was all that I could bear. I started to writhe around begging for it to stop. "Enough," I said, "I can't take it anymore." In response the pleasure began to subside and soon ended. Man if you could only bottle that up and sell it you would be a billionaire.

After the bliss ended I quickly fell back into unconsciousness again, only to be jolted back sometime later in the midst of a laughing fit. Apparently I had just learned the answer to the Great Cosmic Joke. In essence all had been revealed to me. The punch line to the best one-liner I ever heard had been divulged just as I awoke. It was hilarious. Belly laughs continued to roll out unabated as I marvelled at God's great sense of humour. There was only one problem. I couldn't recall the nature of what had been revealed. It was like when you dreamt something amazing only to awaken and find the memory of it had vanished. Apparently I had *gotten* the joke. I just couldn't recall what it was! All that lingered were the after-effects. That God, what a trickster, ever the consummate practical joker. Much later I received the full punch line once again and that time it was unforgettable. In fact that's what I opened this book with.

More often than not ayahuasca and mushrooms produced moments of great wonder, joy and even bliss occasionally. Though I did have to learn to get used to the creepy, distasteful sometimes even vile feeling that welled up during the coming up phase. It lasted about five to ten minutes and was simply something I had to pass through. The feeling was quite unsettling at first. Sometimes I saw strange brightly attired harlequin characters, both men and women, which gave me the chills. I did not enjoy being in their presence whatsoever. These simulacra tried to entice me to join them in their nasty frivolities, but I refused to have anything to do with them. Instead I choose to simply tune them out. This phase was usually accompanied with the feeling that some electronic contraption was being recalibrated and stabilized. Quite often a visual depiction of some mysterious circular electro-mechanical piece of high technology accompanied these weird feelings. Despite seeing it many times, I can't describe it to you clearly. Though, if I were to take ayahuasca again, it would be as familiar to me as an old friend. That is how state-specific memory works

This feeling may have been elicited as a result of DMT slotting into neural receptors normally occupied by serotonin. Once the brain accustomed itself to the newly-generated tryptamine state, all was well. Before reaching this new steady state, my perceptions were flooded with feelings of dread and alien presence. I think these impressions were simply artefacts created by the process of the normal serotonin-generated reality being replaced by one that was decidedly *Other*. The case was not, *I am meeting an alien* but rather *I am becoming one*.

You may recall that the term *psychedelic* means *mind manifesting*. This implies that the mind has unrecognized levels of consciousness waiting to be discovered. William James is credited with first introducing the psychological concept *stream of consciousness* into the vernacular. He described consciousness as being like a stream, in the sense that a continuous succession of unending concepts, emotions, feelings, images, ideas, sensations and thoughts flows by our awareness as a stream would.

The function of consciousness is, he believed, to select what object of perception one pays attention to. Whatever that particular thing is, the awareness of it arises and falls in linear succession, just as our awareness of individual twigs floating down a river would. These mental objects of perception appear to be separate and distinct from each other but in reality there is an association forged between them by the presence of awareness itself. In the same way that everything floating on top of the river is actually linked together by the never-ending river current itself. Awareness functions in a sense as a *river of reality*. It is the one thing that does not arise and fall away. It is as constant and steady in flow as the mighty Nile. If the things we apprehend were actually distinct and separate from each other, as we might suppose, reality would be a chaotic mess of random unrelated experience, and we would be thrashing about in utter confusion. The border separating objects of perception is not well defined at all.

Instead of experiencing a chaotic hodgepodge of unrelated mental constructs, our consciousness ensures that awareness forges associations and relationships amongst thoughts, both past and future. In this way a semblance of comprehensibility is created. Perceptions overlap so that each experience has a *fringe* of the upcoming perception and a tailing-off of the previous perception. In that way, James viewed reality as composed of the present moment being forefront in our minds, with the preceding last few experiences rapidly fading from memory, while our next few experiences are already entering into our awareness stream. This occurs seamlessly and goes unnoticed unless you pay attention to the mechanics of it, as in meditation. Psychedelics disrupt this normal flow of consciousness and replace it with a non-ordinary perceptual modality. What was the foundation of this novel way of experiencing things?

Let's stick with the stream of consciousness analogy a little bit longer to figure this out. Perhaps it is as if the normally functioning linear stream of consciousness sprouts several new tributaries when it is exposed to psychedelics. Each tributary becomes capable of forming its own autonomous self-referential *mind stream*. It seems that this multiplicity of viewpoints is what arises when the domineering ego is forced to relinquish control. In a sense, the ordinary state of consciousness loses coherence and thus arises a much more chaotic, though hugely creative, way of perceiving things. Awareness is no longer focused in a single, narrow, laser-like point of attention. Once it is decoupled, a perceptual *flood-light* is switched on that now illuminates huge swaths of reality all at once. Consequently novel patterns of thought and associations arise much more readily.

To use a computer analogy, I think normal mind function, versus the psychedelically engendered one, could be compared to the difference between serial and parallel, or non-linear, computer processing. The first basic computers could only carry out one simple process at a time. For example, a basic punch-card reader might only be able to tabulate numbers. As parallel processing capability arose, more and more functions or processes could be carried out simultaneously. Crudely put but I think that is what may be occurring to consciousness while on psychedelics.

Heaven and Hell

The sacred as well as the profane can turn up at any time during a psychedelic excursion. With that in mind I now wish to present two final ayahuasca anecdotes that encapsulate these antipodal possibilities. The first is really a bit of a cautionary tale, the last my most cherished and revelatory ayahuasca experience ever.

To set the stage let me explain that this particular ayahuasca episode was the first that occurred outside the safe confines of the hostel. The ninth time was definitely not the charm, I guess. I thought by that point I had accumulated enough experience to know what I was doing. Naïveté has a tendency to do that. I had met this older guy at the previous hostel we both stayed at for awhile. When we reconnected, Serge told me that he was up for an ayahuasca journey.

A well-built man for his age, he sported a clean-shaven head, which made him appear younger than his years. He seemed reserved and soft spoken in a quirky sort of way, with a subtle undertone of anxiety and nervousness about him. His past history of psychedelic use met my criteria for joining my bandwagon. In retrospect I should have been more careful. It is now apparent to me that you should always ascertain someone's state of mental health and possible negative medication interactions before allowing them to partake.

Once I arrived at his apartment, we proceeded to make small talk while he prepared dinner. I explained that we should eat only very lightly, but this fell on deaf ears. He also insisted upon serving wine. Not a good idea, but he was the host. Thankfully I chose not to imbibe and only later recalled that wine was a fermented product which the literature suggested should be avoided prior to taking ayahuasca. Not an auspicious start.

Conversation turned to several odd topics that should have apprised me of the fact that this guy should not be allowed anywhere near ayahuasca. He related that at the age of 13 he dropped acid in the group home he was living in as well as mentioned some *extreme* sexual proclivities. He assured me that the mark of an experienced psychedelic pro, which he considered himself to be, was the ability to *take any hallucinogen at the drop of a hat.* I would later have to correct him on that account by adding my own little rejoinder ... *and not have a full blown psychotic episode at the same time!*

Things began to really go pear-shaped when he insisted that we drink the brew outside on the banks of a nearby river. This did not sit well with me at all, but he was insistent. My experience was that unless the venue was private, for example your home or a natural secluded setting far from the masses, you would just be inviting mishap to befall you. I suggested that we could start there, but my wish was to return to his place once the effects really kicked in.

We drank what I hoped would be a moderate dose while seated on a park bench, just as the sun dropped below the horizon. It took about twenty minutes for the DMT to take hold at which point he decided to go for a stroll. That was a bad idea; we should have returned to his place instead. I suggested we turn back, since walking would soon become difficult. At this point it was getting quite dark. Navigating the path became progressively more difficult until I was forced to reach out for his arm to steady myself. He recoiled in horror and wanted to know, "What the fuck are you doing?" A few days later when we had a chance to debrief he admitted to being very homophobic, so that explained his disconcerting reaction to my innocent attempt at remaining upright. Perhaps this fear was originally instilled during his time spent in the group home or some later correctional facility.

We made it back along the river bank to a spot near the road which led to his place. A mature weeping willow sat in front of me by the riverside. By now it was clear something was severely wrong with this guy. Questions sent him off on peculiar tangents and were often greeted with hostility. Let's just say he had *issues.* He even wondered if I had actually drunk any ayahuasca with him. He was skeptical when I replied of course I had. The hallucinations were just starting to kick in for me. The majesty of the willow in front of me was outstanding. Ethereal *energy rays* emanated upwards from all its branches. Or was it rather downwards from the heavens above, I could not be sure. The projected light appeared quite intense and from my perspective seemed to illuminate the entire surroundings. I was tempted to remain basking in that lovely aura, but I knew I would never make it back to his place unless I acted now. He refused.

He was quite off his rocker at this point. It has been said that ayahuasca can promote a deeper bond, even psychic union between practitioners. I had previously found this to indeed be the case. But this character was projecting the strangest aberrant vibes I recall anyone ever giving off. Lots of confusion and also a sense of cold malevolence and perverseness could be sensed. I feared for what was about to be unleashed upon the neighbourhood. He abandoned me with a mischievous grin and started to make his way into the darkness. After a few steps he turned and added, "Have a good trrrrrriiipp." The last word drawn out with a sinister chuckle for effect. With that Serge scurried off into the neighbourhood like a malevolent gremlin. I sure hoped no ill would befall anyone that evening.

Later, when we met up again, Serge matter-of-factly told me that he had indeed experienced a full-blown psychotic break with reality. It was obvious to me that he was still suffering after-effects some three days later. He wanted to know if I worked for the CIA and whether I had planted some kind of surveillance bug on his computer during dinner. He told me that after we parted he then went back to his place, but an unknown van was parked outside. He wondered whether he was under surveillance, so spent the rest of his time wandering around. I didn't sense any negative repercussions to his antics so counted myself fortunate this time. I had learned an important lesson and would be vigilant to never repeat it. With regards to the conclusion of this story, I still had to make it back across town to the hostel.

By the time the bus had arrived I was starting to *trip my balls off,* which according to definition meant you were seeing pronounced open-eyed hallucinations. Open-eye visuals—OEV—were rarer than the closed-eyed variety. Certainly a public bus was not an appropriate environment to be experiencing this highly esteemed phenomenon. It all seems quite amusing now but the moment the bus doors swung open, I knew it was going to be an exceptionally challenging ride home.

I would have to rally every shred of sanity and composure I was so desperately trying to hold on to, if any chance of misadventure was to be avoided. I certainly didn't want to regain consciousness in a hospital or worse ....

I stepped onto the bus and was greeted by a uniformed correctional officer sitting at the wheel. "Holy fuck this is gonna get interesting," I thought. Of course there was not actually a guard waiting for me to drop my fare into his box, but he sure the hell looked like one.

My first inclination was to read the patch on his wide-brimmed cap in order to figure out what joint he came from, but I immediately curtailed that train of thought and looked away. To continue to do so would only invite disaster. Just like Nobel Prize winner John Nash, who suffered most of his life with debilitating schizophrenia, I too had learned that one could control visions by simply paying them no heed. Nash had said of his hallucinations, "I just choose not to acknowledge them. Like a diet of the mind, I just choose not to indulge certain appetites." He thought ordinary dreams and nightmares were examples of similar phenomena. "We've got to keep feeding them for them to stay alive," he said. I did my utmost to prevent this. There was no way that I wanted to freak out in the confines of some city bus that every second resembled more and more a penal transport spaceship! Sticking to my strategy, I calmly averted my eyes from the *officer* and threw whatever change I had in my pocket into the fare box. Given the circumstances, just managing this simple act was extraordinary—there was no way I could have possibly counted whatever coins came up in my fist. He said it wasn't enough but let me pass anyhow.

I am sure he was aware of my distress and could not help but note my widely dilated pupils. While I was still coherent enough, I asked him to let me know when we got to the stop closest to City Hall. If I could just make it to that landmark, I had a pretty good chance of navigating my way home from there. But it remained to be seen if I could hold it together the twenty minutes required to get there. Very realistic and insistent hallucinations were threatening to overwhelm me at every instant.

After getting seated, I could not help but make furtive glances towards the other passengers. They appeared to lack solidity and definition to quite a degree, being almost ghost-like in their washed-out spectral appearance. The ship, for that was how the bus's futuristic interior now appeared, seemed to be a modest-sized utilitarian transport craft with lots of shiny chrome accents and vibrant colours galore. Its function was apparent, though I wasn't buying any of this prisoner nonsense. I knew exactly where I was and what was going on. Well sort of ....

All the passengers appeared to be held in a form of stasis. They looked like frozen corpses, the blood drained from their bodies. I turned away as it was a very perplexing vision best not dwelt upon too long. Looking down to my feet, a grey open mesh industrial grating could be seen covering the floor. Incredibly, I could vaguely see through the small openings into the hold below. I certainly had no inclination to discover what was down there. I noted an impressive high-tech weapon securely locked in place over the driver's head. More and more details were popping into existence, and I really wondered how much longer I could successfully keep insanity at bay.

I looked across the aisle to where the far side windows lay and was startled by the view of hyperspace. The vista was exactly like that featured in a sci-fi movie like *Star Wars*, where space whipped by at light speed. If I looked out the window immediately adjacent to me I could barely discern buildings flashing by. As a cityscape it was almost unrecognizable, but at least it wasn't the confusion created by stars darting across the emptiness of space.

"That's right," I reassured myself. We are all just passengers riding on a normal bus, nothing to get anxious about here. But I was fooling myself. I was anxious, terribly so, for I worried that very soon there would be no more moments of clarity. It seemed I was now sitting on some kind of red leather upholstered swivel chair that hydraulically rotated whichever way I cared to look out into hyperspace.

The ship, or rather the bus, halted. No problem, just a momentary bus stop I reasoned. But soon I became concerned. The stop seemed to be taking too long. Much too long. What the heck was going on I wondered? This stop should only take a second or two. What was causing the delay? My mind started spinning. I became really anxious and considered abandoning ship while I still had the chance.

From my perspective, it felt like a full fifteen minutes had elapsed. Everybody was still frozen in time, even the driver. It seemed like I was the only living creature in the cosmos. It was all very unsettling. I started to panic. I arose from my seat to leave, then thought better of it and sat down again. Something was horribly wrong. I had to get off the damn spaceship … or bus … or whatever the hell it was—right now!

I took a step towards the door but regained enough composure to once again sit down. Before I had to endure any more of this turmoil, the bus lurched forward and we were on our merry way again. That was a huge relief. I had heard about such time dilations before. An extreme case that comes to mind featured the chap who lived an entire life, got married and grew old and infirm, all within the course of a single LSD trip. I never could ascertain to my satisfaction if the bus had actually made a long stop or rather I had perceived a couple of seconds as an eternity, but I suspect the latter was the case.

The rest of the trip was relatively uneventful. The driver eventually called out, "City Hall," and I got off. I was so relieved to have gotten that far without falling to pieces. A few more blocks on foot and I would be home free. Some of the pedestrians I passed looked rather odd, but I tried to pay them no heed. Just two more blocks remained to my goal.

The next block proved challenging as time started to slow down again, which caused my progress to became increasingly more difficult with each footfall. My legs felt very heavy, my balance unsteady. I now knew for sure that some of these pedestrians were not human. The *fleeting improvised* men once again revealed themselves. These phantoms, frequently appearing in pairs, were dressed for the most part in gothic attire. Big black outlandish hairstyles and bright red lipstick seemed to be favoured by both sexes. Though I never had the impression that these creatures were malevolent, they started to vie for my attention by jeering at me or occasionally jabbing a hand in my direction. By this time my legs felt like they were encased in concrete. I made a big effort to get across the last intersection safely. Just one more block remained to my goal.

Time continued to slow. I kept my gaze restricted as much as possible to what was below my feet. The hostel was within shouting distance now, but I barely seemed to be making any headway. Walking past a single shop or restaurant front felt like it took hours to accomplish. Most bizarrely, the closer I got to my destination the greater time seemed to lag. At one point I started to despair, wondering if I was ever going to make my goal. Finally but one store façade remained between me and home. As climbers do when they prepare for final ascent to the summit of Everest, I tried as best I could to clear my mind and rally all my energy for the last big push. Though I had no flag to plant, I believe my ebullient jubilation was on par with an Everest conqueror. I had made it!

I opened the door to my room and was quite taken aback. Had I made a mistake? Was this really my room? Somehow it appeared transfigured. I had spent an entire winter there, yet had never really seen it, at least not through these *new eyes* Proust had spoken of. I looked back into the hall satisfied that I was indeed at the correct doorway. Though nothing of any material nature had changed, everything somehow felt foreign, like I had never laid eyes upon it until this very moment.

Exhausted I flopped into my bunk. What a relief to finally lay back and relax. Then I realized that the Karaoke King was unaccounted for. Looking at the time I noted it was 9:50 p.m. He would have to be back in an hour at the latest in order to get ready for his new pizza parlour job. I decided not to relax too much until he had returned. Growing impatient for his arrival, I looked back at the clock again after perhaps ten minutes had elapsed. I was surprised to see it said 9:50. No matter, I was probably confused the first time I looked so this time I paid careful attention. It was definitely 9:50.

I waited another ten or so minutes and rechecked again—9:50. Okay, this time I was sure something was amiss. I was getting a little worried. Next time I checked after only a few minutes had gone by, and I'll be damned if it didn't still read 9:50!

"What the hell is going on?" I wondered. I struggled to find an explanation. How was it possible that time could be frozen yet consciousness endured? It made no sense at all to me. Struggling for a more plausible explanation, I began to wonder if the whole day was but a figment of my imagination. Perhaps the previous week had been, too. All the days seemingly just gone by could have been merely an illusion created by my last ayahuasca episode.

In reality could I still be under the influence of that trip, I wondered? Perhaps I was actually laid out flat on my back deeply in a DMT trance only imagining that time had stopped. Could that really be possible? In a moment of clarity, I dismissed that idea as being quite preposterous. More ridiculous than the notion that time had ceased to exist. No, it seemed that this experience was legitimate, but I had no way to account for it.

Hardly daring to look, I checked the clock again quite quickly. It still registered the same dreaded 9:50. With that I grew terribly worried. I simply prayed for this awful spell to come to an end. I was very confused but there seemed nothing to do about it but wait and see what transpired. I resolved to be patient and wait at least fifteen minutes before checking again.

As I lay back, matters were made worse by the dreadful images Serge evoked in my mind. To my utter relief a full two minutes had elapsed once I finally consulted the clock again. "Hoorah—time still actually exists," I repeated again and again to myself. If you come to find you suddenly no longer have something that was always taken for granted, something as ubiquitous as mundane time itself, its reappearance is certainly an occasion for celebration.

When The Karaoke King finally showed up, I was relieved but in no shape to engage him in banter. Preparing to inform him of this fact, I turned in his direction only to recoil in shock, for standing right before me was one of McKenna's *elves*. A transformed Karaoke King now appeared resplendent in peaked green hat and shiny black buckle-down shoes and sported a stylish goatee and pointy ears to match. "Man, this ayahuasca is a hoot," I mused. My first and last full-blown DMT elf—cute. Thank God he didn't break into an elvish ditty at that point. Chuckling I turned away and relaxed into the wonder of it all.

The final report about to unfold represents the ethereal side of the *Heaven and Hell* dichotomy. This experience was without doubt the closest I ever got to the Truth solely through the administrations of an entheogen and still remain on terra firma. 5-MeO-DMT facilitated a shockingly profound drug-induced *happening* as well, but there is not much to report. On that occasion I quite simply ceased to exist. I mean classical near-death experience and then beyond. At that point there was no one left to experience or report anything at all. The dream vanished. All that remained was nothing … and everything.

The occasion I now present arrived quite unexpectedly, as all of these moments of transcendence usually did. This one occurred immediately following my first ayahuasca journey, and nothing of the sort ever happened again. It was simply an experience, but still I recall it fondly for it was one of those rare moments of *grace* that spontaneously arose unbidden. For a brief moment, I was allowed to drink deeply the perfumed ambrosia of life. Let me tell you it was sweet beyond compare. I will begin with briefly describing the moments that preceded it.

After the effects of my initial DMT foray wore off, I managed to get several hours of sleep. If you recall this was the episode where I chanced across Śhiva. Upon awaking I felt amazingly refreshed and rejuvenated. I was still so amazed by what had just transpired that I spent the entire morning and most of the afternoon in bed researching further aspects of this wondrous brew. Now that I had actually garnered firsthand experience, the trip reports were so much more compelling. For long periods of time, I laid back on my bunk trying to remember what had happened the previous evening.

By the time mid-afternoon had arrived, more than half a day had elapsed since any remaining DMT vestiges had been flushed from my system. By this point I was completely sober and lucid. Thus, when I broke my studies to take a walk in the park, I was not expecting any aftereffects. Case reports had not mentioned this possibility. All information indicated that the drug would take several hours to run its course and perhaps provide a few more hours of afterglow at the most. So when I walked out into the warm sunshine of a fine spring afternoon, I had no idea that what was about to unfold was even possible. Once outside everything proceeded just like it always had. By this I mean I didn't pay attention to much of anything in particular. The usual chattering monkey mind held court as it usually did. Approaching the main thoroughfare that would eventually lead to the park, a strange sensation emerged. A brief flash of awareness gave me the odd impression that something was different. I paid attention, really nothing more significant than that. For up to that moment I was totally lost in trance, as are most of you presently reading this book. This was a spontaneous natural act, not forced or contrived. In fact I didn't even recognize that this was simply a case of awareness coming to the fore until many months later when that concept became known to me.

I rounded the corner and got on to Main Street, and then it hit me. The first thing I noticed was my vision. It was improved. Things appeared more distinct, vibrant and clear when I looked upon the downtown cityscape. It amazed me. Later research and practical experience indicated that this was a fairly common temporary phenomenon related to both psychedelic exposure as well as meditation. The effects seemed to stem from the fact that certain perceptual filters had been weakened or just due to attention or awareness increasing. Whatever the case might have been, at this moment all of my senses were sharpened.

The more I paid attention, the more I noticed that reality had been subtly transmuted. Apparently, through no efforts of my own, the world had become a kinder and gentler place. Everything was imbued equally with a charming *presence* that invited me to take notice. The more I became aware of this, the further pronounced the effect became. The world had become an exceedingly delightful place to be in, and, most unexpectedly, so were the people who inhabited it. And I do mean everybody. One and all were now seen to be my *brothers and sisters*. It had suddenly become ridiculously obvious that we all belonged to the same fraternity. These were *my people*. Why had I never understood this before I wondered? These were not strangers to be wary or suspicious of, these were folks that I loved!

By this time I had made it halfway down the street to the park. The biggest goofiest grin imaginable was plastered across my face. I had no idea why I was so jolly. I felt like Scrooge did when he awoke from his nightmare. At times I tried to tone it down for fear people would perceive me as odd. Little details amazed me like how interesting the sidewalk pavers looked or how marvellously sinuously the flow of the curb spilled out onto the main thoroughfare in certain places. Glass storefronts vied for my attention as well. In fact everything did, as the novelty of it all proved irresistible. This episode was yet another example of Cézanne's carrot manifesting itself. The world was a good, a very good, place, but I had not the slightest clue why. The parade of wonder continued unabated until, before the majesty of the park opened up, I got to the last corner lot remaining on the street. It was there that I totally lost it.

Tucked into this final lot was an old abandoned motel. I could see plywood-shuttered windows about fifty feet away. Right next to me stood a little untended yard. For the most part it was a tangled mess of withered grass and old weeds, but here and there fresh spring flowers had somehow managed to poke their heads up. A stately old deciduous tree took centre stage and was in the middle of breaking its buds. These charming little flowers and tree bursting forth with the promise of life took my breath away. I broke down weeping huge tears. It was all too beautiful to bear. To witness such splendour, to actually see reality as it really is, cannot be put down in words. But they are all the conceptual mind understands, so I will make a slight attempt in hopes it may satisfy your curiosity.

To any and all around me, this lot would have appeared simply as an ugly neglected mess. To my present state of mind, and here I stress the word present, it was without doubt the most beautiful thing I had ever beheld. Ever, ever, ever!

Waves of gratitude sweep over me for being granted the opportunity to *see* these simple, tender and innocent pleasures that Life had to offer. Such was my adoration that I stumbled and almost fell to the ground. I tried to regain my composure. For a moment I thought I must be appearing quite the fool. I managed to stop the flow of tears only to break down again as soon as I glanced over at all the grandeur before me. There was a recognition. I can't tell you what it was that moved me so. I can only tell you that it did. In truth it is not something that has any characteristics at all but nonetheless is instantly recognizable if you happen upon it. A few neglected spring flowers and a half-dead tree. Nothing special at all, and yet they meant the world to me. Huxley's doors of perception had been entirely knocked off their hinges! At long last I was actually seeing reality as it actually appeared— unfiltered, conditioned or refined in any way. What a marvellous world we all lived in. You may be heartened to hear that my teacher says all of you can and will see it as such one day. Enlightenment may be put off for awhile but can never be postponed indefinitely.

I tried to recall if I had ever seen things from this perspective before. The best I could come up with was the sensation I got upon seeing something brand new during a backpacking adventure. On the order of the Angkor Wat ruins or the Great Wall, for example. During those occasions there was a brief moment of recognition. I could detect beauty and something even greater in the novelty of the experience, but, as the shock of the new quickly faded from awareness, everything dropped back to the level of ordinary mundane reality. That experience then became just one more to add to the mouldering dust heap of all past memories. If I were to behold such sights again, there was no more interest there. The thrill such experiences generated were fleeting at best.

What I was experiencing now was quite different since there was no end to the joy. And there was no end to my appetite either. I kept looking again and again and again and still the feeling held. All I wanted to do was keep lapping up all the deliciousness life had to offer. To a sugar fiend, the experience was comparable to enjoying a never ending procession of the best banana splits I had ever tasted.

Yet some part of me, which I now identify as my ego, kept interjecting from time to time. Exactly like an annoying back-seat driver. Too bad spiritual maturity was lacking at that point for, while this episode was nothing more than a momentary awakening, it could have progressed into something much greater if only the ego hadn't kept getting in the way. But it really was of no consequence. All would be revealed according to some mysterious agenda not of my own making.

Once again my ego suggested that I was looking foolish and made it clear it wanted me to stop this nonsense and get on with it. After all, wasn't there a park to be visited? Quite amazing—there I was holding the world in the palm of my hand, and the good old ego wanted me to go see some greenery. Taking the ego's admonishment to heart, I crossed the road and entered the park. I regained my composure enough to head over to the alpine area, which was my favourite section of the park. Cresting its highest spot, I broke down once again as I was carried back into the moment. John Keats' famous words rang out clear and strong, "Beauty is truth, truth beauty—that is ... all ye need to know!" From the high vantage, I heard the joyous hoots and howls of some kind of unseen party game going on. Perhaps Frisbee or volleyball was being enjoyed by a group of friends. Music played, food was being prepared. How sublime such seemingly mundane reality truly was. I marvelled again and again that such simple enjoyment like this was even possible. It had become utterly apparent to me—we were all living a lie. What we had here was a *heaven on earth*, if we only dared open our eyes to behold it. I wandered through the park as if it were a wonderland with unimaginable treasures to be revealed around every corner. Yet it was not to last.

After about twenty minutes of this, my ego had enough and once again piped in with its own agenda. This time it told me that I could not possibly continue to live life like this. Incredibly, I believed it without even pausing for a moment to consider whether or not this was actually true. With less thought than it took to brush my teeth, I accepted the notion it presented wholeheartedly, and it was a done deal. My fall from grace was simply unavoidable, I was informed. An hour or two more of aftereffects was all I could expect before everything would be put properly back in its place. And so it came to pass. Paradise lost on the strength of a single goddamn thought. How absurd!

Why we always tend to accept whatever the ego projects at us, with so little regard, is hard to fathom. This quandary only surfaced in my awareness when I began to realize how trapped in illusion I really was. The ego is such a bullshit artist. I think it all boils down to conditioning and self-preservation. The system seems designed such that very few ever take a moment to seriously examine what the hell the all-powerful *voice of reason* (at least that is how it views itself) is actually up to—what its agenda really is. When I finally did, it shocked me to the depths of my being.

Transformation

I hope my ayahuasca reports have given you a sense of the range of experience open to you while on the path of spiritual investigation. It is important to understand the complexity and range of phenomena. Results are unpredictable. The effects are so variable and inconsistent, so dependent on set and setting and the practitioner's own psyche, as to make almost any experience within the realm of possibility. The fun, the frivolous, the fantastic and the spiritually significant may all arise at some point or another. What happened to me should not be expected to happen to you. But it could.

One thing that was readily apparent to me after several encounters was the fact that each experience took up where the last one had ended. It was like I was in some kind of school, and the lesson I was about to receive depended upon my present level of consciousness and spiritual maturity. If the previous *lesson* hadn't been grokked fully enough, I often had to wait until it became completely incorporated before continuing on. Sometimes I had to repeat it. Ayahuasca was very gentle, patient and wise in that regard. It never demanded more of me than I was capable of dealing with at the time. Its method of imparting wisdom might be compared to the slow, methodical, progressive path of Buddhism. Though paradox being its very nature, it was also equally capable of revealing great big chunks of reality to me in an instant.

Ayahuasca could function as a wonderful spiritual tonic if used wisely. It never failed to invigorate my spiritual aspirations. The positive outlook the brew instilled lasted for weeks between sessions. As nature's natural corollary to Prozac, it seemed capable of treating a range of mental health problems, raising spirits and even possibly combating drug-and alcohol-related addictions. Psychologically cathartic and abreactive healing frequently resulted from ayahuasca therapy.

People have reported that one ayahuasca experience was more beneficial to them than numerous sessions on their psychiatrist's couch. I found the psychological effect extraordinarily beneficial. Powerfully repressed material emanating from deep within the subconscious was recognized and dealt with accordingly. To a significant degree, unhealthy perceptions and behaviours were brought to the fore. Being honest with myself was key in this regard. I realized I could no longer afford to remain in ignorance and self-deception if any chance of moving forward was desired. It was very difficult to experience reality as it really was, but it was important that I never flinch when given the opportunity to see the cold hard facts laid out naked before me.

The realizations I garnered had to be actively and intentionally incorporated into my normal waking reality if change were to be permanently effected. Many had wonderfully instructional sessions while under the tutelage of ayahuasca but most failed to implement them in any meaningful way upon sobering up. This can be seen as a major weakness of psychedelics in their function as a spiritual aid. People rarely effect permanent positive change in their lives as a result of taking a drug. Let's face it; conditioning is exceptionally ingrained in most individuals so the chance of significantly busting out of the old, tried-and-true, familiar routine is slight. Radical spiritual transformation is rarer still.

If you recall the earlier chapter on turn-of-the-century writers of mysticism, you may remember Richard Maurice Bucke. We learned that his treatise called *Cosmic Consciousness: A Study in the Evolution of the Human Mind* outlined nine characteristics that he felt marked authentic spiritual experience. The last one you may remember was *definite moment or period of transformation*. As I see it, this factor is paramount. I think the most important question you can ask of psychedelics is, "Can the experience lead me to a full and abiding spiritual transformation?"

I am not speaking here of a momentary glimpse or passing experience like Bucke chronicled. Permanent enlightenment is the goal. The short answer in my estimation is *not very likely*. Though anything is possible so nothing can be ruled out entirely. My eyes were opened to the possibilities greater consciousness has to offer and a taste of the transpersonal realm was experienced from time to time, but a permanent radical shift proved elusive. The high point of all my drug moments was undoubtedly the full-blown awakening experience I just spoke of. The message I received from that experience was—yes, awakening really is that easy! Though, try as I might, I could never figure out what was necessary to cause that reality to return. Much later I learned, through meditation, that the secret is to do nothing at all. It is all the *doing* that actually gets in the way.

In many respects, the less conceptual and philosophical garbage ... er, I mean grounding, you have accumulated, the better. At that time I knew nothing of the ego and the tricks it could get up to. Meditation and non-duality were not even a blip on my radar screen. The notion of *mindfulness practice* and *awareness* had never come up. Apparently my spiritual naïveté allowed ayahuasca to sufficiently erode my ego such that the world was offered my undivided attention for a little while.

The chance encounter with Bucke's *Cosmic Consciousness* was, as all those occasions really were, only a kind of premonition. It arose and then passed away just as all transitory phenomena do. Moments of bliss, oneness, being in the eternal now and receiving great wisdom are other examples of temporary experiences ayahuasca afforded me.

Don't get me wrong—these spiritual moments were wonderful, just not of much enduring spiritual value. In Catholic circles, these episodes might be known as *gratuitous grace*, which were seen as unnecessary for salvation but to be cherished in the manner in which Paul extolled us to accept them: "Thanks be to God for His indescribable gift!" (2 Corinthians 9:15). During the meditative phase of my quest, additional profound moments of grace were experienced. I have no idea why or where this kind of grace originated. I certainly didn't feel God deemed me a special chosen one. Nor was I some kind of spiritual lottery winner, nor had I been in a position of somehow earning it. It was just another one of those mysteries best not contemplated too much.

I think entheogens are most useful in prying open what the Zen folks call the *gateless gate* of Reality. They may even nudge you down it a bit from time to time, but they can't do much more than that. In the book *Zig Zag Zen: Buddhism and Psychedelics*, Zen priest and writer Peter Matthiessen said as much when he commented about his own past psychedelic drug use:

> Drugs can clear away the past,
> enhance the present;
> toward the inner garden,
> they can point the way.

This reminds me of an anecdote.

It's been postulated that the successful development of the atomic bomb by the Soviets advanced so much more quickly than the American project had simply because the Russians knew that their goal was attainable. Not, as a person might reason, because they had gathered American secrets or acquired special high-tech equipment. It was simply the fact that they were assured that *their horse would be a winner* long before it ever left the gate—that made all the difference. Ram Dass points out the same thing: "Knowing that it is possible changes the meaning of all spiritual practice that follows because you go in with a perspective that's not just from here, but from there as well." The chances of waking up were that much greater due to the foretaste of Reality such drugs engendered. That is not conjecture. It definitely proved to be SWIM'S experience.

Though Matthiessen did have a fairly positive view of psychedelics, he added the following caveat, "Lacking the temper of ascetic discipline, the drug vision remains a sort of dream that cannot be brought over into daily life." That is a very important point. A tremendous desire and heartfelt passion to realize the absolute nature of all, and more importantly abide in it, must be present at every moment. If that level of commitment is found wanting, success will likely be limited. It really boils down to whether or not you are willing and able to reorient your life at every possible opportunity away from its present *endarkened* state. Drugs can't do that.

Religious scholar Huston Smith once informed us that while psychedelic use was all about *altered states*, Buddhism was actually more about *altered traits*. One does not necessarily lead to the other, he assured us. I do recognize the validity of this statement but would not negate the potential of entheogens entirely. Smith himself noted that valuable spiritual insight might well arise from their use. It turned out that many Western spiritual seekers, including Buddhists, got the impetus to set out down the path as a direct result of their psychedelic experimentation. Let's take a look at the present situation for a moment.

In the West, interest in Buddhism is on the rise. This resurgence during the last fifty years has not been equalled since it was first introduced to China two millennia ago. Similarly, Advaita Vedanta, a philosophical branch of Hinduism which embraces the principal of *non-duality*, is also creating quite a stir among the spiritual crowds in Europe, America and elsewhere. Concomitantly, non-recreational, spiritually edifying, psychedelic use is also increasing. Largely, the frivolity of the Sixties has been cast aside in favour of a healthier, more mature and informed drug practice. It certainly is possible that the two trends are related. Many seem to be tiring of the largely decrepit, *straw-dog* traditional religious practices that are commonly foisted upon them. There is a longing in many hearts for the real thing.

Apparently the personal histories of almost all first-generation Buddhist teachers in Europe and America are rife with psychedelic use, whether they care to admit it or not. I once heard an American Zen master say that but for the effects of LSD, his realization would never have occurred. Dr. Strassman reports that the majority of the monks and teachers at his Zen centre had significant LSD experience as well. For many it was originally what spurred them on to seek Buddhist refuge in the first place.

One of the first well-known Western expounders of Buddhism was Alan Watts, who, among other things, became a popular author and speaker during the sixties. He viewed Buddhism and psychedelics as mutually harmonious and recommended that they be employed in a syncretic fashion. His views were certainly less rigid than some of his more scripturally uptight Buddhist peers. Watts took psychedelics so that he might find, as he called it, the *essential* or *active ingredients* of the mystical experience. On this count he tells us he found much success.

Dr. W. T. Stace, professor and leading authority on mysticism, had this to say about psychedelically induced mystical states: "It is not a matter of its being similar to mystical experience; it is mystical experience!"

Similarly, in *Zig Zag Zen*, Ram Dass weighed in with:

It's a great gift, a profound sacrament ... You can't put

it down. We just don't know how to use it. I don't see psychedelics as an enlightening vehicle, but I do see it [sic] as an awakening vehicle. I see them beginning a process that awakens you to the possibility.

This accolade, though, is tempered with meditation teacher Michele McDonald-Smith's more critical view, also from *Zig Zag Zen*, in which he says of psychedelics:

> They bring all this energy into the system so that it catapults you into a different state of consciousness at the same time that it taxes your body, mind and heart. You get a sort of beatific view, but actually you're farther down the mountain.

On the other hand when Terence McKenna was questioned about whether meditation could get you to the same revelatory position as psychedelics could, he definitely said no. For him all mainstream spiritual techniques, other than drug taking, "were not substitutions for the psychedelic experience but mere trade-offs." It's very murky water indeed.

If you really want to know the truth of the matter, find out for yourself. My psychedelic pilgrimage was very rewarding. Could I say, like the American Zen master had, that my very awakening depended on the use of hallucinogens? I really don't know, but I suspect not. I do know one thing. Apparently the Buddha never needed them. They just happened to resonate with me, as they have for countless others, and in all probability sped up the process for me significantly.

When Alan Watts was asked what was the best way to reach enlightenment, through meditation or psychedelic drugs, he responded, "Well, I don't know about a 'best' way, but perhaps you want to think of it like this, you can walk to New York or you can fly." There are many paths to the top of the mountain, but only one view.

Making progress should be your main concern. Welcome clarity and awareness into your life. Remember, entertainment and feeling good are not your goal. If your practice is not working, be honest about it and get rid of it pronto. Similarly, if you once found the psychedelic experience rewarding but now it has lost its allure, you must abandon it as surely as you ditch the boat that gets you to a far shore. There is no choice but to move on. Alan Watts put it another way: "Once you get the message, you hang up the phone."

I freely admit the value of ayahuasca and other psychedelics was drastically reduced once I took up meditation. At that juncture I used them very infrequently, if at all. Though I still found some slight merit in them even at the later stages of my quest, since the two types of experience seemed to inform each other to some degree. Using ayahuasca from time to time was an interesting way to gauge my spiritual progress.

At the tail end of my journey, when I did happen to check in with it, *not much happened at all*. This was actually quite wonderful. Mostly I just experienced equanimity and a quiet mind. This was evidence that meditation was really working its magic. That indeed I was really *waking up* to reality, which was not a state at all but a new way of being. This fact contrasted sharply with the myriad possible states of consciousness psychedelics produced when I first experienced them.

Let's now take a look at psychedelics from a strictly doctrinal approach. Particularly let's see if Buddhism has any scriptural prohibitions against the use of drugs. This was of interest to me as that would be the direction I would soon turn.

It became ever more apparent to me, as I delved deeper into the literature, that spiritual and religious organizations, which date back to preliterate times and continue right up to the present, incorporate mind-altering substances into their practice. As previously chronicled, shamans use common psychedelic plants such as ayahuasca, peyote and psilocybin mushrooms, but there are also lesser known ones like the colourful amanita toadstool, the LSD-containing seeds of the morning glory flower and even the venom of certain poisonous toads. It seems that human beings have always been hardwired to get loaded, but, unlike modern man's predilection to get wasted on booze and a good ball game, the ancients sought to alter their consciousness for a higher spiritual purpose.

One only has to look to the ancient Greek mystery religion, with its use of the fabled *kykeon*, to get a sense of what I am talking about. The Eleusinian Mysteries were ancient Greek initiation ceremonies held every year for the cult of Demeter and Persephone. Of all the mysteries celebrated in ancient times, these were held to be the ones of greatest Eurocentric importance. Many scholars believe that the power and longevity of the Eleusinian Mysteries stemmed directly from the initiates' use of the psychedelic kykeon. Its exact composition and use has been lost over time, though some speculate that LSD-containing ergotized barley may have been responsible for its psychoactive effects.

Other religious practices have employed mind-altering substances. Hinduism has its *Soma*—a God, a plant and a drink, which was the focus of the Rigveda. Judaism has, at one time or another, included the spiritual use of alcohol and possibly cannabis. Islamic Sufis have a strong tradition of the spiritual use of cannabis. Christianity seems to be one of the few exceptions. What about Buddhism?

According to Jack Kornfield, renowned vipassana teacher of American Theravada Buddhism:

> The Zen, Vajrayana, and the Theravada traditions had very little to say about the subject. They were rarely, if at all, mentioned points of view we understanding of and teachers based experience. But there body of knowledge in substances that I know of. in the texts. What have come from our Buddhist masters on contemporary is not a traditional relationship to these

The basic "Zen Commandments" contain the following five precepts:
1. not to kill,
2. not to steal,
3. not to speak falsely,
4. not to engage in sexual misconduct and finally
5. to refrain from using intoxicants to the point of heedlessness, loss of mindfulness or loss of awareness.

It did not prohibit intoxicants, merely cautioned practitioners from using them excessively to the point that they interfered with mindful attention or awareness. This point was very explicit. It was left up to the individual to determine if they were a help or a hindrance. Often, though, modern interpreters of this last tenet felt obliged to add their own spin. Contemporary Zen Master, Thich Nhat Hanh, is a case in point.

He advised in his book *The Five Wonderful Precepts* that the readers should all commit to the following personal vow:

"I vow to ingest only items that preserve peace, well-being and joy in my body, in my consciousness, and in the collective body and consciousness of my family and society."

That ideal seemed to reflect the spirit of the original precept well enough, but then he added the following: "I am determined not to use alcohol or any other intoxicants, or to ingest foods or other items that contain toxins, such as certain T.V. programs, magazines, books, films and conversations."

While it was true that the huge canon of Buddhist texts as a whole were largely bereft of passages pertaining to psychedelics, still enough historical references remained to convince certain scholars (I have found reference to over fifteen) that some schools, namely the Vajrayana tradition, had indeed employed entheogens to some extent throughout their history.

According to R. C. Parker's investigation, which focused primarily on the use of entheogens in the anuttara-yoga-tantra materials, especially the Yogini-tantras, datura and cannabis were employed. Of great interest to me was the mention of the Tibetan use of entheogens in the Vajrayana Tibetan Kagyu School of wisdom since I hoped to soon become tutored in its ways at the Buddhist centre. Parker stated that references to psychedelics may be found in texts of Tibetan or Newar origin as well as Tibetan commentarial literature.

It is clear that evidence exists to show that some Buddhists had used drugs in the past.

Keeping my focus primarily on Tibetan Buddhism (which some say is just as much *Tibetanism* as it is pure Buddhism), I also discovered that a huge influence on its modern expression came about as a result of incorporation of certain practices of the ancient indigenous shamanic practice called Bon Po. In general these practices ranged from divination, magic, spiritual guidance regarding death and the attainment of altered states of consciousness. Terence McKenna has stated that the Bon tradition used plant-based drugs like datura and hashish as part of their rituals. Several researchers have also linked the use of the psychedelic *Amanita muscaria* mushrooms to the Himalayan shamanic tradition. Soma, more commonly called *amrita* by modern Tibetan Buddhists, is still apparently employed today.

The late Chogyam Trungpa Rinpoche, Kagyu and Nyingma lineage holder and major disseminator of Tibetan Buddhism to the West during the 1960-70s, once explained the function of *amrita*:

> Amrita dissolves the student's mind into the mind of the teacher of the lineage. In general, amrita is the principle of intoxicating extreme beliefs, belief in ego, and dissolving the boundary between confusion and sanity so that coemergence can be realized.

There was little doubt in my mind that what is being described here was a psychedelic trip—complete with ego loss and dissolution of the ordinary state of being such that access to the transpersonal realm opened up. It seemed undeniable that certain Buddhist schools, like the kagyu lineage for example, had once been and apparently still were to some degree, influenced by psychedelic practice. Yet in a contemporary sense, mind-expanding compounds generally seemed to be eschewed due to a personal bias of the teacher. As best I could determine, there was no absolute prohibition against their use. I would continue to employ them as long as they were useful. They had served me well up to that point, but it was time to look elsewhere—Buddhism awaited.

Moving On

This juncture seems as good a point as any to set aside this story for the time being. There is more to be said, in the book to follow, but I feel some silence is welcomed at this point. Let's take a break to allow things to assimilate. I hope I have provided enough detail (though hopefully not too much as to bore the pants off of you!) to show you what went into the making of a 21st century mystic. Though, to be clear, the continuing journey would become more of an *unmaking* or undoing in its terminal stages. It was then that I experienced the dissolution of everything I ever took to be real. It's become evident to me, as this tale was being exposited, that it was a longer and far more convoluted path than I had first thought. Certainly stretching back to childhood, perhaps even before then. If you decide to, or already have taken up such a journey yourself, don't expect it to resemble mine.

Remember you don't want to emulate Christ or Buddha—rather you want to realize who you are. When The Awakened One set out to determine the ultimate nature of reality, he had no models to copy. No true mystics ever seemed to. They always blazed their own unique way to the Truth. My best advice is to encourage you to defer to your own tender heart and wise inner guru. Those two will never lead you astray since they are the only real arbiters of reality that actually exist. Entheogens may help point that out to you. Undoubtedly drugs could provide you with a new, though short-lived way to perceive reality that does not rely solely on your thoughts and emotions. That, in itself, is a terribly important thing to understand.

A Fleeting Improvised Man

At best all I hoped to offer you in this book were a few spiritual pointers, maybe a shortcut or two and perhaps a little light entertainment. Don't ever expect me to tell you the *Truth*. That remains for you to discover yourself. I do however guarantee that I always endeavoured to be *truthful* in the telling of this tale. I despise bullshit artists and have tried my best to never have that stink associated with me. To put it simply, I am just an ordinary guy who woke up one day and thought there were perhaps a few people out there who wanted to hear the *good news*. As you can see, this story is far from complete. It was during the next phase that all the hard work would really begin. Suffice it to say that the world of Buddhism and non-duality presented concepts so radical in nature and foreign to my normal sensibilities that often all I was left with was a sense of incomprehensibility. Which, by the way, is actually a very desirable state to be in.

When I was first told by a monk that *I didn't really exist*, I wasn't sure whether I should laugh in his face or slap it to bring him back to his senses. Of course, in the end, I found his statement to be entirely accurate. But that was a yet. At that time my level despite the ministrations of long way down the path of ignorance still ran deep entheogens.

To iterate, psychedelics I dove into their strange intensely for some months and could only bring me so far. and illuminating world very then moved on. They yanked at my heart strings and successfully *cracked open my head*, which was no small feat. It was a privilege to experience their illuminating power.

The results of the 2002 Johns Hopkins study on psilocybin and mysticism, which I mentioned briefly, included administering a follow-up questionnaire to the participants several months after the study concluded. Most respondents indicated that the effects of the drug were still spiritually relevant and continued to positively affect them and impact their lives at that point. You may recall the original participants of the Good Friday experiment still reported positive effects decades later. By way of offering a summary of sorts, the following six points of reflection detail answers to some of the same areas of interest that the questionnaire addressed. These reflections represent my state of mind during the time I packed up and left the hostel for greener pastures ahead. By this point I had experienced at least ten tryptamine-induced altered states of consciousness.

Positive attitudes about life and/or self

Moving On

Everything became just that much sweeter, vibrant and poignant. I was definitely upbeat at this time. Demonstrable changes for the better in both outlook and behaviour had already occurred by this point. There was also a sense of mystery to life and less separation from it. Perhaps I was a little less entranced in the dream state than I previously had been. I could hardly wait for the next session to arrive, such was my curiosity to discover what new profound insights ayahuasca might have in store for me.

Positive mood changes

My spirits were certainly uplifted. Ayahuasca, in particular, was a great long-lasting natural antidepressant. Its positive mood-altering affects lasted long after the session was over. It wasn't often clear to me why I felt better, just that I did. I realized deep healing was occurring at the subconscious level. All I can say is this medicine may very well heal that which ails you and certainly won't ever harm you in the process.

Altruistic positive social effects

I lent the Karaoke King money several times during this period. Surprisingly I had come to develop strong positive feelings for that character and entertain the possibility that ayahuasca could have at least been partially responsible for fostering those feelings. Despite his being one of the most self-centred individuals I had ever met, we parted ways calling each other friend. My outlook towards humanity in general was less critical than it had ever been before.

Positive behaviour changes

One of the most important effects of ayahuasca was its capacity to show me, using a kind of *fierce grace*, all the character flaws that I constantly expended so much energy in concealing. I think most of those I ever hurt or offended percolated into my awareness at some point or another. At times it was difficult to endure. Lots of tears were spilled during those kinds of sessions. In forging a new-found spirit of forgiveness towards myself and others, real transformation did ensue.

Indication of how personally meaningful the experience was

If considered solely from the point of view of how well it (ayahuasca) improved my lot in life, aside from spiritually enriching it, I would not hesitate to say that this class of substance succeeded. After all who didn't want to be happier and healthier? I have heard one ayahuasca user declare unequivocally that it made him "a better father, husband and all around healthier human being." That's about as fine a testimonial as you will likely ever get, and it was not at all uncommon. The thousands of ayahuasca drinkers who have returned from Peru and Brazil over the last decade have made similar claims. I would place myself in that camp as well.

Indication of how spiritually significant the experience was

Wow! Up to that point ayahuasca had been the single most significantly spiritual practice I had ever done. Of course it was also the only one, but that does not negate its significance. Some real truths were revealed while on that drug. I don't care what any naysayer may try to lead you to believe. My own experience proved that these compounds are spiritually relevant. They just couldn't quite get me to the mountain top. By this I mean get me high enough up into the rarefied air to realize that there was not actually anyone to ascend the peak anyhow. With that I conclude my post-ayahuasca review, and, lest you have forgotten about SWIM, remember it was really that character who did all those horrible drugs, not I.

Before I began my journey, I had a rather unfavourable opinion of drug use. I guess I still do towards their recreational use. But through my own experience, I now know that not all drugs are good—some are really really great! Without doubt a huge propaganda effort has been kept running throughout the ages designed to taint and discredit the image of valuable mind-altering substances. The powers-that-be have simply poisoned our minds with ludicrous lies.

The time had come to leave plant-based medicines and mind manifesting substances behind me for the most part, but they would not be soon forgotten. It was merely time to change my focus. Now that I had a taste of the numinous, I was bound and determined to see this thing through to the end. A chapter was closing, a new one just beginning. The moment was pregnant with possibility. I checked the old backpack into storage once again and climbed aboard the bus on the continuing journey to complete my quest. I would not be returning to the farm just yet. Rather, I would be going someplace far more recognizable and familiar to me—*Home*. For that was how many described the sensation of returning to their original point of origin. Home. There's no place like it.

We shall not cease from exploration, and the end of all our exploring will be to arrive where we started and know the place for the first time.
T. S. Eliot - "Little Gidding"

That they all may be made ONE. Like thou Father art in me, I in thee, that they may be ONE in us. I in them, they in me, that they may be perfect in ONE. [emphasis added]
John 17:23